Homeowners Insurance Basics

Homeowners insurance provides financial protection against disasters. It is a package policy, which means that it covers both damage to property and liability, or legal responsibility, for any injuries and property damage policyholders or their families cause to other people. This includes damage caused by household pets. Damage caused by most disasters is covered but there are exceptions. Standard homeowners policies do not cover flooding, earthquakes or poor maintenance. Flood coverage, however, is available in the form of a separate policy both from the National Flood Insurance Program (NFIP) and from a few private insurers. Earthquake coverage is available either in the form of an endorsement or as a separate policy. Most maintenance-related problems are the homeowners' responsibility.

A standard homeowners insurance policy includes four essential types of coverage. They include:

1. Coverage for the Structure of the Home

This part of a policy pays to repair or rebuild a home if it is damaged or destroyed by fire, hurricane, hail, lightning or other disaster listed in the policy. It will not pay for damage caused by a flood, earthquake or routine wear and tear. Most standard policies also cover structures that are not attached to a house such as a garage, tool shed or gazebo. Generally, these structures are covered for about 10 percent of the total amount of insurance on the structure of the home.

2. Coverage for Personal Belongings

Furniture, clothes, sports equipment and other personal items are covered if they are stolen or destroyed by fire, hurricane or other insured disaster. Most companies provide coverage for 50 to 70 percent of the amount of insurance on the structure of a home. This part of the policy includes off-premises coverage. This means that belongings are covered anywhere in the world, unless the policyholder has decided against off-premises coverage. Expensive items like jewelry, furs and silverware are covered, but there are usually dollar limits if they are stolen. To insure these items to their full value, individuals can purchase a special personal property endorsement or floater and insure the item for its appraised value.

Trees, plants and shrubs are also covered under standard homeowners insurance—generally up to about $500 per item. Perils covered are theft, fire, lightning, explosion, vandalism, riot and even falling aircraft. They are not covered for damage by wind or disease.

3. Liability Protection

Liability coverage protects against the cost of lawsuits for bodily injury or property damage that policyholders or family members cause to other people. It also pays for damage caused by pets. The liability portion of the policy pays for both the cost of defending the policyholder in court and any court awards—up to the limit of the policy. Coverage is not just in the home but extends to anywhere in the world. Liability limits generally start at about $100,000. However, experts recommend that homeowners purchase at least $300,000 worth of protection. An umbrella or excess liability policy, which provides broader coverage, including claims for libel and slander, as well as higher liability limits, can be added to the policy. Generally, umbrella policies cost between $200 to $350 for $1 million of additional liability protection.

Homeowners policies also provide no-fault medical coverage. In the event that someone is injured in a policyholder's home, the injured person can simply submit medical bills to the policyholder's insurance company. In this way expenses are paid without a liability claim being filed. This coverage, however, does not pay the medical bills for the policyholder's own family or pets.

4. Additional Living Expenses

This pays the additional costs of living away from home if a house is inhabitable due to damage from a fire, storm or other insured disaster. It covers hotel bills, restaurant meals and other extra living expenses incurred while the home is being rebuilt. Coverage for additional living expenses differs from company to company. Many policies provide coverage for about 20 percent of the insurance on a house. The coverage can be increased for an additional premium. Some companies sell a policy that provides an unlimited amount of loss-of-use coverage, but for a limited amount of time.

Additional living expense coverage also reimburses homeowners who rent out part of their home for the rent that would have been collected from a tenant if the home had not been destroyed.

Types of Homeowners Insurance Policies

There are several types of homeowners insurance policies that differ in the amount of insurance coverage they provide. The different types are fairly standard throughout the country. However, individual states and companies may offer policies that are slightly different or go by other names such as "standard" or "deluxe." People who rent the homes they live in have specific renters policies.

The various types of homeowners insurance policies are listed below.

- **HO-3:** This is the most common policy and protects the home from all perils except those specifically excluded.

- **HO-1:** Limited coverage policy
  This "bare bones" policy provides coverage against the first 10 disasters. It is no longer available in most states.

- **HO-2:** Basic policy
  A basic policy provides protection against all 16 disasters. There is a version of HO-2 designed for mobile homes.

- **HO-8:** Older home
  Designed for older homes, this policy usually reimburses for damage on an actual cash value basis, which means replacement cost less depreciation. Full replacement cost policies may not be available for some older homes.

- **HO4:** Renter
  Created specifically for people who rent the home they live in, this policy protects personal possessions and any parts of the apartment that the policyholder owns, such as newly installed kitchen cabinets, against all 16 disasters.

- **H0-6:** Condo/Co-op
  A policy for people who own a condo or co-op, it provides coverage for belongings and the structural parts of the building that they own. It protects against all 16 disasters.

What Type of Disasters Are Covered?

Most homeowners policies cover the 16 disasters listed below. Some "bare bones" policies only cover the first 10:

- Fire or lightning
- Windstorm or hail
- Explosion
- Riot or civil commotion
- Damage caused by aircraft
- Damage caused by vehicles

- Smoke

- Vandalism or malicious mischief

- Theft

- Volcanic eruption

- Falling object

- Weight of ice, snow or sleet

- Accidental discharge or overflow of water or steam from within a plumbing, heating, air conditioning, or automatic fire-protective sprinkler system, or from a household appliance

- Sudden and accidental tearing apart, cracking, burning, or bulging of a steam or hot water heating system, an air conditioning or automatic fire-protective system

- Freezing of a plumbing, heating, air conditioning or automatic, fire-protective sprinkler system, or of a household appliance

- Sudden and accidental damage from artificially generated electrical current (does not include loss to a tube, transistor or similar electronic component)

Standard Homeowners Policy Exclusions

Standard homeowners policies exclude coverage for flood, earthquake, war, nuclear accident, landslide, mudslide, sinkhole. Some of these exclusions are discussed below.

1. Floods

Flood damage is excluded under standard homeowners and renters insurance policies. Flood coverage, however, is available in the form of a separate policy both from the National Flood Insurance Program (NFIP) and from a few private insurers. Additional information on flood insurance can be found on the FloodSmart.gov Web site or by calling 888-379-9531. For coverage over and above the $250,000 limit for property and $100,000 for contents provided by the NFIP, excess flood insurance is available from private insurance companies. (See Topic on Flood Insurance on page 47 for further information.)

Tsunamis cause flood damage and are therefore only covered by a flood policy.

2. Earthquakes

Earthquake coverage can be a separate policy or an endorsement to a homeowners or renters policy. It is available from most insurance companies. In

California, it is also available from the California Earthquake Authority, a privately funded, publically managed organization. In earthquake prone states like California, the policy comes with a high deductible.

3. Damage Resulting from "Faulty, Defective or Inadequate" Maintenance, Workmanship, Construction or Materials

Defective products can include construction materials. An insurance policy will not cover damage due to lack of maintenance, mold, termite infestation and infestation from other pests. It is the policyholder's responsibility to take reasonable precautions to protect the home from damage.

Levels of Coverage

There are three coverage options.

1. Actual Cash Value

This type of coverage pays to replace the home or possessions minus a deduction for depreciation.

2. Replacement Cost

This type of coverage pays the cost of rebuilding or repairing the home or replacing possessions without a deduction for depreciation.

3. Guaranteed/Extended Replacement Cost

An extended replacement cost policy pays a certain percentage, generally 20-25 percent, over the coverage limit to rebuild the home in the event that materials and labor costs are pushed up by a widespread disaster, for example. For example, if homeowners take out a policy for $100,000, they can get up to an extra $20,000 or $25,000 of coverage.

Some companies offer a guaranteed replacement cost policy, which pays whatever it costs to rebuild the home as it was before the fire or other disaster, even if it exceeds the policy limit. This gives protection against sudden increases in construction costs due to a shortage of building materials after a widespread disaster or other unexpected situations. It generally does not cover the cost of upgrading the house to comply with current building codes. However, an endorsement (or an addition to) the policy called Ordinance or Law can help pay for these additional costs.

Guaranteed and extended replacement cost policies are more expensive; but can offer excellent financial protection against disasters. This type of coverage, however, may not be available in all states or from all companies.

Business Insurance Basics

Most businesses need to purchase at least the following four types of insurance:

1. Property Insurance

Property insurance compensates a business if the property used in the business is lost or damaged as the result of various types of common perils, such as fire or theft. Property insurance covers not just a building or structure but also the contents, including office furnishings, inventory, raw materials, machinery, computers and other items vital to a business's operations. Depending on the type of policy, property insurance may include coverage for equipment breakdown, removal of debris after a fire or other destructive event, some types of water damage and other losses.

Business Interruption Insurance

Also known as business income insurance, business interruption insurance is a type of property insurance. A business whose property has sustained a direct physical loss such as fire damage or a damaged roof due to a tree falling on it in a windstorm and has to close down completely while the premises are being repaired may lose out to competitors. A quick resumption of business after a disaster is essential. That is why business interruption insurance is so important.

There are typically three types of business interruption insurance. A business can purchase any one or combination of these.

- **Business Income Coverage:** Compensates for lost income if a company has to vacate its premises due to disaster-related damage that is covered under the property insurance policy. Business income insurance covers the profits the company would have earned, based on financial records, had the disaster not occurred. The policy also covers operating expenses, such as electricity, that continue even though business activities have come to a temporary halt.

- **Extra Income Coverage:** Reimburses the company for a reasonable sum of money that it spends, over and above normal operating expenses, to avoid having to shut down during the restoration period.

- **Contingent Business Interruption Insurance:** Protects a businessowner's earnings following physical loss or damage to the property of the insured's suppliers or customers, as opposed to its own property.

Damage due to floods, earthquakes and acts of terrorism are generally not covered by standard business property insurance but can be purchased through various markets.

Protection Against Flood Damage

Property insurance policies usually exclude coverage for flood damage. Businesses should find out from their local government office or commercial bank whether their business is located in a flood zone and whether their location has been flooded in the past. Flood insurance is available through the federal government's National Flood Insurance Program (www.FloodSmart.gov), which is serviced by private carriers, and from a few specialty insurers.

Protection Against Earthquake Damage

Coverage for earthquake damage is excluded in most property insurance policies, including businessowners package policies. Businesses in an earthquake-prone area will need a special earthquake insurance policy or commercial property earthquake endorsement.

Protection Against Terrorist Attack Losses

Under the Terrorism Risk Insurance Act of 2002 and its extensions, only businesses that purchase optional terrorism coverage are covered for losses arising from terrorist acts. The exception is workers compensation, which covers work-related injuries and deaths including those due to acts of terrorism.

2. Liability Insurance

Any enterprise can be sued. Customers may claim that the business caused them harm as the result of, for example, a defective product, an error in a service or disregard for another person's property. Or a claimant may allege that the business created a hazardous environment. Liability insurance pays damages for which the business is found liable, up to the policy limits, as well as attorneys' fees and other legal defense expenses. It also pays the medical bills of any people injured by, or on the premises of, the business.

A Commercial General Liability (CGL) insurance policy is the first line of defense against many common claims. CGL policies cover claims in four basic categories of business liability:

- Bodily injury
- Property damage
- Personal injury (including slander or libel)
- Advertising injury (damage from slander or false advertising)

In addition to covering claims listed above, CGL policies also cover the cost of defending or settling claims. General liability insurance policies always state the maximum amount that the insurer will pay during the policy period.

There are two major forms of liability insurance policies a business can select: occurrence and claims made. Both types of policies have their advantages.

- **Occurrence Policy:** An occurrence policy covers a business for harm to others caused by incidents that occurred while a policy is in force, no matter when the claim is filed. For example, a person might sue a business in 2010 for an injury stemming from a fall in 1999. The policy that was in place when the incident occurred (i.e. 1999) will apply, even if the company now has a policy in place with higher limits. Occurrence coverage may not be available in some states or for some industries or professions.

- **Claims Made Policy:** A claims made policy covers the business based on the policy that is in force when the claim is made, regardless of when the incident occurred. In the above example, the limits in the policy in effect in 2010 would apply. Businesses with claims made policies can purchase optional "tail coverage." Tail coverage enables a business to report claims after the policy has ended for alleged injuries that occurred while the policy was in effect.

3. Commercial Vehicle Insurance

A commercial auto policy provides coverage for vehicles that are used primarily in connection with commercial establishments or business activities. The insurance pays any costs to third parties resulting from bodily injury or property damage for which the business is legally liable up to the policy limits.

While the major coverages are the same, commercial auto policies differs from a personal auto policy in a number of technical respects. They may have higher limits and/or provisions that cover rented and other non-owned vehicles, including employees' cars driven for company business. Several insurers offer business auto policies geared to owners of small businesses or specific types of businesses.

4. Workers Compensation Insurance

Employers have a legal responsibility to their employees to make the workplace safe. However, despite precautions, accidents can occur. To protect employers from lawsuits resulting from workplace accidents and to provide medical care and compensation for lost income to employees hurt in workplace accidents, in almost every state businesses are required by law to buy workers compensation insurance. Workers compensation insurance covers workers injured on the job, whether they are hurt on the workplace premises or elsewhere, or in auto accidents while on business. It also covers work-related illnesses. Workers compensation provides payments to injured workers, without regard to who was at fault in the accident, for time lost from work and for medical and rehabilitation services. It also provides death benefits to surviving spouses and dependents. Each state has different laws governing the amount and duration of lost income benefits, the provision of medical and rehabilitation services and how the system is administered. For example, in most states there are regulations that cover whether the worker or employer can choose the doctor who treats the injuries and how disputes about benefits are resolved.

Workers compensation insurance must be bought as a separate policy. In-home business and businessowners policies (BOPs) are sold as package policies but do not include coverage for workers' injuries.

Other Types of Business Coverages

The first four coverages discussed below are different types of liability insurance policies available to businesses. The fifth is a form of life insurance. There are also specialized liability policies geared to specific types of businesses.

1. Errors and Omissions Insurance/Professional Liability

Some businesses involve services such as giving advice, making recommendations, designing things, providing physical care or representing the needs of others, which can lead to being sued by customers, clients or patients claiming that the business' failure to perform a job properly has injured them. Errors and omissions or professional liability insurance covers these situations. The policy will pay any judgment for which the insured is legally liable, up to the policy limit. It also provides legal defense costs, even when there has been no wrongdoing.

2. Employment Practices Liability Insurance

Employment practices liability insurance covers, up to the policy limits, damages for which an employer is legally liable such as violating an employee's civil or other legal rights. In addition to paying a judgment for which the insured is liable, it also provides legal defense costs, which can be substantial even when there has been no wrongdoing.

3. Directors and Officers Liability Insurance

Directors and officers liability insurance protects directors and officers of corporations or nonprofit organizations if there is a lawsuit claiming they managed the business or organization without proper regard for the rights of others. The policy will pay any judgment for which the insured is legally liable, up to the policy limit. It also provides for legal defense costs, even where there has been no wrongdoing.

4. Umbrella or Excess Policies

As the name implies, an umbrella liability policy provides coverage over and above a business's other liability coverages. It is designed to protect against unusually high losses, providing protection when the policy limits of one of the underlying policies have been used up. For a typical business, an umbrella policy would provide protection beyond Its general liability and auto liability policies. If a company has employment practices liability insurance, directors and officers liability, or other types of liability insurance, the umbrella could provide protection beyond those policy limits as well. Cost depends on the nature of the business, its size, the type of risks the business faces and the ways the business implements risk reduction.

5. Key Person Life Insurance

The loss of a key person can be a major blow to a small business if that person is the founder of the business or is the key contact for customers and suppliers and the management of the business. Loss of the key person may also make the running of the business less efficient and result in a loss of capital. Losses caused by the death of a key employee are insurable. Such policies compensate the business against significant losses that result from that person's death or disability. The amount and cost of insurance needed for a particular business depends on the situation and the age, health and role of the key employee. Key employee life insurance pays a death benefit to the company when the key employee dies. The policy is normally owned by the company, which pays the premiums and is the beneficiary. The monies from key person insurance can be used to buy back shares in a company from the estate of the deceased, pay a head hunting firm to find a suitable replacement and cover costs or expenses while the business adjusts to the loss.

Package Policies

Commercial insurers sell coverages separately and/or offer policies that combine protection from most major property and liability risks in one package. Package policies are created for types of businesses that generally face the same kind and degree of risk.

1. Packages for Small Businesses

Smaller companies often purchase a package policy known as the Businessowners Policy, or BOP. A BOP is recommended for most small businesses (usually 100 employees or less), as it is often the most affordable way to obtain broad coverage. BOPs are "off the shelf" policies combining many of the basic coverages needed by a typical small business into a standard package at a premium that is generally less than would be required to purchase these coverages separately. Combining both property and liability insurance, a BOP will cover a business in the event of property damage, suspended operations, lawsuits resulting from bodily injury or property damage to others, etc. BOPs do not cover professional liability, auto insurance, workers compensation or health and disability insurance. Small businesses will need separate insurance policies to cover professional services, vehicles and employees.

2. Commercial Multiple Peril Policies
Larger companies might purchase a commercial package policy or customize their policies to meet the special risks they face. Commercial multiple peril policies, often purchased by corporations, bundle property, boiler and machinery, crime and general liability coverage together. Larger firms employee a risk manager to help determine the company's exposure to certain risks.

3. In-Home Business Policies
There are several insurance options designed to address the special needs of home businesses.

- **Homeowners Policy Endorsement:** Homeowners may be able to add a simple endorsement or rider to their existing homeowners policy to increase coverage.

- **In-Home Business Policy:** An in-home business policy provides more comprehensive coverage for business equipment and liability than a homeowners policy endorsement. Many insurance companies offer insurance policies specifically tailored to small business.

- **Businessowners Policy (BOP):** The home business might be eligible for The Businessowners Policy (BOP), see above. The key to whether a business owner is eligible for a BOP is the size of the premises, the limits of liability required, the type of commercial operation it is and the extent of its off-premises servicing and processing activities. A BOP, like an in-home business policy, covers business property and equipment, loss of income, extra expense and liability; however, the BOP provides these coverages on a much broader scale.

Life Insurance Basics

Many financial experts consider life insurance to be the cornerstone of sound financial planning. It can be an important tool in the following situations:

1. Replace Income for Dependents

If people depend on an individual's income, life insurance can replace that income if the person dies. The most common example of this is parents with young children. Insurance to replace income can be especially useful if the government- or employer-sponsored benefits of the surviving spouse or domestic partner will be reduced after he or she dies.

2. Pay Final Expenses

Life insurance can pay funeral and burial costs, probate and other estate administration costs, debts and medical expenses not covered by health insurance.

3. Create an Inheritance for Heirs

Even those with no other assets to pass on, can create an inheritance by buying a life insurance policy and naming their heirs as beneficiaries.

4. Pay Federal "Death" Taxes and State "Death" Taxes

Life insurance benefits can pay for estate taxes so that heirs will not have to liquidate other assets or take a smaller inheritance. Changes in the federal "death" tax rules through January 1, 2011 will likely lessen the impact of this tax on some people, but some states are offsetting those federal decreases with increases in their state-level estate taxes.

5. Make Significant Charitable Contributions

By making a charity the beneficiary of their life insurance policies, individuals can make a much larger contribution than if they donated the cash equivalent of the policy's premiums.

6. Create a Source of Savings

Some types of life insurance create a cash value that, if not paid out as a death benefit, can be borrowed or withdrawn on the owner's request. Since most people make paying their life insurance policy premiums a high priority, buying a cash-value type policy can create a kind of "forced" savings plan. Furthermore, the interest credited is tax deferred (and tax exempt if the money is paid as a death claim).

Types of Life Insurance

There are two major types of life insurance: term and whole life.

1. Term Life

Term insurance is the simplest form of life insurance. It pays only if death occurs during the term of the policy, which is usually from one to 30 years. Most term policies have no other benefit provisions. There are two basic types of term life insurance policies: level term and decreasing term. Level term means that the death benefit stays the same throughout the duration of the policy. Decreasing term means that the death benefit drops, usually in one-year increments, over the course of the policy's term.

2. Whole Life/Permanent Life

Whole life or permanent insurance pays a death benefit whenever the policyholder dies. There are three major types of whole life or permanent life insurance—traditional whole life, universal life, and variable universal life, and there are variations within each type.

In the case of traditional whole life, both the death benefit and the premium are designed to stay the same (level) throughout the life of the policy. The cost per $1,000 of benefit increases as the insured person ages, and it obviously gets very high when the insured lives to 80 and beyond. The insurance company keeps the premium level by charging a premium that, in the early years, is higher than what is needed to pay claims, investing that money, and then using it to supplement the level premium to help pay the cost of life insurance for older people.

By law, when these "overpayments" reach a certain amount, they must be available to the policyholder as a cash value if he or she decides not to continue with the original plan. The cash value is an alternative, not an additional, benefit under the policy. In the 1970s and 1980s, life insurance companies introduced two variations on the traditional whole life product: universal life insurance and variable universal life insurance.

Some varieties of whole life/permanent life insurance are discussed below.

- **Universal Life:** Universal life, also known as adjustable life, allows more flexibility than traditional whole life policies. The savings vehicle (called a cash value account) generally earns a money market rate of interest. After money has accumulated in the account, the policyholder will also have the option of altering premium payments—providing there is enough money in the account to cover the costs.

- **Variable Life:** Variable life policies combine death protection with a savings account that can be invested in stocks, bonds and money market mutual funds. The value of the policy may grow more quickly, but involves more risk. If investments do not perform well, the cash value and death benefit may decrease. Some policies, however, guarantee that the death benefit will not fall below a minimum level.

- **Variable Universal Life:** This type of policy combines the features of variable and universal life policies, including the investment risks and rewards characteristic of variable life insurance and the ability to adjust premiums and the death benefit that is characteristic of universal life insurance.

Annuities Basics

Annuities are financial products intended to enhance retirement security. An annuity is an agreement for one person or organization to pay another a series of payments. Usually the term "annuity" relates to a contract between an individual and a life insurance company.

There are many categories of annuities. They can be classified by:

- **Nature of the underlying investment:** fixed or variable

- **Primary purpose:** accumulation or pay-out (deferred or immediate)

- **Nature of payout commitment:** fixed period, fixed amount or lifetime

- **Tax status:** qualified or nonqualified

- **Premium payment arrangement:** single premium or flexible premium

An annuity can be classified in several of these categories at once. For example, an individual might buy a nonqualified single premium deferred variable annuity.

In general, annuities have the following features:

1. Tax Deferral on Investment Earnings

Many investments are taxed year by year, but the investment earnings—capital gains and investment income—in annuities are not taxable until the investor withdraws money. This tax deferral is also true of 401(k)s and IRAs; however, unlike these products, there are no limits on the amount one can put into an annuity. Moreover, the minimum withdrawal requirements for annuities are much more liberal than they are for 401(k)s and IRAs.

2. Protection from Creditors

People who own an immediate annuity (that is, who are receiving money from an insurance company), are afforded some protection from creditors. Generally the most that creditors can access is the payments as they are made, since the money the annuity owner gave the insurance company now belongs to the company. Some state statutes and court decisions also protect some or all of the payments from those annuities.

3. A Variety of Investment Options

Many annuity companies offer an array of investment options. For example, individuals can invest in a fixed annuity that credits a specified interest rate, similar to a bank Certificate of Deposit (CD). If they buy a variable annuity, their money can be invested in stocks, bonds or mutual funds. In recent years, annuity companies have created various types of "floors" that limit the extent of investment decline from an increasing reference point.

4. Taxfree Transfers Among Investment Options

In contrast to mutual funds and other investments made with aftertax money, with annuities there are no tax consequences if owners change how their funds are invested. This can be particularly valuable if they are using a strategy called "rebalancing," which is recommended by many financial advisors. Under rebalancing, investors shift their investments periodically to return them to the proportions that represent the risk/return combination most appropriate for the investor's situation.

5. Lifetime Income

A lifetime immediate annuity converts an investment into a stream of payments that last until the annuity owner dies. In concept, the payments come from three "pockets": The original investment, investment earnings and money from a pool of people in the investors group who do not live as long as actuarial tables forecast. The pooling is unique to annuities, and it is what enables annuity companies to be able to guarantee a lifetime income.

6. Benefits to Heirs

There is a common apprehension that if an individual starts an immediate lifetime annuity and dies soon after that, the insurance company keeps all of the investment in the annuity. To prevent this situation individuals can buy a "guaranteed period" with the immediate annuity. A guaranteed period commits the insurance company to continue payments after the owner dies to one or more designated beneficiaries; the payments continue to the end of the stated guaranteed period—usually 10 or 20 years (measured from when the owner started receiving the annuity payments). Moreover, annuity benefits that pass to beneficiaries do not go through probate and are not governed by the annuity owner's will.

Types of Annuities

There are two major types of annuities: fixed and variable. Fixed annuities guarantee the principal and a minimum rate of interest. Generally, interest credited and payments made from a fixed annuity are based on rates declared by the company, which can change only yearly. Fixed annuities are considered "general account" assets. In contrast, variable annuity account values and payments are based on the performance of a separate investment portfolio, thus their value may fluctuate daily. Variable annuities are considered "separate account" assets.

There are a variety of fixed annuities and variable annuities. One example, the equity indexed annuity, is a hybrid of the features of fixed and variable annuities. It credits a minimum rate of interest, just as other fixed annuities do, but its value is also based on the performance of a specified stock index—usually computed as a fraction of that index's total return. In December 2008 the Securities and Exchange Commission voted to reclassify indexed annuities (with some exceptions) as securities, not insurance products. Annuities can also be classified by marketing channel, in other words whether they are sold to groups or individuals.

Annuities can be deferred or immediate. Deferred annuities generally accumulate assets over a long period of time, with withdrawals usually as a single sum or as an income payment beginning at retirement. Immediate annuities allow purchasers to convert a lump sum payment into a stream of income that the policyholder begins to receive right away.

Long-Term Care Insurance Basics

Long-term care insurance pays for services to help individuals who are unable to perform certain activities of daily living without assistance, or require supervision due to a cognitive impairment such as Alzheimer's disease.

Features of Long-Term Care Policies

The best policies pay for care in a nursing home, assisted living facility, or at home. Benefits are typically expressed in daily amounts, with a lifetime maximum. Some policies pay half as much per day for at-home care as for nursing home care. Others pay the same amount, or have a "pool of benefits" that can be used as needed.

Criteria for the Beginning of Payments

The policy should state the various conditions that must be met. They can include:

1. The Inability to Perform Two or Three Specific "Activities of Daily Living" Without Help

These include bathing, dressing, eating, toileting and "transferring" or being able to move from place to place or between a bed and a chair.

2. Cognitive Impairment

Most policies cover stroke and Alzheimer's and Parkinson's disease, but other forms of mental incapacity may be excluded.

3. Medical Necessity or Certification by a Doctor that Long-Term Care is Necessary

Most policies have a "waiting period" or "elimination" period. This is a period that begins when an individual first needs long-term care and lasts as long as the policy provides. During the waiting period, the policy will not pay benefits. The policy pays only for expenses that occur after the waiting period is over, if the policyholder continues to need care. In general, the longer the waiting period, the lower the premium for the long-term care policy.

Benefit periods for long-term care may range from two years to a lifetime. Premiums can be kept down by electing coverage for three to four years—longer than the average nursing home stay—instead of a lifetime.

Most long-term care policies pay on a reimbursement (or expense-incurred) basis, up to the policy limits. In other words, if the policy has a $150 per day benefit, but the policyholder spends only $130 per day for a home long-term care provider, the policy will pay only $130. The "extra" $20 each day will, in some policies, go into a "pool" of unused funds that can be used to extend the length of time for which the policy will pay benefits. Other policies pay on an indemnity basis. Using the same example as above, an indemnity policy would pay $150 per day as long as the insured needs and receives long-term care services, regardless of the actual outlay.

Inflation protection is an important feature, especially for people under the age of 65, who are buying benefits that they may not use for 20 years or more. A good inflation provision compounds benefits at 5 percent a year. Without inflation protection, even 3 percent annual inflation will, over 24 years, reduce the purchasing power of a $150 daily benefit to the equivalent of $75.

Six Other Important Policy Provisions

1. Elimination Period

Under some policies, if the insured has qualifying long-term care expenses on one day during a seven-day period, he or she will be credited with having satisfied seven days toward the elimination period: i.e., the time between an injury and the receipt of payments. This type of provision reflects the way home care is often delivered—some days by professionals and some days by family members.

2. Guaranteed Renewable Policies

These must be renewed by the insurance company, although premiums can go up if they are increased for an entire class of policyholders.

3. Waiver of Premium

This provision ensures that no further premiums are due once the policyholder starts to receive benefits.

4. Third-Party Notification

This provision stipulates that a relative, friend or professional adviser will be notified if the policyholder forgets to pay a premium.

5. Nonforfeiture Benefits

These benefits keep a lesser amount of insurance in force if the policyholder lets the coverage lapse. This provision is required by some states.

6. Restoration of Benefits

This provision ensures that maximum benefits are put back in place if the policyholder receives benefits for a time, then recovers and goes for a specified period (typically six months) without receiving benefits.

Disability Insurance Basics

Disabling injuries affect millions of Americans each year. Disability insurance, which complements health insurance, helps replace lost income if an individual is unable to work due to a disability.

There are three basic ways to replace income.

1. Employer-Paid Disability Insurance

This is required in most states. Most employers provide some short-term sick leave. Many larger employers provide long-term disability coverage as well, typically with benefits of up to 60 percent of salary lasting for a period of up to five years until the age of 65, and in some cases extended for life.

2. Social Security Disability Benefits

This is paid to workers whose disability is expected to last at least 12 months and is so severe that no gainful employment can be expected.

3. Individual Disability Income Insurance Policies

Other limited replacement income is available for workers under some circumstances from workers compensation (if the injury or illness is job-related), auto insurance (if disability results from an auto accident) and the Department of Veterans Affairs. For most workers, even those with some employer-paid coverage, an individual disability income policy is the best way to ensure adequate income in the event of disability. Workers who buy a private disability income policy can expect to replace from 50 percent to 70 percent of income. Disability benefits paid out on individual disability policies are not taxed; benefits from employer-paid policies are subject to income tax.

Types of Disability Insurance

There are two types of disability policies: Short-term disability and Long-term disability. Short-term policies have a waiting period of 0 to 14 days with a maximum benefit period of no longer than two years. Long-term policies have a waiting period of several weeks to several months with a maximum benefit period ranging from a few years to a lifetime.

Disability policies have two different protection features: noncancelable and guaranteed renewable. Noncancelable means that the policy cannot be canceled by the insurance company, except for nonpayment of premiums. This gives the policyholder the right to renew the policy every year without an increase in the premium or a reduction in benefits. Guaranteed renewable gives the policyholder the right to renew the policy with the same benefits and not have the policy canceled by the company. However, the insurer has the right to increase premiums as long as it does so for all other policyholders in the same rating class.

There are several options and factors to consider when purchasing a disability policy.

1. Additional Purchase Options
The insurance company gives the policyholder the right to buy additional insurance at a later time.

2. Coordination of Benefits
The amount of benefits policyholders receive from their insurance companies is dependent on other benefits they receive because of the disability. The policy specifies a target amount the policyholder will receive from all the policies combined and will make up the difference not paid by other policies.

3. Cost of Living Adjustment (COLA)
The COLA increases disability benefits over time based on the increased cost of living measured by the Consumer Price Index. Policyholders will pay a higher premium if they select the COLA.

4. Residual or Partial Disability Rider
This provision allows workers to return to work part-time, collecting part of their salaries and receiving a partial disability payment if they are still partially disabled.

5. Return of Premium
This provision requires the insurance company to refund part of the premium if no claims are made for a specific period of time declared in the policy.

6. Waiver of Premium Provision
This clause means that the policyholder does not have to pay premiums on the policy after he or she is disabled for 90 days.

Factors Affecting the Choice of a Disability Policy

1. Definition of Disability
Some policies pay benefits if workers are unable to perform the customary duties of their own occupation. Others pay only if workers are unable to perform any job suitable for their level of education and experience. Some policies define disability in terms of workers' occupations for an initial period of two or three years and then continue to pay benefits only if they are unable to perform any occupation. "Own occupation" policies are more desirable, but more expensive.

2. Benefit Period

The benefit period is the amount of time policyholders will receive monthly benefits during their lifetimes. Experts usually recommend that the policy pay benefits until at least age 65, at which point Social Security disability will take over. Young people may consider buying a policy offering lifetime benefits because it will still be relatively inexpensive.

3. Replacement Percentage

A policy that will replace from 60 percent to 70 percent of total taxable earnings is advisable. A higher replacement percentage, if available, is more expensive. Other sources of income should be evaluated before deciding how much disability coverage is needed.

4. Coverage for Disability Resulting from Either Accidental Injury or Illness

An accident-only policy is less expensive but does not provide adequate protection. Ideally, both accident and illness coverage should be purchased.

5. A Cost-of-Living Increase in Benefits

Policies may not pay benefits for a decade or more and should keep pace with increases in the cost of living. (Some companies also offer "indexed" benefits, keeping pace with inflation after benefit payments begin.)

6. A Policy Paying "Residual" or Partial Benefits

This type of policy is available so that people can work part-time and still receive a benefit making up for lost income. A standard feature in some policies, and added by a rider to others, a residual benefits policy pays partial benefits based on loss of income without an initial period of total disability.

7. Transition Benefits

Offered by some companies, it can offset financial loss during a post-disability period of rebuilding a business or professional practice.

8. Ongoing Coverage

A noncancelable policy will continue in-force as long as the premiums are paid; neither the benefit nor the premium can change. A guaranteed renewable policy keeps the same benefits but may cost more over time since the insurer can increase the premium if it is increased for an entire class of policyholders.

9. Financial Stability

Check the financial stability of insurers through an agent or a ratings firm.

These Topics are adapted from papers
regularly updated at www.iii.org/issues_updates.

Captives and Other Risk-Financing Options

Traditionally, businesses and other organizations have handled risk by transferring it to an insurance company through the purchase of an insurance policy or, alternatively, by retaining the risk and allocating funds to meet expected losses through an arrangement known as "self insurance," in which firms retain rather than transfer risk.

During the liability crisis of the 1980s, when businesses had trouble obtaining some types of commercial insurance coverage, new mechanisms for transferring risk developed, facilitated by passage of the Product Liability Risk Retention Act of 1981. These so-called alternative risk transfer (ART) arrangements blend risk transfer and risk retention mechanisms and, together with self insurance, form the alternative market.

Captives—a special type of insurance company set up by a parent company, trade association or group of companies to insure the risks of its owner or owners—and risk-retention groups—in which entities in a common industry join together to provide members with liability insurance—were the first mechanisms to appear. Other options, including risk retention pools and large deductible plans, a form of self insurance, followed.

ART products, such as catastrophe bonds, weather derivatives and microinsurance programs are also emerging as an alternative to traditional insurance and reinsurance products.

Alternative Market Mechanisms

I. Captives

Wholly owned captives are companies set up by large corporations to finance or administer their risk financing needs. If such a captive insures only the risks of its parent or subsidiaries it is called a "pure" captive.

Captives may be established to provide insurance to more than one entity. An association or group of companies may band together to form a captive to provide insurance coverage. Professionals—doctors, lawyers, accountants—have formed many captives over the years. Captives may, in turn, use a variety of reinsurance mechanisms to provide the coverage. In particular, many offshore captives use a "fronting" insurer to provide the basic insurance policy. Fronting typically means that underwriting, claims and administrative functions are handled in the United States by an experienced commercial insurance company, since a captive generally will not want to get involved directly in running the insurance operation. Also, fronting allows a company to show it has an insurance policy with a U.S.-licensed insurance company, which it may need to do for legal and business reasons.

The rent-a-captive concept was introduced in Bermuda 20 years ago and remains a popular alternative market mechanism. Rent-a-captives serve businesses that are unable to capitalize a captive but are willing to assume a portion of their own risk and share in the underwriting profits and investment income. Generally sponsored by insurers or reinsurers, which essentially "rent out" their capital for a fee, the mechanism allows users to obtain some of the advantages of a captive without having the expense of setting up a single parent captive and meeting minimum capital and surplus requirements.

Captives have been expanding into the employee benefits arena since 2003, the year in which the Department of Labor gave final approval to Archer Daniels Midland Co.'s plan to use its Vermont captive to reinsure group life insurance benefits.

While the leading domicile for captives in the U.S. is Vermont, offshore captives covering U.S. risks are predominantly located in Bermuda, where they enjoy tax advantages and relative freedom from regulation. The Cayman Islands, Guernsey, the British Virgin Islands, Luxembourg and Barbados are also significant centers for captives. Vermont is the leading domicile for captives in the United States.

II. Self Insurance

Self insurance can be undertaken by single companies wishing to retain risk or by entities in similar industries or geographic locations that pool resources to insure each other's risks.

The use of higher retentions/deductibles is increasing in most lines of insurance. In workers compensation many companies are opting to retain a larger portion of their exposure through policies with large deductible amounts of $100,000 or higher. Large deductible programs, which were first introduced in 1989, now account for a sizable portion of the market.

III. Risk Retention Groups

A risk retention group (RRG) is a corporation owned and operated by its members. It must be chartered and licensed as a liability insurance company under the laws of at least one state. The group can then write insurance in all other states. It need not obtain a license in a state other than its chartering states.

IV. Risk Purchasing Groups

Like risk retention groups (RRGs), purchasing groups must be made up of persons or entities with like exposures and in a common business. However, whereas RRGs are liability insurance companies owned by their members, purchasing groups purchase liability coverage for their members from admitted insurers, surplus lines carriers or RRGs. Laws in some states prohibit insurers from giving groups formed to purchase insurance advantages over individuals. However, purchasing groups are not subject to so-called "fictitious group" laws, which require a group to have been in existence for a certain period of time or require a group to have a certain minimum number of members. The Risk Retention Act of 1986 specifically provided for purchasing groups to be created to purchase liability insurance for members of the sponsoring groups.

V. Catastrophe Bonds and other Alternative Risk Transfer (ART) Products

A number of alternative risk transfer (ART) products, such as insurance-linked securities and weather derivatives have developed to meet the financial risk transfer needs of businesses. One such product, catastrophe (cat) bonds, risk-based securities sold via the capital markets, developed in the wake of hurricanes Andrew and Iniki in 1992 and the Northridge earthquake in 1994—mega-catastrophes that resulted in a global shortage of reinsurance (insurance for insurers) for such disasters. Tapping into the capital markets allowed insurers to diversify their risk and expand the amount of insurance available in catastrophe-prone areas. Zurich Financial's Kamp Re was the first major catastrophe bond to be triggered. The $190 million bond was triggered by 2005's Hurricane Katrina, and resulted in a total loss of principal. Catastrophe bonds are now a multibillion dollar industry.

Catastrophes: Insurance Issues

The term "catastrophe" in the property insurance industry denotes a natural or man-made disaster that is unusually severe. An event is designated a catastrophe by the industry when claims are expected to reach a certain dollar threshold, currently set at $25 million, and more than a certain number of policyholders and insurance companies are affected.

The magnitude of the damage caused by Katrina and the potential damage Hurricane Rita might have caused had it not weakened from an intense Category 5 hurricane has triggered a reexamination, not just among insurers and reinsurers but also among public policy and political leaders, of how the United States deals with the financial consequences of such massive property damage and personal loss.

Disaster losses along the coast are likely to escalate in the coming years, in part because of huge increases in development. One catastrophe modeling company predicts that catastrophe losses will double every decade or so due to growing residential and commercial density and more expensive buildings. Data from the Census Bureau, collected by USA Today, show that in 2006, 34.9 million people were seriously threatened by Atlantic hurricanes, compared with 10.2 million in 1950. Before the 2005 hurricane season, Hurricane Andrew ranked as the single most costly U.S. natural disaster.

Man-made catastrophes such as the attacks on the World Trade Center can also cause huge losses. The attacks led Congress to pass the Terrorism Risk Insurance Act (TRIA) in November 2002. Since then, TRIA has been reauthorized twice. The latest reauthorization, passed at the end of 2007, extends the law to 2014. TRIA provides a federal backstop for commercial insurance losses from terrorist acts, making it easier for insurers to calculate their maximum losses for such a catastrophe and thus to underwrite the coverage, see the topic on Terrorism Risk and Insurance.

The typical homeowners insurance policy covers damage from a fire, windstorms, hail, riots and explosions—as well as other types of loss such as theft and the cost of living elsewhere while the structure is being repaired or rebuilt after being damaged. Commercial property insurance policies generally cover the same causes of loss with some variation, depending on the coverages selected. Flood and earthquake damage are excluded under homeowners policies—separate policies are available—but are covered under the comprehensive portion of the standard auto policy, which more than 75 percent of drivers who buy auto liability insurance purchase.

The insurance industry tracks catastrophes to monitor claim costs, assigning a number to each catastrophe. Each claim arising from the event is tagged so that total industrywide losses can be tabulated. The term catastrophe is often used in the property insurance industry in a narrow way to mean a catastrophic event that exceeds a dollar threshold in claims payouts. This figure has changed over the years with inflation and the increase in development of areas subject to natural disasters. Starting in 1997 the catastrophe definition was raised from $5 million to $25 million in insured damage.

There have been four catastrophes that fall into the megacatastrophe category, greatly exceeding the $25 million threshold. The first two, Hurricane Andrew (1992) and the Northridge earthquake (1994), were both watershed events in that they were far more destructive than most experts had predicted a disaster of this type would be. The third, the terrorist attack on the World Trade Center in 2001, altered insurers' attitudes about man-made risks worldwide. Hurricane Katrina (2005), the fourth catastrophe, is not only the most expensive natural disaster on record but also an event that intensified discussion nationwide about the way disasters, natural and man-made, are managed. It also focused attention on the federal flood insurance program, see the topic on Flood Insurance.

Cellphones and Driving

Increased reliance on cellphones has led to a rise in the number of people who use the devices while driving. There are two dangers associated with driving and cellphone use, including text messaging. First, drivers must take their eyes off the road while dialing. Second, people can become so absorbed in their conversations that their ability to concentrate on the act of driving is severely impaired, jeopardizing the safety of vehicle occupants and pedestrians. Since the first law was passed in New York in 2001 banning hand-held cellphone use while driving, there has been debate as to the exact nature and degree of hazard. The latest research shows that while using a cellphone when driving may not be the most dangerous distraction, because it is so prevalent it is by far the most common distraction in crashes and near crashes.

Research: Studies about cellphone use while driving have focused on several different aspects of the problem. Some have looked at its prevalence as the leading cause of driver distraction. Others have looked at the different risks associated with hand-held and hands-free devices. Still others have focused on the seriousness of injuries in crashes involving cellphone users and the demographics of drivers who use cellphones. Of increasing concern is the practice of texting.

In January 2010 the National Safety Council (NSC) released a report that estimates that at least 1.6 million crashes (28 percent of all crashes) are caused each year by drivers talking on cellphones (1.4 million crashes) and texting (200,000 crashes). The estimate is based on data of driver cellphone use from the National Highway Traffic Safety Administration and from peer-reviewed research that quantifies the risks using cellphones and texting while driving.

In July 2009 Virginia Tech Transportation Institute released a study showing that the risk of texting while driving is far greater than previous estimates showed and far exceeds the hazards associated with other driving distractions. Researchers used cameras in the cabs of trucks traveling long distances over a period of 18 months and found that the collision risk became 23 times higher when the drivers were texting. The research also measured the time drivers stopped looking at the road and used their eyes to send or receive texts. Drivers generally spent nearly five seconds looking at their devices before a crash or near crash, a period long enough for a vehicle to travel more than 100 yards at typical highway speeds.

Climate Change: Insurance Issues

There is now a consensus among the scientific community that the climate is changing, with potential risk to the global economy, ecology, and human health and well being. But how much of this is due to natural phenomena and how much to the effects of human activity is a matter of debate. Also unknown is the extent to which weather patterns have already been affected.

As assumers of risk, insurers seek to mitigate potential losses every day through a process known as risk management. Since climate change could lead to losses on a scale never before experienced, insurers are not waiting for researchers to produce all the answers. A 2009 report by Ceres, a network of companies concerned about global warming, identified some 244 insurance-related organizations in 29 countries that were working in 2008 to find solutions to the threat posed by greenhouse gas emissions, up from 190 groups in 26 countries in 2007. Insurers are also redoubling their efforts in the more traditional areas of risk management, including alerting policyholders to the potential for lawsuits for failure to protect against or disclose possible harm to the environment.

Meanwhile, society's concern about climate change offers insurers new avenues for leadership and new opportunities for innovative products.

Global Warming: When fossil fuels—coal, oil and natural gas—are burned to produce energy, so-called greenhouse gases, largely carbon dioxide, are emitted into the atmosphere where they trap heat. Forests and oceans can absorb some of the carbon. But to avoid the most catastrophic effects of what is predicted to occur, researchers say, carbon emissions must be greatly reduced, hence the push to reduce overall energy use, boost the use of energy from renewable sources such as solar heat and curb the use of paper and other products made from trees, which absorb carbon dioxide in the process of photosynthesis.

Global warming has the potential to affect most segments of the insurance business, including life insurance if rising temperatures lead to an up-tick in death rates. Property losses of all kinds are most likely to increase, and there is the potential for much higher commercial liability losses if shareholders and consumers try to hold businesses responsible for changes to the environment.

Insurers' Contribution to Lowering Greenhouse Gases: Insurers, like companies in other industries, are promoting strategies to lower greenhouse gas emissions. Some insurers have been warning public policy leaders and the general public about the threat of climate change for years, and others were among the first to adopt public statements on the environment and climate change and to join business coalitions calling on the federal government to enact legislation to reduce greenhouse gases. Some, particularly reinsurers, are sponsoring research and working with others interested in the same kind of solutions, such as finding ways for individuals and society to adapt to extreme weather, particularly in developing countries.

Many insurance companies are committed to reducing their own total greenhouse gas emissions and offsetting the remainder through contributions to reforestation and renewable energy projects. They also encourage their employees to adopt "green" policies in their private lives. Some were involved in projects to reduce greenhouse gases even before such efforts gained widespread public attention, and many are now reinforcing their policyholders' desire to reduce their carbon footprints by offering them paperless billing and documentation. Some have upgraded the quality of their Web sites to encourage policyholders to transact business electronically. At least one auto insurer sells policies exclusively online.

Insurers are also working on another front: seeking to reduce the incidence and cost of property damage caused by those events that still occur, despite society's best efforts to reduce greenhouse gases.

New Products and Business Opportunities: Without insurance the economy could not function. Insurers essentially enable new products and services to be created by assuming the risk of loss. Just as they quickly adapted existing liability insurance policies for horse-drawn carriages, or teams of horses, to automobiles towards the end of the nineteenth century, so they are responding to climate change initiatives at the beginning of the twenty-first century.

Opportunities exist on several fronts. First, there are new risks to insure, including new industries such as wind farms and other alternative fuel facilities, and emerging financial risks such as those involved in carbon trading. Insurance policies related to carbon trading protect those that invest in clean technology projects against failure of the project to deliver the agreed-upon emission rights. A number of companies are also offering their clients carbon project risk management consulting services. A carbon credit permits the holder to emit one ton of carbon. The Kyoto Protocol and other cap and trade systems now under discussion set ceilings for carbon output and allow those that produce less than the limit to sell credits to those that exceed it. Investors in clean technology projects such as reforestation and renewable energy buy the rights to credits and sell them in the international carbon trading market. Among the risks associated with purchasing carbon trading rights is that the technology/project designed to reduce carbon emissions will not meet expectations or that the company will become insolvent before it is able to fulfill its contract, leaving the investor without the necessary carbon offsets.

Second, the need to curb global warming has spurred the creation of insurance policies that provide incentives to policyholders to contribute to these efforts. These include discounts on auto insurance policies for owning a hybrid car and for driving fewer miles and policies for green building construction.

Auto Insurance Initiatives: Motor vehicles account for more than 25 percent of all U.S. greenhouse gas emissions. Insurance policies such as pay-as-you-drive, which factors mileage driven into the price of insurance, and hybrid car discounts could reduce that amount by more than 10 percent if broadly implemented, according to Ceres, a network of companies concerned about global warming. A study by the Brookings Institution suggests that if drivers paid by the mile, driving would drop by about 8 percent.

There are two ways to reduce the greenhouse gas emissions associated with driving. One is to encourage people to purchase vehicles that emit less carbon dioxide into the environment and get more miles per gallon of gasoline. A number of companies offer discounts to people who drive hybrid vehicles— some believe that people who are socially responsible are also more responsible behind the wheel. The other way is to reward people for driving fewer miles, known as pay-as-you-drive (PAYD) auto insurance. Several insurers have developed technology-based discount programs that provide financial incentives to drive fewer miles. Mileage information comes from a special device. In some, it is linked to the car's odometer and in others it is a wireless sensor that can monitor speed as well as mileage. These programs are offered in a growing number of states. In addition, California and several other states are encouraging the development of PAYD programs.

Insurers are helping to promote sustainable building practices by offering green homeowners and commercial property policies. In addition, they are responding to the growing demand for assistance with energy and emissions-reduction projects with risk management services that address global warming.

"Green" Building Insurance Coverage: Increasingly, homeowners at the leading edge of the environmental sustainability movement are generating their own geothermal, solar or wind power and selling any surplus energy back to the local power grid. Several insurers are supporting this trend by offering a homeowners policy that covers both the income lost when there is a power outage from a covered peril and the extra expense to the homeowner of buying electricity from another source. Policies generally cover the cost of getting back online, such as utility charges for inspection and reconnection.

Some insurers offer homeowners insurance policies that, in the event of a fire or other disaster, allow policyholders to rebuild to environmentally responsible "green" standards, even if they had not purchased such a policy originally. Green standards, part of the sustainability movement, include energy conservation benchmarks and the use of renewable construction materials. The Green Building Council introduced its Leadership in Energy and Environmental Design (LEED) certification program in 2001. According to Ceres, buildings account for more than one-third of greenhouse gas emissions and green building practices can reduce energy use and emissions by more than 50 percent.

With green commercial building construction expected to rise significantly over the next few years, a growing number of insurers are offering green commercial property insurance policies and endorsements, some of which are directed at specific segments of the business community such as manufacturers. The first green commercial policy was introduced in 2006.

In general, the policies allow building owners to replace damaged buildings, whether or not they are already certified green, with green alternatives including energy efficient electrical equipment and interior lighting, water conserving plumbing, and nontoxic and low odor paints and carpeting. They also may pay for engineering inspections of heating, ventilation, air conditioning systems, building recertification fees, the replacement of vegetative or plant covered roofs and debris recycling. Some cover the income lost and costs incurred when alternative energy generating equipment is damaged.

Credit Scoring

The goal of every insurance company is to correlate rates for insurance policies as closely as possible with the actual cost of claims. If insurers set rates too high they will lose market share to competitors who have more accurately matched rates to expected costs. If they set rates too low they will lose money. This continuous search for accuracy is good for consumers as well as insurance companies. The majority of consumers benefit because they are not subsidizing people who are worse insurance risks—people who are more likely to file claims than they are.

The computerization of data has brought more accuracy, speed and efficiency to businesses of all kinds. In the insurance arena, credit information has been used for decades to help underwriters decide whether to accept or reject applications for insurance. New advances in information technology have led to the development of insurance scores, which enable insurers to better assess the risk of future claims.

An insurance score is a numerical ranking based on a person's credit history. Actuarial studies show that how a person manages his or her financial affairs, which is what an insurance score indicates, is a good predictor of insurance claims. Insurance scores are used to help insurers differentiate between lower and higher insurance risks and thus charge a premium equal to the risk they are assuming. Statistically, people who have a poor insurance score are more likely to file a claim.

Insurance scores do not include data on race or income because insurers do not collect this information from applicants for insurance.

The Poor Economy Has Not Had a Negative Impact on Credit Scores:
According to an April 2009 Property Casualty Insurers of America (PCI) release, the recent economic downturn did not have the negative effect on credit scores that some people predicted. Major consumer credit reporting agencies such as Fair Isaac and TransUnion have reported that average scores remain steady or have improved, possibly because consumers are saving more and paying off debt. Despite the economy and credit crisis, no state has made regulatory changes to insurers' use of insurance scores, PCI notes.

Federal Activities: The Federal Trade Commission (FTC) has asked nine of the largest homeowners insurance companies to provide information that it says will allow it to determine how consumer credit data are used by the companies in underwriting and rate setting. The Fair and Accurate Credit Transactions Act, passed in 2003, directed the FTC to consult with the Office of Fair Housing and

Equal Opportunity on how the use of credit information may affect the availability and affordability of property/casualty insurance, whether the use of certain factors by credit scoring systems could have a disparate impact on minorities and, if so, whether the computer models used could be modified to produce
comparable results with less negative impact. The study is expected to be final-
ized sometime 2010.

In a similar study, the FTC found that auto insurers' use of insurance credit
scores leads to more accurate underwriting of auto insurance policies in that
there is a correlation between insurance scores and the likelihood of filing an
insurance claim. The FTC report, Credit-Based Insurance Scores: Impacts on
Consumers of Automobile Insurance, released in July 2007, also states that
credit scores cannot easily be used as a proxy for race and ethnic origin. In other
words, credit scoring predicted risk for members of minority groups in much the
same way that it predicted risk for members of nonminority groups.

The Fair and Accurate Credit Transaction Act of 2003 directed the FTC to
address the issue of whether the use of credit had a disparate impact on the
availability and affordability of insurance for minorities. Based on a poll of consumers, the General Accountability Office has recommended that the Treasury
and FTC take steps to improve consumers' understanding of credit scoring and
how credit histories are used, targeting in particular those with less education
and less experience in obtaining credit.

The Federal Reserve also studied the use of credit scoring. Although looking
at credit scoring to quantify risk posed by a borrower rather than an applicant
for insurance or a policyholder, the Federal Reserve said in a report issued at the
end of August 2007 that credit scores were predictive of credit risk and were not
proxies or substitutes for race ethnicity or gender, underscoring the FTC study.

Insurance Scores: Insurance scores are confidential rankings based on credit
history information. They are a measure of how a person manages his or her
financial affairs. People who manage their finances well tend to also manage
other important aspects of their lives responsibly, such as driving a car. Combined with factors such as geographical area, previous crashes, age and gender,
insurance scores enable auto insurers to price more accurately, so that people
less likely to file a claim pay less for their insurance than people who are more
likely to file a claim. For homeowners insurance, insurers use other factors combined with credit such as the home's construction, location and proximity to
water supplies for fighting fires.

Insurance scores predict the average claim behavior of a group of people
with essentially the same credit history. A good score is typically above 760 and

a bad score is below 600. People with low insurance scores tend to file more claims. But there are exceptions. Within that group, there may be individuals who have stellar driving records and have never filed a claim just as there are teenager drivers who have never had a crash although teenagers as a group have more accidents than people in other age groups.

Credit Report Information—Who Wants It? It is becoming increasingly important to have an acceptable credit record. Whether we like it or not, society equates the ability to manage credit responsibly with responsible behavior, even if individuals have a bad credit record through no fault of their own. Landlords often look at applicants' credit records before renting apartments to see whether they manage their finances responsibly and are therefore likely to pay their rent on time. Banks and other lenders look at the credit records of loan applicants to find out whether they are likely to have loans repaid. Some employers also look at credit records, especially where employees handle money, and view a good credit record as a measure of maturity and stability.

In some insurance companies, underwriters have long used credit records in cases where additional information was needed. Before the development of automated scoring systems, underwriters would look at the data and make decisions, often erring on the overly cautious side that disadvantaged many more people. Automated insurance scoring and underwriting systems eliminate the weaknesses inherent in someone's personal judgment and have allowed more drivers to be placed in preferred and standard rating classifications, saving them money. With the development of these scoring models, the use of credit-related information in underwriting and rating for many insurers has become routine. Insurers use insurance scores to different extents and in different ways. Most use them to screen new applicants for insurance and price new business.

Why Insurers Need It: Insurers need to be able to assess the risk of loss—the possibility that a driver or a homeowner will have an accident and file a claim—in order to decide whether to insure that individual and what rate to set for the coverage provided. The more accurate the information, the closer the insurance company can come to making appropriate decisions. Where information is insufficient, applicants for insurance may be placed in the wrong risk classification. That means that some good drivers will pay more than they should for coverage and some bad drivers will pay less than they should. The insurance company will probably collect enough premiums between the two groups to pay claims and expenses, but the good drivers will be subsidizing the bad.

By law in every state, insurers are prohibited from setting rates that unfairly discriminate against any individual. But the underwriting and rating processes are geared specifically to differentiate good risks from bad risks. Since insurance is a business, insurers favor those applicants that are least likely to suffer a loss. One of the key competitive aspects of the personal lines insurance business is the ability to segment risks and price policies accurately according to the likely cost of claims generated by those policies. Insurance scores help insurers accomplish these objectives.

Earthquakes: Risk and Insurance Issues

An earthquake is a sudden and rapid shaking of the earth caused by the breaking and shifting of rock beneath the earth's surface. This shaking can sometimes trigger landslides, avalanches, flash floods, fires and tsunamis. Unlike other natural disasters such as hurricanes, there are no specific seasons for earthquakes.

Earthquakes in the United States are not covered under standard homeowners or business insurance policies. Coverage is usually available for earthquake damage in the form of an endorsement to a home or business insurance policy. However, insurers that do not sell earthquake insurance may still be impacted by these catastrophes due to losses from fire following a quake. These losses could involve claims for business interruption and additional living expenses as well. Cars and other vehicles are covered for earthquake damage under the comprehensive part of the auto insurance policy.

In the United States about 5,000 quakes strike each year. Since 1900, earthquakes have occurred in 39 states and caused damage in all 50. One of the worst catastrophes in U.S. history, the San Francisco Earthquake of 1906, would have caused insured losses of $96 billion, were the quake to hit under current economic and demographic conditions, according to AIR Worldwide.

The potential cost of earthquakes has been growing because of increasing urban development in seismically active areas and the vulnerability of older buildings, which may not have been built or upgraded to current building codes.

The Northridge earthquake, which struck Southern California on January 17, 1994, was the most costly quake in U.S. history, causing an estimated $20 billion in total property damage, including $12.5 billion in insured losses. In its wake the California Earthquake Authority (CEA) was created in 1996. Fearing insolvency from another massive earthquake, the vast majority of insurers in the state's homeowners insurance market had severely restricted or ceased writing coverage altogether after Northridge. To ensure the availability of homeowners coverage and end a serious threat to the vitality of the state's housing market, the California Legislature established the CEA as a publicly managed, largely privately funded entity.

Only about 12 percent of Californians now purchase earthquake coverage, down from about 30 percent in 1996 when the devastating 1994 Northridge quake was still fresh in people's minds. To encourage more Californians to buy the coverage, the CEA, approved an average 22 percent rate cut, which went into effect July 1, 2006. The CEA says that a sharp drop in the cost of reinsurance and several years without a major quake, allowing the buildup reserves, made the cut possible.

Losses from Major Recent Earthquakes: At the beginning of 2010 there were two major earthquakes: a 7.0 magnitude quake in Haiti in January and a 8.8 magnitude quake in Chile in February. The Haiti quake killed over 220,000 people and caused $8 billion dollars in damages, most of it uninsured. The Chile quake, though more powerful, was far less deadly as its epicenter was located in a region with relatively low population density and because Chile's history of damaging quakes has led to strict building codes. The Chile quake and its associated tsunami caused over $4 billion in insured losses and more than $20 billion in total damages (including insured and uninsured losses), according to Munich Re. It caused about 500 deaths.

Financial and Market Conditions

Many forces affect the price, availability and security of the insurance product. Some are external, such as the state of the economy, changes in interest rates and the stock market, regulatory activity, the number and severity of natural disasters, growth in litigation and rising medical costs. Others are internal, such as the level of competition.

Fortunately, insurance companies run their businesses conservatively, as if every day might bring some new disaster, so despite current economic and financial conditions, the industry has been able to function normally. Unlike banks, insurers are not highly leveraged (they generally do not borrow to make investments or to pay claims); they limit the amount of risk they assume to the capital they have on hand; and because they do not sell the risks they assume to another party—they have some "skin in the game"—they must underwrite carefully or suffer the consequences.

The insurance industry is cyclical. Rates and profits fluctuate depending on the phase of the cycle, particularly in commercial coverages. The profitability cycle may be somewhat different for different types of insurance.

The cycle of the early and mid-1980s was among the most severe that the industry has experienced. That cycle centered on liability insurance. The most recent hard market began early in about 2001 and peaked in early 2004. The industry has been experiencing a soft market due to the poor economy. While there had been some indication that rates were flattening out, industry analysts expect to soft market to continue well into 2010.

The Insurance Cycle: The property/casualty insurance industry has exhibited cyclical behavior for many years, as far back as the 1920s. These cycles are characterized by periods of rising rates leading to increased profitability. Following a period of solid but not spectacular rates of return, the industry enters a down phase where prices soften, supply of insurance becomes plentiful and, eventually, profitability diminishes or vanishes completely. In the cycle's down phase, as results deteriorate, the basic ability of insurance companies to underwrite new business or, for some companies even to renew some existing policies, can be impaired because the capital needed to support the underwriting of risk has been depleted through losses. Cycles vary in their severity.

The insurance industry cycle is not unlike the cycle that occurs in agriculture, for example, in the wheat and beef markets. Demand for the product in both industries is relatively stable and is relatively unresponsive to price changes, while supply can vary from year to year. This means that when supply increases, lowering the price will not instantly "clear" the market of excess supply. If the price of auto insurance is cut in half, people will still buy only one policy, although they may increase the amount of coverage they purchase.

In the 1950s and 1960s cycles were regular, with a three-year period of soft pricing followed by a three-year period of hard pricing in practically all lines of property/casualty insurance. In the 1970s and 1980s, there were only two cycles, one mainly affecting auto insurance in the mid-1970s and the other in the mid-1980s, affecting commercial liability insurance. The commercial liability insurance cycle gave rise to the "liability crisis," when certain types of commercial liability coverages, such as insurance for daycare centers, municipalities, ski resorts and any establishment selling liquor, became difficult to obtain. Since that time, with the exception of the difficulty in obtaining medical malpractice insurance in the early part of the last decade, the insurance cycle has had less of an impact on the public.

Flood Insurance

Because of frequent flooding of the Mississippi River during the 1960s and the rising cost of taxpayer funded disaster relief for flood victims, in 1968 Congress created the National Flood Insurance Program (NFIP). It has three mandates: to provide residential and commercial insurance coverage for flood damage, to improve floodplain management and to develop maps of flood hazard zones.

While the comprehensive section of an auto insurance policy covers flood damage to vehicles, there is no coverage for flooding in standard homeowners, renters or commercial property insurance policies. It is available in a separate policy from the NFIP and from a few private insurers. Despite efforts to publicize this, many people exposed to the risk of floods still fail to purchase flood insurance.

It was the widespread flooding associated with Hurricane Katrina in 2005 that drew attention to the NFIP and set in motion debate about how to improve it. So far, Congress has not taken steps to significantly revamp the program.

Federal flood insurance is only available where local governments have adopted adequate flood plain management regulations for their floodplain areas as set out by NFIP. About 20,400 communities across the country participate in the program. NFIP coverage is also available outside of the high-hazard areas.

The NFIP law was amended in 1969 to provide coverage for mudslides and again in 1973. Until then, the purchase of flood insurance had been voluntary, with only about one million policies in force. The 1973 amendment put constraints on the use of federal funds in high-risk floodplains, a measure that was expected to lead to almost universal flood coverage in these zones. The law prohibits lenders that are federally regulated, supervised or insured by federal agencies from lending money on a property in a floodplain zone when a community is participating in the NFIP, unless the property is covered by flood insurance.

Legislation was enacted in 1994 to tighten enforcement of flood insurance requirements. Regulators can now fine banks with a pattern of failure to enforce the law and lenders can purchase flood insurance on behalf of homeowners who fail to buy it themselves, then bill them for coverage. The law includes a provision that denies federal disaster aid to people who have been flooded twice and have failed to purchase insurance after the first flood.

Buildings constructed in a floodplain after a community has met regulations must conform to elevation requirements. When repair, reconstruction or improvement to an older building equals or exceeds 50 percent of its market value, the structure must be updated to conform to current building codes. A 2007 NFIP study on the benefits of elevating buildings showed that due to significantly lower premiums homeowners can usually recover the higher construction costs in less than five years for homes built in a "velocity" zone, where the structure is likely to be subject to wave damage, and in five to 15 years in a standard flood zone. The Federal Emergency Management Agency (FEMA) estimates that buildings constructed to NFIP standards suffer about 80 percent less damage annually that those not built in compliance.

How It Works: The NFIP is administered by FEMA, now part of the Department of Homeland Security. Flood insurance was initially only available through insurance agents who dealt directly with the federal program. The "direct" policy program has been supplemented since 1983 with a private/public cooperative arrangement, known as "Write Your Own," through which a pool of insurance companies issue policies and adjust flood claims on behalf of the federal government under their own names, charging the same premium as the direct program. Participating insurers receive an expense allowance for policies written and claims processed. The federal government retains responsibility for underwriting losses. Today, most policies are issued through the Write-Your-Own program but some nonfederally backed coverage is available from the private market.

The NFIP is expected to be self-supporting (i.e., premiums are set at an actuarially sound level) in an average loss year, as reflected in past experience. In an extraordinary year, as Hurricane Katrina demonstrated, losses can greatly exceed premiums, leaving the NFIP with a huge debt to the U.S. Treasury that it is unlikely to be able to pay back. Hurricane Katrina losses and the percentage of flood damage that was uninsured led to calls for a revamping of the entire flood program.

As with other types of insurance, rates for flood insurance are based on the degree of risk. FEMA assesses flood risk for all the participating communities, resulting in the publication of thousands of individual flood rate maps. High-risk areas are known as Special Flood Hazard Areas, or SFHAs.

Flood plain maps are redrawn periodically, removing some properties previously designated as high hazard and adding new ones. New technology enables flood mitigation programs to more accurately pinpoint areas vulnerable to flooding. As development in and around flood plains increases, run off patterns can change, causing flooding in areas that were formerly not considered high risk and vice versa.

People tend to underestimate the risk of flooding. The highest-risk areas (Zone A) have an annual flood risk of 1 percent and a 26 percent chance of flooding over the lifetime of a 30-year mortgage, compared with a 9 percent risk of fire over the same period. In addition, people who live in areas adjacent to high-risk zones may still be exposed to floods on occasion. Ninety percent of all natural disasters in this country involve flooding, the NFIP says. Since the inception of the federal program, some 25 to 30 percent of all paid losses were for damage in areas not officially designated at the time of loss as special flood hazard areas. NFIP coverage is available outside high-risk zones at a lower premium.

To prevent people putting off the purchase of coverage until waters are rising and flooding is inevitable, policyholders must wait 30 days before their policy takes effect. In 1993, 7,800 policies purchased at the last minute resulted in $48 million in claims against only $625,000 in premiums.

Proposals for Change: The NFIP has four major goals: to decrease the risk of flood losses; reduce the costs and consequences of flooding; reduce the demand for federal assistance; and preserve and restore beneficial floodplain functions. In a final report published in 2006 by the American Institutes for Research (AIR), which conducted an evaluation of the federal flood insurance program, AIR said that although much had been accomplished, the program fell short of meeting its goals in part because the NFIP did not have the ability to guide development away from floodplains and cannot restore beneficial floodplain functions once they have been impaired. In addition, AIR said, many people still are not covered or not adequately covered for flood damage. AIR also noted that the NFIP was hampered in reaching its goals by insufficient Congressional funding, lack of pertinent data, misperceptions about the nature of the program and the breakdown in coordination among its three major sectors.

A report published by FEMA in 2007 suggests that development patterns should be changed to protect environmentally sensitive areas and that communities in the flood program should be encouraged or required to ban development in these locations.

Another criticism of the NFIP is that it does not charge enough for coverage. Among the reasons for the premium shortfall is that the cost of coverage on dwellings that were built before floodplain management regulations were established in their communities is subsidized. As a result, the premiums paid for flood coverage by the owners of these properties reflect only 30 to 40 percent of the true risk of loss. In January 2006 FEMA estimated an annual shortfall in premium income of $750 million due to these subsidies. Some subsidized properties also suffer repetitive losses. Repetitive loss properties accounted for about $4.6 billion in claims payments between 1978 and 2004. The AIR report acknowledged that the current system is not eliminating existing damage-prone buildings as quickly as expected.

Insurance Fraud

The Insurance Information Institute estimates that fraud accounts for 10 percent of the property/casualty insurance industry's incurred losses and loss adjustment expenses, or about $30 billion a year. This fraud results in higher premiums.

Fraud may be committed at different points in the insurance transaction by different parties: applicants for insurance, policyholders, third-party claimants and professionals who provide services to claimants. Common frauds include "padding," or inflating actual claims; misrepresenting facts on an insurance application; submitting claims for injuries or damage that never occurred; and "staging" accidents.

Prompted by the incidence of insurance fraud, 41 states and the District of Columbia have set up fraud bureaus (some bureaus have limited powers, and some states have more than one bureau to address fraud in different lines of insurance). These agencies have reported increases in referrals (tips about suspected fraud), cases opened, convictions and court-ordered restitution.

Insurance fraud can be "hard" or "soft." Hard fraud occurs when someone deliberately fabricates claims or fakes an accident. Soft insurance fraud, also known as opportunistic fraud, occurs when people pad legitimate claims, for example, or, in the case of business owners, list fewer employees or misrepresent the work they do to pay lower workers compensation premiums.

People who commit insurance fraud range from organized criminals, who steal large sums through fraudulent business activities and insurance claim mills, to professionals and technicians, who inflate the cost of services or charge for services not rendered, to ordinary people who want to cover their deductible or view filing a claim as an opportunity to make a little money.

Some lines of insurance are more vulnerable to fraud than others. Healthcare, workers compensation and auto insurance are believed to be the sectors most affected.

Insurance fraud received little attention until the 1980s when the rising price of insurance and the growth in organized fraud spurred efforts to pass stronger antifraud laws. Allied with insurers were parties affected by fraud—consumers who pay higher insurance premiums to compensate for losses from fraud; direct victims of organized fraud groups; and chiropractors and other medical professionals who are concerned that their reputations will be tarnished.

One out of five Americans think it is acceptable to defraud insurance companies under certain conditions, according to the Coalition Against Insurance Fraud. The organization released the findings in a 2008 study, "The Four Faces of Insurance Fraud." It found that the public is consistently more tolerant of specific insurance frauds today than it was 10 years before.

In addition, studies by the Insurance Research Council show that significant numbers of Americans think it is all right to inflate their insurance claims to make up for insurance premiums they have paid in previous years when they have had no claims or to pad a claim to make up for the deductible they would have to pay.

Insurers must preserve the fine line between investigating suspicious claims and harassing legitimate claimants and the need to comply with the time requirements for paying claims imposed by fair claim practice regulations. All states have unfair claim settlement practice laws on their books to ensure that the parties involved are informed of the progress of investigations and that investigators settle the claim promptly or within a specified amount of time. About 19 states have provisions that provide guidance and protection for investigators by allowing time limit extensions or waivers and detailing what evidence is required and to whom the evidence should be made available.

Insurers' Antifraud Measures: The legal options of an insurance company that suspects fraud are limited. The insurer can only inform law enforcement agencies of suspicious claims, withhold payment and collect evidence for use in a court. The success of the battle against insurance fraud therefore depends on two elements: the level of priority assigned by legislators, regulators, law enforcement agencies and society as a whole to the problem and the resources devoted by the insurance industry itself. To that end most insurers have established special investigation units (SIUs). These entities help identify and investigate suspicious claims.

Insurers have also created a national fraud academy. A joint initiative of the Property Casualty Insurers Association of America, the FBI, National Insurance Crime Bureau (NICB) and the International Association of Special Investigating Units, it is designed to fight insurance claims fraud by educating and training fraud investigators. It offers online classes under the leadership of the NICB.

The Liability System and Medical Malpractice Insurance Issues

Litigiousness has become a societal problem in the United States. The tort system cost $254.7 billion in 2008 in direct costs, which translates into $838 per person, and many billions of dollars more in indirect costs, according to Towers Perrin's most recent tort costs study. U.S. consumers pay directly for the high cost of going to court through higher liability insurance premiums because liability insurance rates reflect what insurance companies pay out for their policyholders' legal defense and any judgments against them. And they pay indirectly in higher prices for goods and services since businesses pass on to consumers the expenses they incur in protecting themselves against lawsuits, including the cost of commercial liability insurance.

Beginning in the 1980s, in an effort to reduce litigation costs, business groups and others mounted a campaign to reform tort law. Tort law is the basis for the U.S. liability system. Most reforms have taken place on the state level and during the last decade all but a handful of states passed significant tort law reforms. However, some have been overturned by the courts.

Many reform efforts have focused on medical malpractice issues. Medical malpractice insurance covers doctors and other professionals in the medical field for liability claims arising from their treatment of patients.

The cost of medical malpractice insurance began to rise in the early 2000s after a period of essentially flat prices. Rate increases were precipitated in part by the growing size of claims, particularly in urban areas. Among the other factors driving up prices was a reduced supply of available coverage as several major insurers exited the medical malpractice business because of the difficulty of making a profit.

New research suggests that premium increases may be moderating but, for any significant turnaround to take root, major reforms in the delivery of medical care that focus on patient safety need to occur, industry observers say.

State Tort Reform Issues

Caps in Noneconomic Damages: According to the National Conference of State Legislatures, 30 states, the Virgin Islands and Puerto Rico limit jury awards in malpractice cases. In the past few years, a number court have ruled against such limits. In Georgia, the Supreme Court ruled that a 2005 state law that limited jury awards for pain and suffering in malpractice cases to $350,000 improperly interfered with a jury's duty to determine damages in a civil lawsuit. In the decision Chief Justice Carol Hunstein said that limits in any amount violate the right to trial by jury. In Illinois, the Supreme Court overturned the state's 2005 medical malpractice statute, which capped noneconomic (pain and suffering) medical malpractice awards at $500,000 in lawsuits against physicians and $1 million for hospitals. The court ruled that the law violated the state's constitutional principle of separation of powers in that lawmakers had made decisions that should be made by judges and juries.

Some states, such as Maryland, are deciding to retain their caps when challenged.

Arbitration: To keep small disputes out of the courts, insurers are increasingly turning to arbitration. The nation's largest arbitration provider, nonprofit Arbitration Forums, resolved more than 520,000 inter-insurance disputes in 2009 valued at $2.5 billion, for a savings in litigation costs of $700 million. Disputes leading to arbitration typically arise when insurance or self-insured companies believe their policyholders or employees are not at fault or due to disagreement over the percentage of liability or the amount of damages. More than 85 percent of these disputes involve auto collisions.

Tort Liability Environment: In December 2009 the American Tort Reform Association (ATRA) released its annual list of states and counties characterized as "Judicial Hellholes," places with courts that have a disproportionately harmful impact on civil litigation. ATRA explains that personal injury lawyers seek out these places as targets for their efforts to expand liability and develop new opportunities for litigation. ATRA's newest list includes six Judicial Hellholes, including holdovers South Florida; West Virginia; Cook County, Illinois; and Atlantic County, New Jersey, and New Mexico appellate courts and New York City, which are new on the list. ATRA highlights several reforms that can help restore balance to these jurisdictions. They include stopping venue shopping (looking for jurisdictions where juries are favorable to plaintiffs), imposing sanctions for bringing frivolous lawsuits, stemming abuse of consumer laws, ensuring that noneconomic damage awards serve a compensatory purpose, and strengthening rules to promote sound science in the courtroom.

Microinsurance

A growing number of insurers are tapping into markets in developing countries through microinsurance projects, which provide low-cost insurance to individuals generally not covered by traditional insurance or government programs. Microinsurance products tend to be much less costly than traditional products and thus extend protection to a much wider market. The approach is an outgrowth of the microfinancing projects developed by Bangladeshi Nobel Prize-winning banker and economist Muhammad Yunus, which helped millions of low-income individuals in Asia and Africa to set up businesses and buy houses. American International Group Inc. (AIG) was one of the first companies to offer microinsurance and began selling policies in Uganda in 1997. Swiss Re, Munich Re, Allianz and Zurich Financial Services have also entered the microinsurance arena. Disasters such as the 2005 tsunami in Indonesia and the 2010 Haiti earthquake have demonstrated the need for insurance in many regions, prompting insurers to develop new products. While the coverage is often geared to protection from natural disasters, there are also programs covering life/health risks as well.

With limited growth prospects in the insurance markets of developed countries, which are largely saturated, insurers see microinsurance in emerging economies as presenting significant potential for growth and profitability. A 2009 Swiss Re report on world insurance markets found that premium growth in emerging markets far outpaced growth in industrialized countries in 2008. The study identified the following regions as "emerging markets": Latin America, Central and Eastern Europe, South and East Asia, the Middle East (excluding Israel) and Central Asia, Turkey and Africa.

In 2009 the International Association of Insurance Supervisors, the World Bank, the International Labor Organization and other multilateral groups launched a program to improve access to insurance in emerging and underserved markets called the "Access to Insurance Initiative." Also in 2009 representatives from over 60 countries participated in the Fifth International Microinsurance Conference, which was organized by the reinsurer Munich Re and the Microinsurance Network, a joint effort of aid organizations, multilateral agencies, insurers, policymakers and academics.

No-Fault Auto Insurance and Other Auto Liability Systems

State auto liability insurance laws fall into four broad categories: no-fault, choice no-fault, tort liability and add-on. The major differences are whether there are restrictions on the right to sue and whether the policyholder's own insurer pays first-party benefits, up to the state maximum amount, regardless of who is at fault in the accident. These alternative systems have evolved over time as consumers, regulators and insurers have sought ways to lower the cost and speed up the delivery of compensation for auto accidents.

The term "no-fault" auto insurance is often used loosely to denote any auto insurance program that allows policyholders to recover financial losses from their own insurance company, regardless of fault. But in its strictest form no-fault applies only to state laws that both provide for the payment of no-fault first-party benefits and restrict the right to sue, the so-called "limited tort" option. The first-party (policyholder) benefit coverage is known as personal injury protection (PIP).

Under current no-fault laws, motorists may sue for severe injuries and for pain and suffering only if the case meets certain conditions. These conditions, known as a threshold, relate to the severity of injury. They may be expressed in verbal terms (a descriptive or verbal threshold) or in dollar amounts of medical bills, a monetary threshold. Some laws also include minimum requirements for the days of disability incurred as a result of the accident. Because high threshold no-fault systems restrict litigation, they tend to reduce costs and delays in paying claims. Verbal thresholds eliminate the incentive to inflate claims that may exist when there is a dollar "target" for medical expenses. However, in some states the verbal threshold has been eroded over time by broad judicial interpretation of the verbal threshold language, and PIP coverage has become the target of abuse and fraud by dishonest doctors and clinics that bill for unnecessary and expensive medical procedures, pushing up costs.

Currently 12 states and Puerto Rico have no-fault auto insurance laws. Florida, Michigan, New Jersey, New York and Pennsylvania have verbal thresholds. The other seven states—Hawaii, Kansas, Kentucky, Massachusetts, Minnesota, North Dakota and Utah—use a monetary threshold. Three states have a "choice" no-fault law. In New Jersey, Pennsylvania and Kentucky, motorists may reject the lawsuit threshold and retain the right to sue for any auto-related injury.

The Different Auto Insurance Systems

No-fault: The no-fault system is intended to lower the cost of auto insurance by taking small claims out of the courts. Each insurance company compensates its own policyholders (the first party) for the cost of minor injuries, regardless of who was at fault in the accident. (The second party is the insurance company and the third is the other party or parties hurt as a result of the accident.)

These first-party benefits, known as personal injury protection (PIP), are a mandatory coverage in true no-fault states. The extent of coverage varies by state. In states with the most comprehensive benefits, a policyholder receives compensation for medical fees, lost wages, funeral costs and other out-of-pocket expenses. The major variations involve dollar limits on medical and hospital expenses, funeral and burial expenses, lost income and the amount to be paid a person hired to perform essential services that an injured non-income producer is unable to perform.

Drivers in no-fault states may sue for severe injuries if the case meets certain conditions. These conditions are known as the tort liability threshold and may be expressed in verbal terms such as death or significant disfigurement (verbal threshold) or in dollar amounts of medical bills (monetary threshold).

Choice no-fault: In choice no-fault states, drivers may select one of two options: a no-fault auto insurance policy or a traditional tort liability policy. In New Jersey and Pennsylvania the no-fault option has a verbal threshold. In Kentucky there is a monetary threshold.

Tort liability: In traditional tort liability states, there are no restrictions on lawsuits. A policyholder at fault in a car crash can be sued by the other driver and by the other driver's passengers for the pain and suffering the accident caused as well as for out-of-pocket expenses such as medical costs.

Add-on: In add-on states, drivers receive compensation from their own insurance company as they do in no-fault states, but there are no restrictions on lawsuits. The term "add-on" is used because in these states first-party benefits have been added on to the traditional tort liability system. In add-on states, first-party coverage may not be mandatory and the benefits may be lower than in true no-fault states.

Regulation

Insurance is regulated by the individual states. The move to modernize insurance regulation is being driven in part by the globalization of insurance services. Some large U.S. companies that operate in other countries support the concept of a federal system that provides one-stop regulatory approval while others believe the merits of a state system outweigh the virtues of a single national regulator. As a result of discussions about the merits of each system, states are making it easier for insurers to respond quickly to market forces. States monitor insurance company solvency. One important function related to this is overseeing rate changes. Rate making is the process of calculating a price to cover the future cost of insurance claims and expenses, including a margin for profit. To establish rates, insurers look at past trends and changes in the current environment that may affect potential losses in the future. Rates are not the same as premiums. A rate is the price of a given unit of insurance—$2.50 per $1,000 of earthquake coverage, for example. The premium represents the total cost of many units. If the price to rebuild a house is $150,000, the premium would be 150 x $2.50. Rates vary according to the likelihood and potential size of loss. Using the example of earthquake insurance, rates would be higher near a fault line and for a brick house, which is more susceptible to damage, than a frame one.

While the regulatory processes in each state vary, three principles guide every state's rate regulation system: that rates be adequate (to maintain insurance company solvency), but not excessive (not so high as to lead to exorbitant profits), nor unfairly discriminatory (price differences must reflect expected claim and expense differences). Recently, in auto and home insurance, the twin issues of availability and affordability, which are not explicitly included in the guiding principles, have been assuming greater importance in regulatory decisions.

In line with these principles, states have adopted various methods of regulating insurance rates, which fall roughly into two categories: "prior approval" and "competitive." This does not mean there is no competition in states using a prior approval system. Most approved rates in prior approval states are the rates used, but in some cases, particularly in commercial coverages, companies compete at rates below these approved ceilings.

Regulation Modernization

Increasingly, even in the most regulated states, officials are relying on competition among insurance companies to keep rates down and are modernizing and streamlining the rate setting process.

The move to modernize insurance regulation is being driven in part by the globalization of insurance services. Some large U.S. companies that operate in other countries support the concept of a federal system that provides one-stop regulatory approval while others believe the merits of a state system outweigh the virtues of a single national regulator. As a result of discussions about the merits of each system, states are making it easier for insurers to respond quickly to market forces. Since 2009, various pieces of legislation have been introduced in Congress that respond to a number of concerns: lack of an entity at the federal level that can represent insurance interests, particularly in the discussion of international issues; the need for better oversight of systemic risk—the interconnectedness of the risk assumed by a few large financial services companies whose failure could bring down the entire financial system; and the need to streamline the regulation of reinsurers and surplus lines insurers.

For example, in Georgia, a law was signed in May 2008 that allows auto insurance companies to adjust most rates without the prior approval of the insurance commissioner. Georgia joins at least 30 other states that let rates more closely reflect competition in the marketplace

Type of State Rating Laws

Prior Approval: The insurer must file rates, rules, etc. with state regulators. Depending on the statute, the filing becomes effective when a specified waiting period elapses (if the state regulator does not take specific action on the filing, it is deemed approved automatically) or the state regulator formally approves the filing. A state regulator may disapprove a filing at any time if it is not in compliance with the law. The state regulator normally must hold a hearing to establish noncompliance.

Modified Prior Approval: This is a hybrid of "prior approval" and "file and use" laws. If the rate revision is based solely on a change in loss experience then "file and use" may apply. However, if the rate revision is based on a change in expense relationships or rate classifications, then "prior approval" may apply. A state regulator may disapprove a filing at any time if it is not in compliance with the law. The state regulator normally must hold a hearing to establish noncompliance.

Flex Rating: The insurer may increase or decrease a rate within a "flex band," or range, without approval of the state regulator. Generally, either "file and use" or "use and file" provisions apply. Generally, the insurer must file rate increases or decreases that fall outside the established "flex band" with the state regulator for approval. Typically, "prior approval" provisions apply. The "flex band" is set either by statute or by the state regulator. A state regulator may disapprove a filing at any time if it is not in compliance with the law. The state regulator normally must hold a hearing to establish noncompliance.

File and Use: The insurer must file rates, rules, etc. with the state regulator. The filing becomes effective immediately or on a future date specified by the filer. A state regulator may disapprove a filing at any time if it is not in compliance with the law. The state regulator normally must hold a hearing to establish noncompliance.

Use and File: The filing becomes effective when used. The insurer must file rates, rules, etc. with the state regulator within a specified time period after first use. A state regulator may disapprove a filing at any time if it is not in compliance with the law. The state regulator normally must hold a hearing to establish noncompliance.

State-Prescribed: The state regulator determines and promulgates the rates, classifications, forms, etc. to which all insurers must adhere. Insurers are usually permitted to deviate from state prescribed rates, classifications, forms, etc., with the approval of the state regulator.

No File/Record Maintenance: The insurer need not file rates, rules, etc. with the state regulator. Rates, rules, etc. become effective when used. The state regulator may periodically examine insurer(s) to ensure compliance with the law.

Generally, there are record maintenance requirements, under which insurers must make their rating systems available to the state regulator for examination. A state regulator may order discontinuance of the use of the material at any time if it is not in compliance with the law. The state regulator normally must hold a hearing to establish noncompliance.

Reinsurance

Reinsurance is insurance for insurance companies. It is a way of transferring or "ceding" some of the financial risk insurance companies assume in insuring cars, homes and businesses to another insurance company, the reinsurer. Reinsurance, a highly complex global business, accounted for about 9 percent of the U.S. property/casualty insurance industry premiums in 2008, according to the Reinsurance Association of America.

The reinsurance business is evolving. Traditionally, reinsurance transactions were between two insurance entities: the primary insurer that sold the original insurance policies and the reinsurer. Most still are. Primary insurers and reinsurers can share both the premiums and losses or reinsurers may assume the primary company's losses above a certain dollar limit in return for a fee. However, risks of various kinds, particularly of natural disasters, are now being sold by insurers and reinsurers to institutional investors in the form of catastrophe bonds and other alternative risk-spreading mechanisms. Increasingly, new products reflect a gradual blending of reinsurance and investment banking.

After Hurricane Andrew hit Southern Florida in 1992, causing $15.5 billion in insured losses at the time, it became clear that U.S. insurers had seriously underestimated the extent of their liability for property losses in a megadisaster. Until Hurricane Andrew, the industry had thought $8 billion was the largest possible catastrophe loss. Reinsurers subsequently reassessed their position, which in turn caused primary companies to reconsider their catastrophe reinsurance needs.

The shortage and high cost of traditional catastrophe reinsurance precipitated by Hurricane Andrew and declining interest rates, which sent investors looking for higher yields, prompted interest in securitization of insurance risk. Among the precursors to catastrophe bonds and other forms of securitization were contingency financing bonds such as those issued for the Florida Windstorm Association in 1996, which provided cash in the event of a catastrophe but had to be repaid after a loss, and contingent surplus notes—an agreement with a bank or other lender that in the event of a megadisaster that would significantly reduce policyholders' surplus, funds would be made available at a predetermined price. Funds to pay for the transaction should money be needed, are held in U.S. Treasuries. Surplus notes are not considered debt, therefore do not hamper an insurer's ability to write additional insurance. In addition, there were equity puts, through which an insurer would receive a sum of money in the event of a catastrophic loss in exchange for stock or other options.

A catastrophe bond is a specialized security, introduced in 1997, that increases insurers' ability to provide insurance protection by transferring the risk to bond investors. Commercial banks and other lenders have been securitizing mortgages for years, freeing up capital to expand their mortgage business. Insurers and reinsurers issue catastrophe bonds to the securities market through an issuer known as a special purpose reinsurance vehicle (SPRV) set up specifically for this purpose. These bonds have complicated structures and are typically created offshore where tax and regulatory treatment may be more favorable. SPRVs collect the premium from the insurance or reinsurance company and the principal from investors and hold them in a trust in the form of U.S. Treasuries or other highly rated assets, using the investment income to pay interest on the principal. Catastrophe bonds pay high interest rates but if the trigger event occurs, investors lose the interest and sometimes the principal, depending on the structure of the bond, both of which may be used to cover the insurer's disaster losses. Bonds may be issued for a one-year term or multiple years, often three.

The field has gradually evolved to the point where some investors and insurance company issuers are beginning to feel comfortable with the concept, with some coming back to the capital markets each year. In addition to the high interest rates catastrophe bonds pay, their attraction to investors is that they diversify investment portfolio risk, thus reducing the volatility of returns. The returns on most other securities are tied to economic activity rather than natural disasters. Catastrophe bonds have evolved into a multibillion dollar industry. Though pioneered by reinsurers, primary insurers now frequently sponsor new issues.

In addition to catastrophe bonds, catastrophe options were developed but the market for these options never took off. Another alternative is the exchange of risk where individual companies in different parts of the world swap a certain amount of losses. Payment is triggered by the occurrence of an agreed upon event at a certain level of magnitude.

Residual Markets

In a normal competitive market, insurers are free to select from among people applying for insurance those drivers, property owners and commercial operations they wish to insure. They do this by evaluating the risks involved through a process called underwriting.

Applicants who are considered "high risk" may have difficulty obtaining insurance through the regular "voluntary" market channels. (The term "high risk" applies to individuals or individual businesses with a poor loss record due to inadequate safety measures; certain kinds of businesses or professions where the nature of the work is hazardous or where the risk of lawsuits is high; and specific locations where the risk of theft, vandalism or severe storm damage is substantial.) To make basic coverage more readily available to everyone who wants or needs insurance, special insurance plans have been set up by state regulators working with the insurance industry.

The business that insurers do not voluntarily assume is called the residual market. Residual markets may also be called "shared," because the profits and losses of each type of residual market are shared by all insurers in the state selling that type of insurance, or involuntary, because insurers do not choose to underwrite the business, in contrast to the regular voluntary market.

Residual market programs are rarely self-sufficient. Where the rates charged to high-risk policyholders are too low to support the program's operation, insurers are generally assessed to make up the difference. These additional costs are typically passed on to all insurance consumers. However, in a few states, insurers are not able to recoup their residual market losses and political pressure prevents rates from rising to the level they should be actuarially.

The number of drivers and properties insured in the residual market fluctuates as lawmakers and regulators change laws or address availability, rate adequacy and other factors that influence underwriting decisions.

The Automobile Residual Market

The first of the residual market mechanisms for automobile coverage was established in New Hampshire in 1938. As states began to pass laws requiring drivers to furnish proof of insurance, having auto liability insurance became a prerequisite for driving a car. Today, all 50 states and the District of Columbia use one of four systems to guarantee that auto insurance is available to those who need it. All four systems are commonly known as assigned risk plans, although the term technically applies only to the first type of plan, where each insurer is required to assume its share of residual market policyholders or "risks." (The

term "risk" is used in the insurance industry to denote the policyholder or property insured as well as the chance of loss.) Commercial auto insurance is also
available through the residual market.

Automobile Insurance Plans: The assigned risk plan, the most common
type, currently found in 42 states and the District of Columbia, generally is
administered through an office created or supported by the state and governed
by a board representing insurance companies licensed in the state. Massachusetts began a three-year process of changing over to an assigned risk plan, beginning in April 2008. It formerly had a reinsurance pooling facility.

When agents or company representatives are unable to obtain auto insurance for an applicant in the voluntary market, they submit the application to
the assigned risk plan office. These applications are distributed randomly by the
automobile insurance plan to all insurance companies that offer automobile
liability coverage in the state in proportion to the amount of their voluntary
business. Thus, if on a given day the plan receives 100 applications from agents
around the state, a company with 10 percent of that state's regular private pas-
senger automobile insurance business will be assigned 10 of those applicants
and will be responsible for all associated losses.

Assigned risk policies usually are more restricted in the coverage they can
provide and have lower limits than voluntary market policies. In addition, premiums for assigned risk policies usually are significantly higher, although not
always sufficiently high enough to cover the increased costs of insuring high-
risk drivers.

Joint Underwriting Associations (JUAs): Automobile JUAs, found in
four states, Florida, Hawaii, Michigan and Missouri, are state-mandated pooling mechanisms through which all companies doing business in the state share
the premiums of business outside the voluntary market as well as the profits
or losses and expenses incurred. To simplify the policyholder distribution process, insurance agents and company representatives are generally assigned one
of several servicing carriers (companies that have agreed for a fee to issue and
service JUA policies). They submit applications to that company, which then
issues the JUA policy. In Michigan, however, agents submit applications directly
to the JUA office, which then distributes them to the servicing carriers. Coverages offered by JUAs generally are the same as those offered in the voluntary
market but the limits may be lower. Although rates may be higher than in the
voluntary market, they may not be sufficient for the JUA to be self-sustaining.
State statutes setting up the JUA generally permit it to recoup losses by surcharg-

ing policyholders or deducting losses from state premium taxes. (JUAs may be set up for other lines of insurance, including homeowners insurance. JUAs for commercial insurance coverage, such as medical malpractice and liquor liability, may operate somewhat differently in some states, see below.)

Reinsurance Facilities: Reinsurance facilities exist in North Carolina, New Hampshire and Massachusetts. (In Massachusetts, beginning in April 2008, the reinsurance facility which is known as Commonwealth Automobile Insurers, or CAR, began disbanding over a three-year period as the new "managed competition" regulations take effect.) An automobile reinsurance facility is an unincorporated, nonprofit entity, through which auto insurers provide coverage and service claims. After issuing a policy, an insurer decides whether to handle the policy as part of its regular "voluntary business" or transfer it to the reinsurance facility or pool. An insurer is permitted to transfer or "cede" to the pool a percentage of its policies. Premiums for this portion of business are sent to the pool and companies bill the pool for claims payments and expenses. Profits or losses are shared by all auto insurers licensed in the state.

State Fund: One state, Maryland, has a residual market mechanism for auto insurance which is administered by the state. It was created in 1973. Private insurers do not participate directly in the Maryland Automobile Insurance Fund (MAIF) but are required by law to subsidize any losses from the operation, with the cost being charged back against their own policyholders. In years that the fund has a loss, all Maryland insured drivers, including MAIF drivers, help offset the deficit through an assessment mechanism.

Size of the Auto Insurance Market: Together, residual market programs insured about 1.97 million cars in 2007, about 1.06 percent of the total market and a 9.0 percent drop from 2006, according to the Automobile Insurance Plans Service Office, which tracks such data. In 1990 the residual market served 6.3 percent of the total market. In 2007, in a major change from much of the 1990s, only one state, North Carolina, had more than a million cars insured through the residual market. At 1.5 million, the pool insured more than 21.6 percent of the state's total insured vehicles. In South Carolina, which enacted sweeping reforms in 1998, the residual market dropped from 38 percent of all insured cars in 1996 to close to zero in 2007.

The Property Residual Market

Pools: FAIR Plans, Beach and Windstorm Plans, Assigned Risk and Others: A pool is an organization of insurers or reinsurers through which particular types of insurance coverage are provided. The pool acts as a single insuring entity, as opposed to some JUAs and assigned risk plans where the policyholder deals directly with an individual insurance company. Premiums, losses and expenses are shared among pool members in agreed-upon amounts. The range of activities handled by the pool varies. Some pool operations are limited to redistributing premiums and losses, while others have broader functions similar to an insurance company. Some pools use specific insurers as servicing carriers.

In pools composed of primary companies (as opposed to reinsurers), business is placed directly with the pool by the agent. (In a reinsurance pool, a member company underwrites the risk, issues the policy and reinsures the business in the pool, see below.) Pools may be mandated by state legislation or established on a voluntary basis.

Pools assure that insurance is available to property owners in high-risk, generally urban or coastal areas, and businesses with a poor safety record or other high risk characteristics. Among the best-known primary pooling arrangements are property insurance plans, such as Beach and Windstorm Plans, which insure owners of properties vulnerable to severe storm damage.

FAIR Plans: Thirty-two states and the District of Columbia currently have property insurance plans known as FAIR, an acronym for Fair Access to Insurance Requirements Plans. The concept of FAIR Plans was established following passage by Congress of the Housing and Urban Development Act of 1968, a measure designed to address the conditions that led to the 1967 urban riots. This legislation made federal riot reinsurance available to those states that instituted such property insurance pools. One of the plans, Arkansas' Rural Risk Plan, was created in 1988 to provide a market for property insurance in rural areas where fire protection is poor or nonexistent. Mississippi's Rural Plan, which offered fire, extended coverage and vandalism, see below, was expanded to cover the entire state in 2003. (The state's windstorm pool offers wind and hail coverage in coastal counties to the Plan's policyholders.) Georgia's FAIR Plan also provides windstorm and hail coverage in coastal counties as do Plans in Massachusetts and New York. In most states where FAIR Plans are in operation, they are mandatory.

Beach and Windstorm Insurance Plans: Counterparts to the FAIR Plans are Beach and Windstorm Insurance Plans, operated by property insurers in states along the Atlantic and Gulf Coasts to assure that insurance is available for both residences and commercial properties against damage from hurricanes and other windstorms. Established between 1969 and 1971, Beach and Windstorm Plans operate in a manner similar to FAIR Plans, except that properties must be located in a designated area to be eligible for insurance under the Plans.

There are currently five Beach and Windstorm Plans: Alabama, Mississippi, South Carolina, North Carolina and Texas. In 2001 there were seven pools, but Florida's windstorm pool merged with the joint underwriting association in 2002 to create a new type of residual market entity, see below. In a similar move in 2003, Louisiana merged its FAIR Plan with its coastal pool. The Plans are mandatory in all of these states with the exception of Alabama. (In addition, hail and windstorm coverage for homes in coastal counties is available through some FAIR Plans, see above and the WindMap in New Jersey.) Windstorm Plans in Mississippi, South Carolina and Texas offer only wind and hail coverage. Plans in Alabama and North Carolina offer coverage for fire as well. In some states, Plan policyholders must buy flood insurance also.

Property owners who live in areas covered by Beach and Windstorm Plans may be insured for windstorm losses by the Plan or by an individual insurance company. If an insurer has accepted all the windstorm risk it is prepared to assume, an applicant for homeowners insurance may purchase a policy that excludes windstorm coverage from the homeowners insurance company and pay a separate premium for windstorm coverage to the Plan.

One disadvantage of Beach and Windstorm Plans, and the National Flood Insurance Program, is that the availability of insurance encourages development of coastal areas where construction otherwise would not be feasible and where tax money must be spent to protect against continuous erosion to preserve the property.

In the past there was a clear delineation between coastal and urban plans with coastal properties insured under Beach and Windstorm Plans, and urban properties under FAIR Plans. Increasingly, the distinctions are blurring. FAIR Plans are acting as an insurer of last resort for residents who live in shoreline communities in states that do not have a Beach and Windstorm Plan, such as New York State. Beach and Windstorm Plans in some states are being merged with FAIR Plans or joint underwriting associations, as in Florida and Louisiana, or are administering new FAIR Plans, as in Texas. As a result, it is difficult to compare the number of properties insured under any Plan with numbers from earlier years. FAIR Plans have almost doubled in size, pushed up in large part by these mergers and the increase in coastal properties in such states as New York and Massachusetts, but also by more stringent underwriting standards on the part of insurers in the voluntary market.

Residual Market Plan Mergers: In 2002 Florida's two residual market organizations, the JUA and the Florida Windstorm Underwriting Association, merged to become the Citizens' Property Insurance Corporation (CPIC). The Florida CPIC, known as Citizens, has a tax-exempt status. This feature enables it to finance loss payments in the event of a major disaster by issuing tax-exempt bonds that carry low interest rates, thus reducing financing costs over the years by hundreds of millions of dollars. In Louisiana, following Florida's model, the FAIR Plan and the Coastal Plan became the Louisiana Citizens Property Insurance Corporation in 2004.

Other Residual Market Entities

JUAs for Other Lines of Insurance: JUAs are not limited to automobile insurance. At various times, there have been JUAs for residential insurance and workers compensation. A number of states have medical malpractice JUAs, most of which were set up in the 1970s or 1980s when the line was beset by high losses.

Market Assistance Plans (MAPs): A MAP is a temporary, voluntary clearinghouse and referral system designed to put people looking for insurance in touch with insurance companies. They are organized when something happens to cause insurance companies to cut back on the amount of insurance they are willing to provide. MAPs are generally administered by agents' associations, which assign insurance applications to a group of insurers doing business in a state. These companies have agreed to take their share of applicants on a rotating basis.

MAPs may be organized for a single line of insurance, such as daycare liability or homeowners insurance, or for a broad range of liability coverages. Homeowners insurance MAPs have been formed in several East Coast states, including Connecticut and Texas, and medical malpractice MAPs were created in states such as Washington, when the medical community had difficulty finding malpractice insurance.

Workers Compensation Assigned Risk Plans and Pools:
The mechanism used to handle the workers compensation residual market varies from state to state. In the four remaining states with a monopolistic state workers compensation fund (North Dakota, Ohio, Washington and Wyoming switched to a competitive market in July 2008), all businesses are insured through that fund. In most states with a competitive state fund (an entity that competes for business with private insurers), the fund accepts all risks rejected

Residual Markets

by the voluntary market, thus eliminating the need for assigned risk plans. In states without a competitive fund, insurers may be assigned applicants based on their market share and service those employers as they would employers that came to them through the voluntary market, through a system known as direct assignment. They may also participate in the residual market through a reinsurance pooling arrangement.

Second Injury Funds: Second injury funds were created to encourage businesses to hire workers who are physically handicapped by congenital defects or the residual effects of an accident or illness but due to other laws that now protect the physically handicapped worker, such as the Americans With Disabilities Act, some states are disbanding their fund.

Second injury funds receive money from insurance companies and employers as well as from legislative appropriations. Insurance company payments may be based on a percentage of total compensation paid, premiums collected or the nature of the specific injury. The second injury funds may be administered by the state Workers Compensation Commission, Industrial Board or Department of Labor.

Terrorism Risk and Insurance

Prior to September 11, 2001, insurers provided terrorism coverage to their commercial insurance customers essentially free of charge because the chance of property damage from terrorist acts was considered remote. After September 11, which costs insurers about $31.6 billion, insurers began to reassess the risk. For a while terrorism coverage was scarce. Reinsurers were unwilling to reinsure policies in urban areas perceived to be vulnerable to attack. Primary insurers filed requests with their state insurance departments for permission to exclude terrorism coverage from their commercial policies.

Concerned about the limited availability of terrorism coverage in high-risk areas and its impact on the economy, Congress passed the Terrorism Risk Insurance Act (TRIA). The Act provides a temporary program that, in the event of major terrorist attack, allows the insurance industry and federal government to share losses according to a specific formula. TRIA was signed into law on November 26, 2002 and renewed again for two years in December 2005. Passage of TRIA enabled a market for terrorism insurance to begin to develop because the federal backstop effectively limits insurers' losses, greatly simplifying the underwriting process. TRIA was extended for another seven years to 2014 in December 2007. The new law is known as the Terrorism Risk Insurance Program Reauthorization Act (TRIPRA) of 2007.

The Difficulty of Insuring Terrorism Risk: From an insurance viewpoint, terrorism risk is very different from the kind of risks typically insured. To be readily insurable, risks have to have certain characteristics.

The risk must be measurable. Insurers must be able to determine the possible or probable number of events (frequency) likely to result in claims and the maximum size or cost (severity) of these events. For example, insurers know from experience about how many car crashes to expect per 100,000 miles driven for any geographic area and what these crashes are likely to cost. As a result they can charge a premium equal to the risk they are assuming in issuing an auto insurance policy.

A large number of people or businesses must be exposed to the risk of loss but only a few must actually experience one so that the premiums of those that do not file claims can fund the losses of those who do. Losses must be random as regards time, location and magnitude.

Insofar as acts of terrorism are intentional, terrorism risk does not have these characteristics. In addition, no one knows what the worst case scenario might be. There have been very few terrorist attacks, so there is little data on which to base estimates of future losses, either in terms of frequency or severity. Terrorism losses are also likely to be concentrated geographically, since terrorism is usually targeted to produce a significant economic or psychological impact. This leads to a situation known in the insurance industry as adverse selection, where only the people most at risk purchase coverage, the same people who are likely to file claims. Moreover, terrorism losses are never random. They are carefully planned and often coordinated.

Assessing Risk: To underwrite terrorism insurance—to decide whether to offer coverage and what price to charge—insurers must be able to quantify the risk: the likelihood of an event and the amount of damage it would cause. Increasingly, they are using sophisticated modeling tools to assess this risk. According to the modeling firm, AIR Worldwide, the way terrorism risk is measured is not much different from assessments of natural disaster risk, except that the data used for terrorism are more subject to uncertainty. It is easier to project the risk of damage in a particular location from an earthquake of a given intensity or a Category 5 hurricane than a terrorist attack because insurers have had so much more experience with natural disasters than with terrorist attacks and therefore the data to incorporate into models are readily available.

One problem insurers face is the accumulation of risk. They need to know not only the likelihood and extent of damage to a particular building but also the company's accumulated risk from insuring multiple buildings within a given geographical area, including the implications of fire following a terrorist attack. In addition, in the United States, workers compensation insurers face concentrations of risk from injuries to workers caused by terrorism attacks. Workers compensation policies provide coverage for loss of income and medical and rehabilitation treatment from "first dollar," that is without deductibles.

Extending the Terrorism Risk Insurance Act (TRIA): There is general agreement that TRIA has helped insurance companies provide terrorism coverage because the federal government's involvement offers a measure of certainty as to the maximum size of losses insurers would have to pay and allows them to plan for the future. However, when the Act came up for renewal in 2005 and in 2007, there were some who believed that market forces should be allowed to deal with the problem.

Both the U.S. Government Accountability Office and the President's Working Group on Financial Markets published reports on terrorism insurance in September 2006. The two reports essentially supported the insurance industry in its evaluation of nuclear, biological, chemical and radiological (NBCR) risk—that it is uninsurable—but unlike the insurance industry, the President's Working Group said that the existence of TRIA has negatively affected the development of a more robust market for terrorism insurance, a point on which the industry disagrees. TRIA is the reason that coverage is available, insurers say. The structure of the program has encouraged the development of reinsurance for the layers of risk that insurers must bear themselves—deductible amounts and coinsurance—which in turn allows primary insurers to provide coverage.

TRIA and its extensions authorized the creation of a federal reinsurance plan, which is triggered when insured terrorism losses exceed a predetermined amount. The program, a sharing of losses between the insurance industry and the federal government according to a preset formula—a type of reinsurance—has enabled the commercial insurance market to function, even though the threat of terrorism remains.

The law defines an act of terrorism under the 2007 amendment. To be covered by the federal program, an act of terrorism must be committed by individuals acting as part of an effort to influence the policy or conduct of the United States. The law also requires that the act be certified by the Secretary of the Treasury in concurrence with the Secretary of State and the Attorney General. Insurers do not pay the federal government for this reinsurance coverage.

Only commercial insurers and causes of losses specified in the underlying policies are covered. In addition to commercial lines insurers, insurers eligible for coverage include residual market entities such as workers compensation pools, state-licensed captive insurers and risk retention groups, see report on captives. Personal lines insurance companies—those that sell auto and home insurance—and reinsurers are not covered. Neither are group life insurance losses. Most types of commercial insurance losses were covered under the original legislation, except some specialty coverages such as medical malpractice and crop insurance. Some commercial insurance coverages were deleted under the 2005 extension including commercial auto insurance, professional liability except for directors and officers liability, surety, burglary and theft and farmowners multiperil, a coverage similar to homeowners.

In return for the federal backstop, commercial insurers must make terrorism coverage available and conspicuously state the premium charges; policyholders can reject the offer and choose to mitigate this class of risk in other ways. In offering terrorism coverage to their policyholders, commercial insurers must make it available on the same terms and conditions as they offer in their non-TRIA coverage.

After September 11, to minimize the likelihood of a wave of liability claims,

Congress established the Federal Victims Compensation Act, which provided nearly $7 billion in payments to families of September 11 victims. In return, victims' families were required to give up the right to sue those they perceived as responsible parties. This provision is not part of TRIA or its extension.

Mandated Coverages/Exclusions: In some states a doctrine know as "fire following" applies. This means that in the event of a terrorist-caused explosion followed by fire, insurers could be liable to pay out losses attributable to the fire (but not the explosion) even if a commercial property owner had not purchased terrorism coverage. A number of states have amended their standard fire policy laws to exclude such coverage for acts of terrorism.

Injuries in the workplace resulting from terrorist attacks are covered under state workers compensation laws. Workers compensation insurance is a mandatory coverage in all states but Texas.

Workers Compensation

Workers compensation insurance covers the cost of medical care and rehabilitation for workers injured on the job. It also compensates them for lost wages and provides death benefits for their dependents if they are killed in work-related accidents, including terrorist attacks. The workers compensation system is the "exclusive remedy" for on-the-job injuries suffered by employees. As part of the social contract embedded in each state's law, the employee gives up the right to sue the employer for injuries caused by the employer's negligence and in return receives workers compensation benefits regardless of who or what caused the accident, as long as it happened in the workplace as a result of and in the course of workplace activities.

Workers compensation systems vary from state to state. State statutes and court decisions control many aspects, including the handling of claims, the evaluation of impairment and settlement of disputes, the amount of benefits injured workers receive and the strategies used to control costs.

Workers compensation costs are one of the many factors that influence businesses to expand or relocate in a state, generating jobs. When premiums rise sharply, legislators often call for reforms. The last round of widespread reform legislation started in the late 1980s. In general, the reforms enabled employers and insurers to better control medical care costs through coordination and oversight of the treatment plan and return-to-work process and to improve workplace safety. Some states are now approaching a crisis once again as new problems arise.

The Workers Compensation Social Contract: The industrial expansion that took place in the United States during the 19th century was accompanied by a significant increase in workplace accidents. At that time, the only way injured workers could obtain compensation was to sue their employers for negligence. Proving negligence was a costly, time-consuming effort, and often the court ruled in favor of the employer. But by the early 1900s, a state-by-state pattern of legislative proposals designed to compensate injured workers had begun to emerge.

Wisconsin enacted the first permanent workers compensation insurance law in 1911 (New York had enacted a law a year earlier but it was found unconstitutional), and by 1920 all but eight states had enacted similar laws. By 1949 all states had a workers compensation system that provided compensation to workers hurt on the job, regardless of who was at fault. The costs of medical treatment and wage loss benefits were the responsibility of the employer which were paid through the workers compensation system.

Workers Compensation

The scope of workers compensation coverage has broadened considerably since its early beginnings. In 1972, states amended their laws to meet performance standards recommended by the National Commission on State Workmen's Compensation Laws. Many states took action not only to expand benefits but also to make the coverage applicable to classifications of employees not previously covered.

However, compensation levels are not uniform. In some states benefits are still inadequate, while in others, they are overly generous. Some states were slow in adopting the National Commission's guidelines and have still not embraced the entire package of 19 recommendations published in 1972. Many states exempt employers with only a few workers (fewer than five, four or three, depending on the state) from mandatory coverage laws. A major benefits issue still to be resolved in some states is the imbalance between levels of compensation for various degrees of impairment; permanent partial disabilities tend to be overcompensated and permanent total disability undercompensated.

Some coverage for workers compensation is provided by federal programs. For example, the Longshoremen's and Harbor Workers Compensation Act, passed in 1927 and substantially amended in 1984, provides coverage for certain maritime employees and the Federal Employees' Compensation Act protects workers hired by the U.S. government.

Employers can purchase workers compensation coverage from private insurance companies or state-run workers agencies, known as state funds. In 14 states, state funds compete with private insurers (competitive funds) and in four states, the state is the sole provider of workers compensation insurance. State funds also function as the insurer of last resort for businesses that have difficulty getting coverage in the open market.

The only state in which workers compensation coverage is truly optional is Texas, where about one-third of the state's employers are so-called nonsubscribers. Those that opt out of the system can be sued by employees for failure to provide a safe workplace. The nonsubscribers tend to be smaller companies, but the percentage of larger companies opting out has been growing.

Some businesses finance their own workplace injury benefits through a system known as self-insurance. Large organizations with many employees can often estimate the cost of routine types of injuries. Self-insurance, along with large deductibles, which are in effect self-insurance, now account for more than one-third of traditional market premium.

About nine out of 10 people in the nation's workforce are protected by workers compensation insurance.

How the System Works: Workers compensation systems are administered by the individual states, generally by commissions or boards whose responsibility it is to ensure compliance with the laws, investigate and decide disputed cases, and collect data. In most states employers are required to keep records of accidents. Accidents must be reported to the workers compensation board and to the company's insurer within a specified number of days.

Workers compensation covers an injured worker's medical care and attempts to cover his or her economic loss. This includes loss of earnings and the extra expenses associated with the injury. Injured workers receive all medically necessary and appropriate treatment from the first day of injury or illness and rehabilitation when the disability is severe.

To rein in expenditures and improve cost effectiveness, many states have adopted cost control measures, including treatment guidelines that spell out acceptable treatments and diagnostic tests for specific injuries such as lower back injuries and fee schedules that set maximum payment amounts to doctors for certain types of care.

Most claims are medical only, but lost-time claims, those with both medical and lost income payments, though few, consume most resources. Claims are categorized according to the degree of impairment—partial or total disability—and whether the impairment is permanent or temporary. Cash benefits can include impairment benefits and, when the impairment causes a loss of income, disability or wage loss benefits.

Impairment can be defined in several ways. Payments may be based on a schedule or list of body parts covered and the benefits paid for a loss of that part. For injuries not on the schedule, benefit payments may be calculated according to the degree of impairment or the loss of future or current earnings capacity, often using the American Medical Association's definitions.

Most states pay benefits for the duration of the injury. But some specify a maximum number of weeks, particularly for temporary disabilities. For workers with a total disability, the benefit amount is some percentage of the worker's weekly wage (actual or state average). Cash benefits may not be paid until after a waiting period of several days.

Costs to Employers: Costs to employers include premiums, payments made under deductibles and the benefits and administrative costs incurred by employers that self-insure or fund their own benefit program. In the mid-1950s, private sector employers paid an average 0.5 percent of payroll for workers compensation. By 1970 this figure was 1 percent. Employer costs escalated steeply in the 1980s and 1990s, reaching a record high in 1994 of 2.99 percent. Since then they have fluctuated. Estimates by John Burton in the Workers Compensation Policy Review, January/February 2008 put workers compensation costs as a percentage of payroll in 2007 at 2.28, up from a 10-year low of 1.92 in 2001. The NCCI estimates that in 2008 employers' workers compensation insurance costs accounted for 1.7 percent of total compensation costs. However, there is a wide variation in costs among states and industries, so that the highest rated (the inherent riskiest) groups could pay several hundred times that of the lowest rated (safest) groups, as a percentage of payroll. Also taken into account is the firm's own safety record.

Reducing Costs: Workers compensation system costs are rarely static. Reforms are implemented and then, over time, one or more elements in these multifaceted systems get out of balance. Some employers and legislators complain that the cost of coverage is hurting the state's economy by reducing its ability to compete with other states for new job-producing opportunities.

In the 1980s, with a view to increasing competition within the insurance industry in order to bring down rates, legislation was introduced in more than a dozen states to change the method of establishing rates from administered pricing, where rating organizations recommended rates that included expenses and a margin for profit, to open competition. Now insurers base their rate filings on more of their own company's specific data, rather than using industrywide figures in such areas as expenses and profit and contingency allowances. Rating organizations still provide industrywide data on "losses"—the costs associated with work-related accidents, which help small companies that lack access to large amounts of data.

The aim of the workers compensation system is to help workers recover from work-related accidents and illnesses and to return to the workplace. A fast return to work is desirable from the employer and insurer's viewpoint, lowering claim costs for the insurer but benefiting the worker too.

Another factor pushing up costs in some states is the amount of attorney involvement. Workers compensation programs were originally intended to be "no-fault" systems and therefore litigation-free.

However today, attorneys are involved in 5 to 10 percent of all workers compensation claims in most states—but in as much as 20 percent in systems where the number of disputes is high and in roughly a third of claims where the worker was injured seriously.

Although attorney involvement boosts claim costs by 12 to 15 percent, because claimants must pay attorneys' fees there is generally no net gain in the actual benefits received. The involvement of an attorney does not necessarily indicate formal litigation proceedings. Sometimes, injured workers turn to attorneys to help them negotiate what they believe is a confusing and complex system. Increasingly, states are trying to make the system easier to understand and to use.

The workers compensation system plays a major role in improving workplace safety. An employer's workers compensation premium reflects the relative hazards to which workers are exposed and the employer's claim record. About one-half of states allow what is known as "schedule rating," a discount or rate credit for superior workplace safety programs.

Workers Compensation Residual Markets: Residual markets, traditionally the market of last resort, are an important segment of the workers comp market. Workers comp residual plans are administered by the NCCI in 29 jurisdictions. In some states, particularly where rates in the voluntary market are inadequate, the residual market provides coverage for a large portion of policyholders.

Terrorism Coverage: Since the terrorist attacks of September 11, 2001, workers compensation insurers have been taking a closer look at their exposures to catastrophes, both natural and man-made. According to a report by Risk Management Solutions, if the earthquake that shook San Francisco in 1906 were to happen today, it could cause as many as 78,000 injuries, 5,000 deaths and over $7 billion in workers compensation losses.

Workers compensation claims for terrorism could cost an insurer anywhere from $300,000 to $1 million per employee, depending on the state. As a result, firms with a concentration of employees in a single building in major metropolitan areas, such as New York, or near a "trophy building" are now considered high risk, a classification that used to apply only to people in dangerous jobs such as roofing.

STATES WITH A STATE-RUN WORKERS COMPENSATION FUND

Competitive with Private Insurers			Exclusive
Arizona*	Maryland	Oregon	North Dakota
California	Minnesota	Pennsylvania	Ohio
Colorado	Montana	Texas	Washington
Idaho	New York	Utah	Wyoming**
Kentucky	Oklahoma	West Virginia	

*Scheduled to be privatized by 2013.
**Compulsory for extra hazardous operations only. Employers with nonhazardous operations may insure with the state fund or opt to go without coverage.

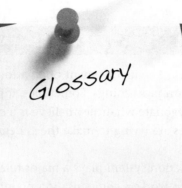

401(K) PLAN

An employer-sponsored retirement savings plan funded by employee contributions, which may or may not be matched by the employer. Federal laws allow employees to invest pretax dollars, up to a stated maximum each year.

*403(B) PLAN

In the United States, an arrangement that allows not-for-profit employers and their employees to make contributions to a tax-deferred retirement savings plan established for the benefit of employees.

529 SAVINGS PLANS

State-administered plans designed to encourage households to save for college education. Named after a part of the Internal Revenue tax code, these saving plans allow earnings to accumulate free of federal income tax and sometimes to be withdrawn to pay for college costs taxfree. There are two types of plans: savings and prepaid tuition. Plan assets are managed either by the state's treasurer or an outside investment company. Most offer a range of investment options.

A

A-SHARE VARIABLE ANNUITY

A form of variable annuity contract where the contract holder pays sales charges up front rather than eventually having to pay a surrender charge.

*ABSOLUTE ASSIGNMENT

An irrevocable transfer of complete ownership of a life insurance policy or an annuity from one party to another. *Contrast with* Collateral assignment. (*See* Assignment)

ACCELERATED DEATH BENEFITS

A life insurance policy option that provides policy proceeds to insured individuals over their lifetimes, in the event of a terminal illness. This is in lieu of a traditional policy that pays beneficiaries after the insured's death. Such benefits kick in if the insured becomes terminally ill, needs extreme medical intervention, or must reside in a nursing home. The payments made while the insured is living are deducted from any death benefits paid to beneficiaries.

ACCIDENT AND HEALTH INSURANCE

Coverage for accidental injury, accidental death, and related health expenses. Benefits will pay for preventative services, medical expenses and catastrophic care, with limits.

*ACCIDENTAL DEATH BENEFIT (ADB)

A supplementary life insurance policy benefit that provides a death benefit in addition to the policy's basic death benefit if the insured's death occurs as the result of an accident. (*See* Double indemnity benefit)

*ACCIDENTAL DEATH AND DISMEMBERMENT (AD&D) BENEFIT

A supplementary life insurance policy benefit that provides for an amount of money in addition to the policy's basic death benefit. This additional amount is payable if the insured dies as the result of an accident or if the insured loses any two limbs or the sight in both eyes as the result of an accident.

ACCOUNT RECEIVABLES

See Receivables.

*ACCUMULATION AT INTEREST DIVIDEND OPTION

An option, available to the owners of participating insurance policies, that allows a policy owner to leave policy dividends on deposit with the insurer and earn interest. (*See* Dividends)

ACTUAL CASH VALUE

A form of insurance that pays damages equal to the replacement value of damaged property minus depreciation. (*See* Replacement cost)

ACTUARY

An insurance professional skilled in the analysis, evaluation and management of statistical information. Evaluates insurance firms' reserves, determines rates and rating methods, and determines other business and financial risks.

ADDITIONAL LIVING EXPENSES

Extra charges covered by homeowners policies over and above the policyholder's customary living expenses. They kick in when the insured requires temporary shelter due to damage by a covered peril that makes the home temporarily uninhabitable.

*ADDITIONAL TERM INSURANCE OPTION

An option available to owners of participating insurance policies under which the insurer uses a policy dividend as a net single premium to purchase one-year term insurance on the insured's life. Also known as fifth dividend option. (*See* Dividend; Policy dividend options)

*ADJUSTABLE LIFE INSURANCE

A form of life insurance that allows policy owners to vary the type of coverage provided by their policies as their insurance needs change.

ADJUSTER

An individual employed by a property/casualty insurer to evaluate losses and settle policyholder claims. These adjusters differ from public adjusters, who negotiate with insurers on behalf of policyholders, and receive a portion of a claims settlement. Independent adjusters are independent contractors who adjust claims for different insurance companies.

ADMITTED ASSETS

Assets recognized and accepted by state insurance laws in determining the solvency of insurers and reinsurers. To make it easier to assess an insurance company's financial position, state statutory accounting rules do not permit certain assets to be included on the balance sheet. Only assets that can be easily sold in the event of liquidation or borrowed against, and receivables for which payment can be reasonably anticipated, are included in admitted assets. (*See* Assets)

ADMITTED COMPANY

An insurance company licensed and authorized to do business in a particular state.

ADVERSE SELECTION

The tendency of those exposed to a higher risk to seek more insurance coverage than those at a lower risk. Insurers react either by charging higher premiums or not insuring at all, as in the case of floods. (Flood insurance is provided by the federal government but sold mostly through the private market.) In the case of natural disasters, such as earthquakes, adverse selection concentrates risk instead of spreading it. Insurance works best when risk is shared among large numbers of policyholders.

AFFINITY SALES

Selling insurance through groups such as professional and business associations.

AFTERMARKET PARTS

See Crash parts; Generic auto parts.

AGENCY COMPANIES

Companies that market and sell products via independent agents.

AGENT

Insurance is sold by two types of agents: independent agents, who are self-employed, represent several insurance companies and are paid on commission; and exclusive or captive agents, who represent only one insurance company and are either salaried or work on commission. Insurance companies that use exclusive or captive agents are called direct writers.

*ALEATORY CONTRACT

A contract in which one party provides something of value to another party in exchange for a conditional promise, which is a promise that the other party will perform a stated act upon the occurrence of an uncertain event. Insurance contracts are aleatory because the policyowner pays premiums to the insurer, and in return the insurer promises to pay benefits if the event insured against occurs. *Contrast with* Commutative contract.

ALIEN INSURANCE COMPANY

An insurance company incorporated under the laws of a foreign country, as opposed to a "foreign" insurance company which does business in states outside its own.

ALLIED LINES

Property insurance that is usually bought in conjunction with fire insurance; it includes wind, water damage and vandalism coverage.

ALTERNATIVE DISPUTE RESOLUTION/ADR

An alternative to going to court to settle disputes. Methods include arbitration, where disputing parties agree to be bound to the decision of an independent third party, and mediation, where a third party tries to arrange a settlement between the two sides.

ALTERNATIVE MARKETS
Nontraditional mechanisms used to finance risk. This includes captives, which are insurers owned by one or more non-insurers to provide owners with coverage. Risk-retention groups, formed by members of similar professions or businesses to obtain liability insurance and self-insurance, are also included.

ANNUAL ANNUITY CONTRACT FEE
Covers the cost of administering an annuity contract.

ANNUAL STATEMENT
Summary of an insurer's or reinsurer's financial operations for a particular year, including a balance sheet. It is filed with the state insurance department of each jurisdiction in which the company is licensed to conduct business.

ANNUITANT
The person who receives the income from an annuity contract. Usually the owner of the contract or his or her spouse.

ANNUITIZATION
The conversion of the account balance of a deferred annuity contract to income payments.

ANNUITY
A life insurance product that pays periodic income benefits for a specific period of time or over the course of the annuitant's lifetime. There are two basic types of annuities: deferred and immediate. Deferred annuities allow assets to grow tax-deferred over time before being converted to payments to the annuitant. Immediate annui-

ties allow payments to begin within about a year of purchase.

ANNUITY ACCUMULATION PHASE OR PERIOD
The period during which the owner of a deferred annuity makes payments to build up assets.

ANNUITY ADMINISTRATIVE CHARGES
Covers the cost of customer services for owners of variable annuities.

ANNUITY BENEFICIARY
In certain types of annuities, a person who receives annuity contract payments if the annuity owner or annuitant dies while payments are still due.

*ANNUITY CERTAIN
A type of annuity contract that pays periodic income benefits for a stated period of time, regardless of whether the annuitant lives or dies. Also known as period certain annuity. *Contrast with* Straight life annuity. (*See* Payout options)

ANNUITY CONTRACT
An agreement similar to an insurance policy for other insurance products such as auto insurance.

ANNUITY CONTRACT OWNER
The person or entity that purchases an annuity and has all rights to the contract. Usually, but not always, the annuitant (the person who receives incomes from the contract).

*ANNUITY COST
A monetary amount that is equal to the present value of future periodic income payments under an annuity. (*See* Gross annuity cost; Income date; Net annuity cost)

*ANNUITY DATE
See Income date.

ANNUITY DEATH BENEFITS

The guarantee that if an annuity contract owner dies before annuitization (the switchover from the savings to the payment phase) the beneficiary will receive the value of the annuity that is due.

ANNUITY INSURANCE CHARGES

Covers administrative and mortality and expense risk costs.

ANNUITY INVESTMENT MANAGEMENT FEE

The fee paid for the management of variable annuity invested assets.

ANNUITY ISSUER

The insurance company that issues the annuity.

ANNUITY PROSPECTUS

Legal document providing detailed information about variable annuity contracts. Must be offered to each prospective buyer.

ANNUITY PURCHASE RATE

The cost of an annuity based on such factors as the age and gender of the contract owner.

*ANTISELECTION

The tendency of individuals who suspect or know they are more likely than average to experience loss to apply for or renew insurance to a greater extent than people who lack such knowledge of probable loss. Also known as adverse selection and selection against the company.

ANTITRUST LAWS

Laws that prohibit companies from working as a group to set prices, restrict supplies or stop competition in the marketplace. The insurance industry is subject to state antitrust laws but has a limited exemption from federal antitrust laws. This exemption, set out in the McCarran-Ferguson Act, permits insurers to jointly develop common insurance forms and share loss data to help them price policies.

APPORTIONMENT

The dividing of a loss proportionately among two or more insurers that cover the same loss.

APPRAISAL

A survey to determine a property's insurable value, or the amount of a loss.

ARBITRATION

Procedure in which an insurance company and the insured or a vendor agree to settle a claim dispute by accepting a decision made by a third party.

ARSON

The deliberate setting of a fire.

ASSET-BACKED SECURITIES

Bonds that represent pools of loans of similar types, duration and interest rates. Almost any loan with regular repayments of principal and interest can be securitized, from auto loans and equipment leases to credit card receivables and mortgages.

ASSETS

Property owned, in this case by an insurance company, including stocks, bonds and real estate. Insurance accounting is concerned with solvency and the ability to pay claims. State insurance laws therefore require a conservative valuation of assets, prohibiting insurance companies from listing assets on their balance sheets whose values are uncertain, such as furniture, fixtures, debit balances and accounts receivable that are more than 90 days past due. (See Admitted assets)

ASSIGNED RISK PLANS

Facilities through which drivers can obtain auto insurance if they are unable to buy it in the regular or voluntary market. These are the most well-known type of residual auto insurance market, which exist in every state. In an assigned risk plan, all insurers selling auto insurance in the state are assigned these drivers to insure, based on the amount of insurance they sell in the regular market. (*See* Residual market)

*ASSIGNMENT

An agreement under which one party—the assignor—transfers some or all of his owner-ship rights in a particular property, such as a life insurance policy or an annuity contract, to another party—the assignee. (*See* Absolute assignment; Collateral assignment)

*ASSOCIATION GROUP

A type of group that generally is eligible for group insurance and that consists of members of an association of individuals formed for a purpose other than to obtain insurance coverage, such as teachers' associations and physicians' associations.

AUTO INSURANCE POLICY

There are basically six different types of coverages. Some may be required by law. Others are optional. They are:
1. Bodily injury liability, for injuries the policyholder causes to someone else.
2. Medical payments or Personal Injury Protection (PIP) for treatment of injuries to the driver and passengers of the policyholder's car.
3. Property damage liability, for damage the policyholder causes to someone else's property.
4. Collision, for damage to the policyholder's car from a collision.
5. Comprehensive, for damage to the policyholder's car not involving a collision with another car (including damage from fire, explosions, earthquakes, floods, and riots), and theft.

6. Uninsured motorists coverage, for costs resulting from an accident involving a hit-and-run driver or a driver who does not have insurance.

AUTO INSURANCE PREMIUM

The price an insurance company charges for coverage, based on the frequency and cost of potential accidents, theft and other losses. Prices vary from company to company, as with any product or service. Premiums also vary depending on the amount and type of coverage purchased; the make and model of the car; and the insured's driving record, years of driving and the number of miles the car is driven per year. Other factors taken into account include the driver's age and gender, where the car is most likely to be driven and the times of day—rush hour in an urban neighborhood or leisure time driving in rural areas, for example. Some insurance companies may also use credit history related information. (*See* Insurance score)

AVIATION INSURANCE

Commercial airlines hold property insurance on airplanes and liability insurance for negligent acts that result in injury or property damage to passengers or others. Damage is covered on the ground and in the air. The policy limits the geographical area and individual pilots covered.

B

B-SHARE VARIABLE ANNUITY

A form of variable annuity contract with no initial sales charge but if the contract is cancelled the holder pays deferred sales charges (usually from 5 to 7 percent the first year, declining to zero after from 5 to 7 years). The most common form of annuity contract.

BALANCE SHEET

Provides a snapshot of a company's financial condition at one point in time. It shows assets, including investments and reinsurance, and liabilities, such as loss reserves to pay claims in the future, as of a certain date. It also states a company's equity, known as policyholder surplus. Changes in that surplus are one indicator of an insurer's financial standing.

BANK HOLDING COMPANY

A company that owns or controls one or more banks. The Federal Reserve has responsibility for regulating and supervising bank holding company activities, such as approving acquisitions and mergers and inspecting the operations of such companies. This authority applies even though a bank owned by a holding company may be under the primary supervision of the Comptroller of the Currency or the FDIC.

BASIS POINT

0.01 percent of the yield of a mortgage, bond or note. The smallest measure used.

BEACH AND WINDSTORM PLANS

State-sponsored insurance pools that sell property coverage for the peril of windstorm to people unable to buy it in the voluntary market because of their high exposure to risk. Several states offer these plans to cover residential and commercial properties against hurricanes and other windstorms. (See Fair access to insurance requirements plans/FAIR plans; Residual market)

*BENEFICIARY

The person or legal entity the owner of an insurance policy names to receive the policy benefit if the event insured against occurs. (See Annuity beneficiary; Contingent beneficiary; Irrevocable beneficiary)

BINDER

Temporary authorization of coverage issued prior to the actual insurance policy.

BLANKET INSURANCE

Coverage for more than one type of property at one location or one type of property at more than one location. Example: chain stores.

BODILY INJURY LIABILITY COVERAGE

Portion of an auto insurance policy that covers injuries the policyholder causes to someone else.

BOILER AND MACHINERY INSURANCE

Often called Equipment Breakdown, or Systems Breakdown insurance. Commercial insurance that covers damage caused by the malfunction or breakdown of boilers, and a vast array of other equipment including air conditioners, heating, electrical, telephone and computer systems.

BOND

A security that obligates the issuer to pay interest at specified intervals and to repay the principal amount of the loan at maturity. In insurance, a form of suretyship. Bonds of various types guarantee a payment or a reimbursement for financial losses resulting from dishonesty, failure to perform and other acts.

BOND RATING

An evaluation of a bond's financial strength, conducted by such major ratings agencies as Standard & Poor's and Moody's Investors Service.

BOOK OF BUSINESS
Total amount of insurance on an insurer's books at a particular point in time.

BROKER
An intermediary between a customer and an insurance company. Brokers typically search the market for coverage appropriate to their clients. They work on commission and usually sell commercial, not personal, insurance. In life insurance, agents must be licensed as securities brokers/dealers to sell variable annuities, which are similar to stock market-based investments.

BURGLARY AND THEFT INSURANCE
Insurance for the loss of property due to burglary, robbery or larceny. It is provided in a standard homeowners policy and in a business multiple peril policy.

BUSINESS INCOME INSURANCE
Commercial coverage that reimburses a business owner for lost profits and continuing fixed expenses during the time that a business must stay closed while the premises are being restored because of physical damage from a covered peril, such as a fire. Business income insurance also may cover financial losses that may occur if civil authorities limit access to an area after a disaster and their actions prevent customers from reaching the business premises. Depending on the policy, civil authorities coverage may start after a waiting period and last for two or more weeks. Also known as business interruption insurance.

BUSINESSOWNERS POLICY/BOP
A policy that combines property, liability and business interruption coverages for small- to medium-sized businesses. Coverage is generally cheaper than if purchased through separate insurance policies.

C

C-SHARE VARIABLE ANNUITIES
A form of variable annuity contract where the contract holder pays no sales fee up front or surrender charges. Owners can claim full liquidity at any time.

CAPACITY
The supply of insurance available to meet demand. Capacity depends on the industry's financial ability to accept risk. For an individual insurer, the maximum amount of risk it can underwrite based on its financial condition. The adequacy of an insurer's capital relative to its exposure to loss is an important measure of solvency. A property/casualty insurer must maintain a certain level of capital and policyholder surplus to underwrite risks. This capital is known as capacity. When the industry is hit by high losses, such as after the World Trade Center terrorist attack, capacity is diminished. It can be restored by increases in net income, favorable investment returns, reinsuring more risk and or raising additional capital. When there is excess capacity, usually because of a high return on investments, premiums tend to decline as insurers compete for market share. As premiums decline, underwriting losses are likely to grow, reducing capacity and causing insurers to raise rates and tighten conditions and limits in an effort to increase profitability. Policyholder surplus is sometimes used as a measure of capacity.

CAPITAL
Shareholder's equity (for publicly traded insurance companies) and retained earnings (for mutual insurance companies). There is no general measure of capital adequacy for property/casualty insurers. Capital adequacy is linked to the riskiness of an insurer's business. A company underwriting medical device manufacturers needs a

larger cushion of capital than a company writing Main Street business, for example. (*See* Risk-based capital; Solvency; Surplus)

CAPITAL MARKETS

The markets in which equities and debt are traded. (*See* Securitization of insurance risk)

CAPTIVE AGENT

A person who represents only one insurance company and is restricted by agreement from submitting business to any other company, unless it is first rejected by the agent's captive company. (*See* Exclusive agent)

CAPTIVES

Insurers that are created and wholly owned by one or more non-insurers, to provide owners with coverage. A form of self-insurance.

CAR YEAR

Equal to 365 days of insured coverage for a single vehicle. It is the standard measurement for automobile insurance.

CASE MANAGEMENT

A system of coordinating medical services to treat a patient, improve care and reduce cost. A case manager coordinates health care delivery for patients.

*CASH DIVIDEND OPTION

For participating insurance policies, a dividend option under which the insurer sends the policy owner a check in the amount of the policy dividend. (*See* Dividend; Policy dividend options)

*CASH PAYMENT OPTION

One of several nonforfeiture options included in life insurance policies and some annuity contracts that allows a policy owner to receive the cash surrender value of a life insurance policy or an annuity contract in a single payment. Also known as

cash surrender option. (*See* Cash surrender value; Nonforfeiture options)

*CASH SURRENDER VALUE

(1) For life insurance, the amount, before adjustments for factors such as policy loans, that the owner of a permanent life insurance policy is entitled to receive if the policy does not remain in force until the insured's death. (2) For annuities, the amount of a deferred annuity's accumulated value, less any surrender charges, that the contract holder is entitled to receive if the policy is surrendered during its accumulation period. Also known as cash value and surrender value.

*CASH VALUE

See Cash surrender value.

CATASTROPHE

Term used for statistical recording purposes to refer to a single incident or a series of closely related incidents causing severe insured property losses totaling more than a given amount, currently $25 million.

CATASTROPHE BONDS

Risk-based securities that pay high interest rates and provide insurance companies with a form of reinsurance to pay losses from a catastrophe such as those caused by a major hurricane. They allow insurance risk to be sold to institutional investors in the form of bonds, thus spreading the risk. (*See* Securitization of insurance risk)

CATASTROPHE DEDUCTIBLE

A percentage or dollar amount that a homeowner must pay before the insurance policy kicks in when a major natural disaster occurs. These large deductibles limit an insurer's potential losses in such cases, allowing it to insure more property. A property insurer may not be able to buy reinsurance to protect its own bottom line unless it keeps its potential maximum losses under a certain level.

CATASTROPHE FACTOR

Probability of catastrophic loss, based on the total number of catastrophes in a state over a 40-year period.

CATASTROPHE MODEL

Using computers, a method to mesh long-term disaster information with current demographic, building and other data to determine the potential cost of natural disasters and other catastrophic losses for a given geographic area.

CATASTROPHE REINSURANCE

Reinsurance for catastrophic losses. The insurance industry is able to absorb the multibillion dollar losses caused by natural and man-made disasters such as hurricanes, earthquakes and terrorist attacks because losses are spread among thousands of companies including catastrophe reinsurers who operate on a global basis. Insurers' ability and willingness to sell insurance fluctuates with the availability and cost of catastrophe reinsurance. After major disasters, such as Hurricane Andrew and the World Trade Center terrorist attack, the availability of catastrophe reinsurance becomes extremely limited. Claims deplete reinsurers' capital and, as a result, companies are more selective in the type and amount of risks they assume. In addition, with available supply limited, prices for reinsurance rise. This contributes to an overall increase in prices for property insurance.

CELLPHONE INSURANCE

Separate insurance provided to cover cell phones for damage or theft. Policies are often sold with the cell phones themselves.

CHARTERED FINANCIAL CONSULTANT/ChFC

A professional designation given by The American College to financial services professionals who complete courses in financial planning.

CHARTERED LIFE UNDERWRITER/CLU

A professional designation by The American College for those who pass business examinations on insurance, investments and taxation, and have life insurance planning experience.

CHARTERED PROPERTY/ CASUALTY UNDERWRITER/CPCU

A professional designation given by the American Institute for Chartered Property Casualty Underwriters. National examinations and three years of work experience are required.

CLAIMS MADE POLICY

A form of insurance that pays claims presented to the insurer during the term of the policy or within a specific term after its expiration. It limits liability insurers' exposure to unknown future liabilities. (*See* Occurrence policy)

COBRA

Short for Consolidated Omnibus Budget Reconciliation Act. A federal law under which group health plans sponsored by employers with 20 or more employees must offer continuation of coverage to employees who leave their jobs and their dependents. The employee must pay the entire premium. Coverage can be extended up to 18 months. Surviving dependents can receive longer coverage.

COINSURANCE

In property insurance, requires the policyholder to carry insurance equal to a specified percentage of the value of property to receive full payment on a loss. For health insurance, it is a percentage of each claim above the deductible paid by the policy-holder. For a 20 percent health insurance coinsurance clause, the policyholder pays for the deductible plus 20 percent of his covered losses. After paying 80 percent of losses up to a specified ceiling, the insurer starts paying 100 percent of losses.

COLLATERAL
Property that is offered to secure a loan or other credit and that becomes subject to seizure on default. Also called security.

*COLLATERAL ASSIGNMENT
A temporary transfer of some of the owner-ship rights in a particular property, such as a life insurance policy or an annuity contract, as collateral for a loan. The transfer is made on the condition that upon payment of the debt for which the contract is collateral, all transferred rights shall revert back to the original owner. *Contrast with* Absolute assign-ment.

COLLISION COVERAGE
Portion of an auto insurance policy that cov-ers the damage to the policyholder's car from a collision.

COMBINED RATIO
Percentage of each premium dollar a prop-erty/casualty insurer spends on claims and expenses. A decrease in the combined ratio means financial results are improving; an increase means they are deteriorating.

COMMERCIAL AUTOMOBILE INSURANCE
Provides coverage for vehicles that are used primarily in connection with commercial establishments or business activities. While the major coverages are the same, commer-cial auto policies differs from a personal auto

policy in a number of technical respects. (*See* Auto Insurance Policy).

COMMERCIAL GENERAL LIABILITY INSURANCE/CGL
A broad commercial policy that covers all liability exposures of a business that are not specifically excluded. Coverage includes product liability, completed operations, premises and operations, and independent contractors.

COMMERCIAL LINES
Products designed for and bought by busi-nesses. Among the major coverages are boiler and machinery, business income, commercial auto, comprehensive general liability, direc-tors and officers liability, fire and allied lines, inland marine, medical malpractice liability, product liability, professional liability, surety and fidelity, and workers compensation. Most of these commercial coverages can be purchased separately except business income, which must be added to a fire insurance (property) policy. (*See* Commercial multiple peril policy)

COMMERCIAL MULTIPLE PERIL POLICY
Package policy that includes property, boiler and machinery, crime and general liability coverages.

COMMERCIAL PAPER
Short-term, unsecured and, usually, discounted promissory note issued by commercial firms and financial companies often to finance current business. Com-mercial paper, which is rated by debt rating agencies, is sold through dealers or directly placed with an investor.

COMMISSION

Fee paid to an agent or insurance salesperson as a percentage of the policy premium. The percentage varies widely depending on coverage, the insurer, and the marketing methods.

COMMUNITY RATING LAWS

Enacted in several states on health insurance policies. Insurers are required to accept all applicants for coverage and charge all applicants the same premium for the same coverage regardless of age or health. Premiums are based on the rate determined by the geographic region's health and demographic profile.

*COMMUTATIVE CONTRACT

An agreement under which the contracting parties specify the values that they will exchange; moreover, the parties generally exchange items or services that they think are of relatively equal value. *Contrast with* Aleatory contract.

COMPETITIVE REPLACEMENT PARTS

See Crash parts; Generic auto parts.

COMPETITIVE STATE FUND

A facility established by a state to sell workers compensation in competition with private insurers.

COMPLAINT RATIO

A measure used by some state insurance departments to track consumer complaints against insurance companies. Generally, it is stated as the number of complaints upheld against an insurance company, as a percentage of premiums written. In some states, complaints from medical providers over the promptness of payments may also be included.

COMPLETED OPERATIONS COVERAGE

Pays for bodily injury or property damage caused by a completed project or job. Protects a business that sells a service against liability claims.

COMPREHENSIVE COVERAGE

Portion of an auto insurance policy that covers damage to the policyholder's car not involving a collision with another car (including damage from fire, explosions, earthquakes, floods and riots), and theft.

COMPULSORY AUTO INSURANCE

The minimum amount of auto liability insurance that meets a state law. Financial responsibility laws in every state require all automobile drivers to show proof, after an accident, of their ability to pay damages up to the state minimum. In compulsory liability states this proof, which is usually in the form of an insurance policy, is required before you can legally drive a car.

*CONTESTABLE PERIOD

The time during which an insurer has the right to cancel or rescind an insurance policy if the application contained a material misrepresentation. (*See* Incontestability provision)

*CONTINGENT BENEFICIARY

The party designated to receive the proceeds of a life insurance policy following the insured's death if the primary beneficiary predeceased the insured. Also known as secondary beneficiary and successor beneficiary. (*See* Primary beneficiary)

CONTINGENT LIABILITY

Liability of individuals, corporations, or partnerships for accidents caused by people other than employees for whose acts or omissions the corporations or partnerships are responsible.

*CONVERTIBLE TERM INSURANCE POLICY

A term life insurance policy that gives the policy owner the right to convert the policy to a permanent plan of insurance.

COVERAGE

Synonym for insurance.

CRASH PARTS

Sheet metal parts that are most often damaged in a car crash. (*See* Generic auto parts)

CREDIT

The promise to pay in the future in order to buy or borrow in the present. The right to defer payment of debt.

CREDIT DERIVATIVES

A contract that enables a user, such as a bank, to better manage its credit risk. A way of transferring credit risk to another party.

CREDIT ENHANCEMENT

A technique to lower the interest payments on a bond by raising the issue's credit rating, often through insurance in the form of a financial guarantee or with standby letters of credit issued by a bank.

CREDIT INSURANCE

Commercial coverage against losses resulting from the failure of business debtors to pay their obligation to the insured, usually due to insolvency. The coverage is geared to manufacturers, wholesalers and service providers who may be dependent on a few accounts and therefore could lose significant income in the event of an insolvency.

CREDIT LIFE INSURANCE

Life insurance coverage on a borrower designed to repay the balance of a loan in the event the borrower dies before the loan is repaid. It may also include disablement

and can be offered as an option in connection with credit cards and auto loans.

CREDIT RATING

See Bond rating.

CREDIT SCORE

The number produced by an analysis of an individual's credit history. The use of credit information affects all consumers in many ways, including getting a job, finding a place to live, securing a loan, getting telephone service and buying insurance. Credit history is routinely reviewed by insurers before issuing a commercial policy because businesses in poor financial condition tend to cut back on safety, which can lead to more accidents and more claims. Auto and home insurers may use information in a credit history to produce an insurance score. Insurance scores may be used in underwriting and rating insurance policies. (*See* Insurance score)

CRIME INSURANCE

Term referring to property coverages for the perils of burglary, theft and robbery.

*CRITICAL ILLNESS (CI) INSURANCE

A type of individual health insurance that pays a lump-sum benefit when the insured is diagnosed with a specified illness. Also known as critical diagnosis insurance. *Contrast with* Specified disease coverage.

CROP-HAIL INSURANCE

Protection against damage to growing crops from hail, fire or lightning provided by the private market. By contrast, multiple peril crop insurance covers a wider range of yield reducing conditions, such as drought and insect infestation, and is subsidized by the federal government.

*CURRENT ASSUMPTION WHOLE LIFE INSURANCE

See Interest-sensitive insurance.

D

*DEATH BENEFIT
(1) For a life insurance contract, the amount of money paid by an insurer to a beneficiary when a person insured under the life insurance policy dies. (2) For an annuity contract, the amount of money paid to a beneficiary if the contract owner dies before the annuity payments begin.

DECLARATION
Part of a property or liability insurance policy that states the name and address of policyholder, property insured, its location and description, the policy period, premiums and supplemental information. Referred to as the "dec page."

*DECLINED RISK CLASS
In insurance underwriting, the group of proposed insureds whose impairments or anticipated extra mortality are so great that an insurer cannot provide insurance coverage to them at an affordable cost. Also known as uninsurable class. *Contrast with* Preferred risk class, Standard risk class and Substandard risk class.

*DECREASING TERM LIFE INSURANCE
Term life insurance that provides a death benefit that decreases in amount over the policy term. *Contrast with* Increasing term life insurance.

DEDUCTIBLE
The amount of loss paid by the policyholder. Either a specified dollar amount, a percentage of the claim amount, or a specified amount of time that must elapse before benefits are paid. The bigger the deductible, the lower the premium charged for the same coverage.

DEFERRED ANNUITY
An annuity contract, also referred to as an investment annuity, that is purchased either with a single tax-deferred premium or with periodic tax-deferred premiums over time. Payments begin at a predetermined point in time, such as retirement. Money contributed to such an annuity is intended primarily to grow tax-deferred for future use.

DEFINED BENEFIT PLAN
A retirement plan under which pension benefits are fixed in advance by a formula based generally on years of service to the company multiplied by a specific percentage of wages, usually average earnings over that period or highest average earnings over the final years with the company.

DEFINED CONTRIBUTION PLAN
An employee benefit plan under which the employer sets up benefit accounts and contributions are made to it by the employer and by the employee. The employer usually matches the employee's contribution up to a stated limit.

DEMAND DEPOSIT
Customer assets that are held in a checking account. Funds can be readily withdrawn by check, "on demand."

DEMUTUALIZATION
The conversion of insurance companies from mutual companies owned by their policyholders into publicly traded stock companies.

DEPENDENT LIFE INSURANCE
See Family benefit coverage.

DEPOSITORY INSTITUTION
Financial institutions that obtain their funds mainly through deposits from the public. They include commercial banks,

savings and loan associations, savings banks and credit unions.

DEREGULATION
In insurance, reducing regulatory control over insurance rates and forms. Commercial insurance for businesses of a certain size has been deregulated in many states.

DERIVATIVES
Contracts that derive their value from an underlying financial asset, such as publicly traded securities and foreign currencies. Often used as a hedge against changes in value.

DIFFERENCE IN CONDITIONS
Policy designed to fill in gaps in a business's commercial property insurance coverage. There is no standard policy. Policies are specifically tailored to the policyholder's needs.

DIMINUTION OF VALUE
The idea that a vehicle loses value after it has been damaged in an accident and repaired.

DIRECT PREMIUMS
Property/casualty premiums collected by the insurer from policyholders, before reinsurance premiums are deducted. Insurers share some direct premiums and the risk involved with their reinsurers.

DIRECT SALES/DIRECT RESPONSE
Method of selling insurance directly to the insured through an insurance company's own employees, through the mail, by telephone or via the Internet. This is in lieu of using captive or exclusive agents.

DIRECT WRITERS
Insurance companies that sell directly to the public using exclusive agents or their own employees, through the mail, by telephone or via the Internet. Large insurers, whether predominately direct writers or agency companies, are increasingly using many different channels to sell insurance. In reinsurance, denotes reinsurers that deal directly with the insurance companies they reinsure without using a broker.

DIRECTORS AND OFFICERS LIABILITY INSURANCE/D&O
Directors and officers liability insurance (D&O) covers directors and officers of a company for negligent acts or omissions and for misleading statements that result in suits against the company. There are a variety of D&O coverages. Corporate reimbursement coverage indemnifies directors and officers of the organization. Side-A coverage provides D&O coverage for personal liability when directors and officers are not indemnified by the firm. Entity coverage, for claims made specifically against the company, is also available. D&O policies may be broadened to include coverage for employment practices liability.

*DISABILITY
In disability insurance, the inability of an insured person to work due to an injury or sickness. Each disability policy has a definition of disability that must be satisfied in order for the insured to receive the policy's benefits. (*See* Residual disability; Total disability)

*DISABILITY INCOME INSURANCE
A type of health insurance designed to compensate an insured person for a portion of the income lost because of a disabling injury or illness. Benefit payments are made either weekly or monthly for a specified period during the continuance of an insured's disability. (*See* Income protection insurance)

*DIVIDEND ACCUMULATIONS OPTION
See Accumulation at interest option.

DIVIDENDS
Money returned to policyholders from an insurance company's earnings. Considered a partial premium refund rather than a taxable distribution, reflecting the difference between the premium charged and actual losses. Many life insurance policies and some property/casualty policies pay dividends to their owners. Life insurance policies that pay dividends are called participating policies.

DOMESTIC INSURANCE COMPANY
Term used by a state to refer to any company incorporated there.

*DOUBLE INDEMNITY BENEFIT
An accidental death benefit that is equal to the face amount of a life insurance policy's basic death benefit and is paid when the insured's death is the result of an accident as defined in the policy. (See Accidental death benefit/ADB)

DREAD DISEASE COVERAGE
See Specified disease coverage.

E

EARLY WARNING SYSTEM
A system of measuring insurers' financial stability set up by insurance industry regulators. An example is the Insurance Regulatory Information System (IRIS), which uses financial ratios to identify insurers in need of regulatory attention.

EARNED PREMIUM
The portion of premium that applies to the expired part of the policy period. Insurance premiums are payable in advance but the insurance company does not fully earn them until the policy period expires.

EARTHQUAKE INSURANCE
Covers a building and its contents, but includes a large percentage deductible on each. A special policy or endorsement exists because earthquakes are not covered by standard homeowners or most business policies.

ECONOMIC LOSS
Total financial loss resulting from the death or disability of a wage earner, or from the destruction of property. Includes the loss of earnings, medical expenses, funeral expenses, the cost of restoring or replacing property and legal expenses. It does not include noneconomic losses, such as pain caused by an injury.

ELECTRONIC COMMERCE/ E-COMMERCE
The sale of products such as insurance over the Internet.

ELIMINATION PERIOD
A kind of deductible or waiting period usually found in disability policies. It is counted in days from the beginning of the illness or injury.

EMPLOYEE DISHONESTY COVERAGE
Covers direct losses and damage to businesses resulting from the dishonest acts of employees. (See Fidelity bond)

EMPLOYEE RETIREMENT INCOME SECURITY ACT/ERISA
Federal legislation that protects employees by establishing minimum standards for private pension and welfare plans.

EMPLOYER'S LIABILITY
Part B of the workers compensation policy that provides coverage for lawsuits filed by injured employees who, under certain circumstances, can sue under common law. (See Exclusive remedy)

EMPLOYMENT PRACTICES LIABILITY COVERAGE

Liability insurance for employers that covers wrongful termination, discrimination and other violations of employees' legal rights.

ENDORSEMENT

A written form attached to an insurance policy that alters the policy's coverage, terms, or conditions. Sometimes called a rider.

*ENDOWMENT INSURANCE

Life insurance that provides a policy benefit payable either when the insured dies or on a stated date if the insured is still alive on that date.

ENVIRONMENTAL IMPAIRMENT LIABILITY COVERAGE

A form of insurance designed to cover losses and liabilities arising from damage to property caused by pollution.

EQUITY

In investments, the ownership interest of shareholders. In a corporation, stocks as opposed to bonds.

EQUITY INDEXED ANNUITY

Nontraditional fixed annuity. The specified rate of interest guarantees a fixed minimum rate of interest like traditional fixed annuities. At the same time, additional interest may be credited to policy values based upon positive changes, if any, in an established index such as the S&P 500. The amount of additional interest depends upon the particular design of the policy. They are sold by licensed insurance agents and regulated by state insurance departments.

ERRORS AND OMISSIONS COVERAGE/E&O

A professional liability policy covering the policyholder for negligent acts and omissions that may harm his or her clients.

ESCROW ACCOUNT

Funds that a lender collects to pay monthly premiums in mortgage and homeowners insurance, and sometimes to pay property taxes.

EXCESS AND SURPLUS LINES

Property/casualty coverage that isn't available from insurers licensed by the state (called admitted insurers) and must be purchased from a nonadmitted carrier.

EXCESS OF LOSS REINSURANCE

A contract between an insurer and a reinsurer, whereby the insurer agrees to pay a specified portion of a claim and the reinsurer to pay all or a part of the claim above that amount.

EXCLUSION

A provision in an insurance policy that eliminates coverage for certain risks, people, property classes, or locations.

EXCLUSIVE AGENT

A captive agent, or a person who represents only one insurance company and is restricted by agreement from submitting business to any other company unless it is first rejected by the agent's company. (*See* Captive agent)

EXCLUSIVE REMEDY

Part of the social contract that forms the basis for workers compensation statutes under which employers are responsible for work-related injury and disease, regardless of whether it was the employee's fault and in return the injured employee gives up the right to sue when the employer's negligence causes the harm.

EXPENSE RATIO
Percentage of each premium dollar that goes to insurers' expenses including overhead, marketing and commissions.

EXPERIENCE
Record of losses.

EXPOSURE
Possibility of loss.

EXTENDED COVERAGE
An endorsement added to an insurance policy, or clause within a policy, that provides additional coverage for risks other than those in a basic policy.

EXTENDED REPLACEMENT COST COVERAGE
Pays a certain amount above the policy limit to replace a damaged home, generally 120 percent or 125 percent. Similar to a guaranteed replacement cost policy, which has no percentage limits. Most homeowner policy limits track inflation in building costs. Guaranteed and extended replacement cost policies are designed to protect the policyholder after a major disaster when the high demand for building contractors and materials can push up the normal cost of reconstruction. (*See* Guaranteed replacement cost coverage)

*EXTENDED TERM INSURANCE OPTION
One of several nonforfeiture options included in life insurance policies that allows the owner of a policy with a cash value to discontinue premium payments and to use the policy's net cash value to purchase term insurance for the full coverage amount provided under the original policy for as long a term as the net cash value can provide. (*See* Nonforfeiture options)

F
For definitions of **401(k) Plan**, **403(b) Plan**, and **529 Savings Plans**, see page 78.

*FACE AMOUNT
For a fixed-amount whole life insurance policy, the amount of the death benefit payable if the insured person dies while the policy is in force.

FACULTATIVE REINSURANCE
A reinsurance policy that provides an insurer with coverage for specific individual risks that are unusual or so large that they aren't covered in the insurance company's reinsurance treaties. This can include policies for jumbo jets or oil rigs. Reinsurers have no obligation to take on facultative reinsurance, but can assess each risk individually. By contrast, under treaty reinsurance, the reinsurer agrees to assume a certain percentage of entire classes of business, such as various kinds of auto, up to preset limits.

FAIR ACCESS TO INSURANCE REQUIREMENTS PLANS/ FAIR PLANS
Insurance pools that sell property insurance to people who can't buy it in the voluntary market because of high risk over which they may have no control. FAIR Plans, which exist in 28 states and the District of Columbia, insure fire, vandalism, riot and windstorm losses, and some sell homeowners insurance which includes liability. Plans vary by state, but all require property insurers licensed in a state to participate in the pool and share in the profits and losses. (*See* Residual market)

*FAMILY BENEFIT COVERAGE
A type of supplementary benefit rider offered in conjunction with a life insurance policy that insures the lives of the

insured's spouse and children. Also known as dependent life insurance and spouse and children's insurance rider.

FARMOWNERS-RANCHOWNERS INSURANCE
Package policy that protects the policyholder against named perils and liabilities and usually covers homes and their contents, along with barns, stables and other structures.

FEDERAL FUNDS
Reserve balances that depository institutions lend each other, usually on an overnight basis. In addition, Federal funds include certain other kinds of borrowing by depository institutions from each other and from federal agencies.

FEDERAL INSURANCE ADMINISTRATION/FIA
Federal agency in charge of administering the National Flood Insurance Program. It does not regulate the insurance industry.

FEDERAL RESERVE BOARD
Seven member board that supervises the banking system by issuing regulations controlling bank holding companies and federal laws over the banking industry. It also controls and oversees the U.S. monetary system and credit supply.

FIDELITY BOND
A form of protection that covers policyholders for losses that they incur as a result of fraudulent acts by specified individuals. It usually insures a business for losses caused by the dishonest acts of its employees.

FIDUCIARY BOND
A type of surety bond, sometimes called a probate bond, which is required of certain fiduciaries, such as executors and trustees,

that guarantees the performance of their responsibilities.

FIDUCIARY LIABILITY
Legal responsibility of a fiduciary to safeguard assets of beneficiaries. A fiduciary, for example a pension fund manager, is required to manage investments held in trust in the best interest of beneficiaries. Fiduciary liability insurance covers breaches of fiduciary duty such as misstatements or misleading statements, errors and omissions.

FILE-AND-USE STATES
States where insurers must file rate changes with their regulators, but don't have to wait for approval to put them into effect.

FINANCIAL GUARANTEE INSURANCE
Covers losses from specific financial transactions and guarantees that investors in debt instruments, such as municipal bonds, receive timely payment of principal and interest if there is a default. Raises the credit rating of debt to which the guarantee is attached. Investment bankers who sell asset-backed securities, securities backed by loan portfolios, use this insurance to enhance marketability. (*See* Municipal bond insurance)

FINANCIAL RESPONSIBILITY LAW
A state law requiring that all automobile drivers show proof that they can pay damages up to a minimum amount if involved in an auto accident. Varies from state to state but can be met by carrying a minimum amount of auto liability insurance. (*See* Compulsory auto insurance)

FINITE RISK REINSURANCE
Contract under which the ultimate liability of the reinsurer is capped and on which anticipated investment income is expressly acknowledged as an underwrit-

ing component. Also known as financial reinsurance because this type of coverage is often bought to improve the balance sheet effects of statutory accounting principles.

FIRE INSURANCE

Coverage protecting property against losses caused by a fire or lightning that is usually included in homeowners or commercial multiple peril policies.

FIRST-PARTY COVERAGE

Coverage for the policyholder's own property or person. In no-fault auto insurance it pays for the cost of injuries. In no-fault states with the broadest coverage, the personal injury protection (PIP) part of the policy pays for medical care, lost income, funeral expenses and, where the injured person is not able to provide services such as child care, for substitute services. (See No-fault; Third-party coverage)

FIXED ANNUITY

An annuity that guarantees a specific rate of return. In the case of a deferred annuity, a minimum rate of interest is guaranteed during the savings phase. During the payment phase, a fixed amount of income, paid on a regular schedule, is guaranteed.

*FLEXIBLE PREMIUM

A premium payment method sometimes offered in connection with annuities and with some types of life insurance that allows the contract owner or policy owner to alter the amount and the frequency of payments, within specified boundaries defined by the insurer and the law.

FLOATER

Attached to a homeowners policy, a floater insures movable property, covering losses wherever they may occur. Among the items often insured with a floater are expensive jewelry, musical instruments and furs. It provides broader coverage than a regular homeowners policy for these items.

FLOOD INSURANCE

Coverage for flood damage is available from the federal government under the National Flood Insurance Program but is sold by licensed insurance agents. Flood coverage is excluded under homeowners policies and many commercial property policies. However, flood damage is covered under the comprehensive portion of an auto insurance policy. (See Adverse selection)

FORCED PLACE INSURANCE

Insurance purchased by a bank or creditor on an uninsured debtor's behalf so if the property is damaged, funding is available to repair it.

FOREIGN INSURANCE COMPANY

Name given to an insurance company based in one state by the other states in which it does business.

FRAUD

Intentional lying or concealment by policyholders to obtain payment of an insurance claim that would otherwise not be paid, or lying or misrepresentation by the insurance company managers, employees, agents and brokers for financial gain.

*FRATERNAL BENEFIT SOCIETY

See Fraternal insurer.

*FRATERNAL INSURER

A nonprofit organization that is operated solely for the benefit of its members and that provides its members with social and insurance benefits. Also known as fraternal benefit society.

FREE-LOOK PERIOD

A period of up to one month during which the purchaser of an annuity can cancel the contract with no penalty. Rules vary by state.

FREQUENCY
Number of times a loss occurs. One of the criteria used in calculating premium rates.

FRONTING
A procedure in which a primary insurer acts as the insurer of record by issuing a policy, but then passes the entire risk to a reinsurer in exchange for a commission. Often, the fronting insurer is licensed to do business in a state or country where the risk is located, but the reinsurer is not. The reinsurer in this scenario is often a captive or an independent insurance company that cannot sell insurance directly in a particular country.

FUTURES
Agreement to buy a security for a set price at a certain date. Futures contracts usually involve commodities, indexes or financial futures.

G

GAP INSURANCE
An automobile insurance option, available in some states, that covers the difference between a car's actual cash value when it is stolen or wrecked and the amount the consumer owes the leasing or finance company. Mainly used for leased cars. (*See* Actual cash value)

*GENERAL ACCOUNT
An undivided investment account in which insurers maintain funds that support contractual obligations for guaranteed insurance products such as whole life insurance or fixed-rate annuities. *Contrast with* Separate account.

GENERALLY ACCEPTED ACCOUNTING PRINCIPLES/GAAP
Generally accepted accounting principles (GAAP) accounting is used in financial statements that publicly held companies prepare for the Securities and Exchange Commission. (*See* Statutory accounting principles/SAP)

GENERIC AUTO PARTS
Auto crash parts produced by firms that are not associated with car manufacturers. Insurers consider these parts, when certified, at least as good as those that come from the original equipment manufacturer (OEM). They are often cheaper than the identical part produced by the OEM. (*See* Crash parts; Aftermarket parts; Competitive replacement parts; Original equipment manufacturer parts/OEM)

GLASS INSURANCE
Coverage for glass breakage caused by all risks; fire and war are sometimes excluded. Insurance can be bought for windows, structural glass, leaded glass and mirrors. Available with or without a deductible.

*GRACE PERIOD
(1) For insurance premium payments, a specified length of time following a premium due date within which the renewal premium may be paid without penalty. The length of the grace period is specified in a grace period provision that is found in a life insurance, health insurance, or annuity policy. (2) For purchases made on credit, a period of time between the date of a purchase and the date the lender begins to charge interest during which no interest accrues.

*GRADED PREMIUM POLICY
A type of modified-premium whole life policy that calls for three or more levels of annual premium payment amounts,

increasing at specified points in time—such as every three years—until reaching the amount to be paid as a level premium for the rest of the life of the policy.

GRADUATED DRIVER LICENSES

Licenses for younger drivers that allow them to improve their skills. Regulations vary by state, but often restrict nighttime driving. Young drivers receive a learner's permit, followed by a provisional license, before they can receive a standard driver's license.

GRAMM-LEACH-BLILEY ACT

Financial services legislation, passed by Congress in 1999, that removed Depression era prohibitions against the combination of commercial banking and investment banking activities. It allows insurance companies, banks and securities firms to engage in each others' activities and own one another.

*GROSS ANNUITY COST

A monetary amount equal to the present value of future periodic income payments under an annuity contract, calculated on a gross basis, with a specific provision for expense loading. *Contrast with* Net annuity cost.

GROUP INSURANCE

A single policy covering a group of individuals, usually employees of the same company or members of the same association and their dependents. Coverage occurs under a master policy issued to the employer or association.

GUARANTEE PERIOD

Period during which the level of interest specified under a fixed annuity is guaranteed.

GUARANTEED DEATH BENEFIT

Basic death benefits guaranteed under variable annuity contracts.

GUARANTEED INCOME CONTRACT/GIC

Often an option in an employer-sponsored retirement savings plan. Contract between an insurance company and the plan that guarantees a stated rate of return on invested capital over the life of the contract.

*GUARANTEED INSURABILITY (GI) BENEFIT

A supplementary life insurance policy benefit often provided through a policy rider that gives the policy owner the right to purchase additional insurance of the same type as the life insurance policy that provides the GI benefit on specified option dates. Also known as guaranteed insurability option (GIO).

GUARANTEED LIVING BENEFIT

A guarantee in a variable annuity that a certain level of annuity payment will be maintained. Serves as a protection against investment risks. Several types exists.

*GUARANTEED RENEWABLE POLICY

An individual health insurance policy that requires the insurer to renew the policy—as long as premium payments are made—at least until the insured attains a specified age. The insurer can change premium rates for broad classes of insureds but not for an individual insured. *Contrast with* Noncancellable and Guaranteed renewable policy.

GUARANTEED REPLACEMENT COST COVERAGE

Homeowners policy that pays the full cost of replacing or repairing a damaged or destroyed home, even if it is above the policy limit. (*See* Extended replacement cost coverage)

GUARANTY FUND

The mechanism by which solvent insurers ensure that some of the policyholder and third-party claims against insurance companies that fail are paid. Such funds are required in all 50 states, the District of Columbia and Puerto Rico, but the type and amount of claim covered by the fund varies from state to state. Some states pay policyholders' unearned premiums—the portion of the premium for which no coverage was provided because the company was insolvent. Some have deductibles. Most states have no limits on workers compensation payments. Guaranty funds are supported by assessments on insurers doing business in the state.

GUN LIABILITY

A legal concept that holds gun manufacturers liable for the cost of injuries caused by guns. Several cities have filed lawsuits based on this concept.

H

HACKER INSURANCE

A coverage that protects businesses engaged in electronic commerce from losses caused by hackers.

HARD MARKET

A seller's market in which insurance is expensive and in short supply. (See Property/casualty insurance cycle)

HOMEOWNERS INSURANCE POLICY

The typical homeowners insurance policy covers the house, the garage and other structures on the property, as well as personal possessions inside the house such as furniture, appliances and clothing, against a wide variety of perils including windstorms, fire and theft. The extent of the perils covered depends on the type of policy. An all-risk policy offers the broadest coverage. This covers all perils except those specifically excluded in the policy. Homeowners insurance also covers additional living expenses. Known as Loss of Use, this provision in the policy reimburses the policyholder for the extra cost of living elsewhere while the house is being restored after a disaster. The liability portion of the policy covers the homeowner for accidental injuries caused to third parties and/or their property, such as a guest slipping and falling down improperly maintained stairs. Coverage for flood and earthquake damage is excluded and must be purchased separately. (See Flood insurance; Earthquake insurance)

HOUSE YEAR

Equal to 365 days of insured coverage for a single dwelling. It is the standard measurement for homeowners insurance.

HURRICANE DEDUCTIBLE

A percentage or dollar amount added to a home-owners insurance policy to limit an insurer's exposure to loss from a hurricane. Higher deductibles are instituted in higher risk areas, such as coastal regions. Specific details, such as the intensity of the storm necessary for the deductible to be triggered and the extent of the high risk area, vary from insurer to insurer and state to state.

HYBRID ANNUITY

An annuity with features of both fixed and variable annuities. (See Fixed annuity; variable annuity)

I

IDENTITY THEFT INSURANCE

Coverage for expenses incurred as the result of an identity theft. Can include costs for notarizing fraud affidavits and certified mail, lost income from time taken off from work to meet with law enforcement personnel or credit agencies, fees for reapplying for loans and attorney's fees to defend against lawsuits and remove criminal or civil judgments.

IMMEDIATE ANNUITY

A product purchased with a lump sum, usually at the time retirement begins or afterwards. Payments begin within about a year. Immediate annuities can be either fixed or variable.

*INCOME DATE

The date on which an insurer begins or is scheduled to begin making annuity benefit payments under an annuity contract. Also known as maturity date and annuity date.

*INCOME PROTECTION INSURANCE

A type of disability income coverage that provides an income benefit both, while the insured is totally disabled and unable to work and while he is able to work, but because of a disability, is earning less than he earned before being disabled. Also known as residual disability insurance.

*INCONTESTABILITY PROVISION

An insurance and annuity policy provision that limits the time within which an insurer has the right to avoid the contract on the ground of material misrepresentation in the application for the policy. Also known as incontestable clause. (See Contestable period; Time limit on certain defenses provision)

*INCREASING TERM LIFE INSURANCE

A type of term life insurance that provides a death benefit that increases by some specified amount or percentage at stated intervals over the policy term. Contrast with Decreasing term life insurance.

INCURRED BUT NOT REPORTED LOSSES/IBNR

Losses that are not filed with the insurer or reinsurer until years after the policy is sold. Some liability claims may be filed long after the event that caused the injury to occur. Asbestos-related diseases, for example, do not show up until decades after the exposure. IBNR also refers to estimates made about claims already reported but where the full extent of the injury is not yet known, such as a workers compensation claim where the degree to which work-related injuries prevents a worker from earning what he or she earned before the injury unfolds over time. Insurance companies regularly adjust reserves for such losses as new information becomes available.

INCURRED LOSSES

Losses occurring within a fixed period, whether or not adjusted or paid during the same period.

INDEMNIFY

Provide financial compensation for losses.

INDEPENDENT AGENT

Agent who is self-employed, is paid on commission, and represents several insurance companies. (See Captive agent)

*INDETERMINATE PREMIUM LIFE INSURANCE POLICY

A type of nonparticipating whole life policy that specifies two premium rates—both a maximum guaranteed rate and a lower rate. The insurer charges the lower premium rate when the policy is purchased and guarantees that rate for at least a stated period of time, after which the insurer uses its actual mortality, interest, and expense experience to establish a new premium rate that may be higher or lower than the previous premium rate. Also known as nonguaranteed premium life insurance policy and variable premium life insurance policy.

INDEXED LIFE INSURANCE CONTRACT

An arrangement similar to a universal life contract. Death benefit amounts are based on the amount selected by the policyholder plus the account value. The policyholder's account value is linked to cumulative returns based on the S&P 500 index or some other tied index. An essential component of the contract is that the cash surrender value is also linked to a tied index. Typically, the tied index doesn't include dividends. There may be additional constraints on the amount that the insurance company will credit as interest under this policy.

INDIVIDUAL RETIREMENT ACCOUNT/IRA

A tax-deductible savings plan for those who are self-employed, or those whose earnings are below a certain level or whose employers do not offer retirement plans. Others may make limited contributions on a tax-deferred basis. The Roth IRA, a special kind of retirement account created in 1997, may offer greater tax benefits to certain individuals.

INFLATION GUARD CLAUSE

A provision added to a homeowners insurance policy that automatically adjusts the coverage limit on the dwelling each time the policy is renewed to reflect current construction costs.

INLAND MARINE INSURANCE

This broad type of coverage was developed for shipments that do not involve ocean transport. Covers articles in transit by all forms of land and air transportation as well as bridges, tunnels and other means of transportation and communication. Floaters that cover expensive personal items

such as fine art and jewelry are included in this category. (See Floater)

INSOLVENCY

Insurer's inability to pay debts. Insurance insolvency standards and the regulatory actions taken vary from state to state. When regulators deem an insurance company is in danger of becoming insolvent, they can take one of three actions: place a company in conservatorship or rehabilitation, if the company can be saved, or in liquidation, if salvage is deemed impossible. The difference between the first two options is one of degree—regulators guide companies in conservatorship but direct those in rehabilitation. Typically the first sign of problems is inability to pass the financial tests regulators administer as a routine procedure. (See Liquidation; Risk-based capital)

INSTITUTIONAL INVESTOR

An organization such as a bank or insurance company that buys and sells large quantities of securities.

*INSURABLE INTEREST

In insurance, a person exhibits an insurable interest in a potential loss if that person will suffer a genuine economic loss if the event insured against occurs. Without the presence of insurable interest, an insurance contract is not formed for a lawful purpose and, thus, is not a valid contract.

INSURABLE RISK

Risks for which it is relatively easy to get insurance and that meet certain criteria. These include being definable, accidental in nature, and part of a group of similar risks large enough to make losses predictable. The insurance company also must be able to come up with a reasonable price for the insurance.

INSURANCE
A system to make large financial losses more affordable by pooling the risks of many individuals and business entities and transferring them to an insurance company or other large group in return for a premium.

INSURANCE POOL
A group of insurance companies that pools its assets, enabling them to provide an amount of insurance substantially more than can be provided by individual companies to ensure large risks such as nuclear power stations. Pools may be formed voluntarily or mandated by the state to insure risks that cannot be covered in the voluntary market such as coastal properties subject to hurricanes. (*See* Beach and windstorm plans; Fair access to insurance requirements plans/FAIR plans; Joint underwriting association/JUA)

INSURANCE REGULATORY INFORMATION SYSTEM/IRIS
Uses financial ratios to measure insurers' financial strength. Developed by the National Association of Insurance Commissioners. Each individual state insurance department chooses how to use IRIS.

INSURANCE SCORE
Insurance scores are confidential rankings based on credit information. This includes whether the consumer has made timely payments on loans, the number of open credit card accounts and whether a bankruptcy filing has been made. An insurance score is a measure of how well consumers manage their financial affairs, not of their financial assets. It does not include information about income or race. Studies have shown that people who manage their money well tend also to manage their most important asset, their home, well. And people who manage their money respon-

sibly also tend to drive a car responsibly. Some insurance companies use insurance scores as an insurance underwriting and rating tool.

INSURANCE-TO-VALUE
Insurance written in an amount approximating the value of the insured property.

INTEGRATED BENEFITS
Coverage where the distinction between job-related and non-occupational illnesses or injuries is eliminated and workers compensation and general health coverage are combined. Legal obstacles exist, however, because the two coverages are administered separately. Previously called twenty-four hour coverage.

*INTEREST-ADJUSTED COST COMPARISON INDEX
A cost comparison index used to compare life insurance policy costs that takes into account the time value of money. By comparing the index numbers derived for similar life insurance policies, a consumer has some basis on which to compare the costs of the policies. (*See* Net payment cost comparison index; Surrender cost comparison index)

*INTEREST-SENSITIVE INSURANCE
A general category of insurance products in which the face amount and/or the cash value vary according to the insurer's investment earnings.

INTERMEDIATION
The process of bringing savers, investors and borrowers together so that savers and investors can obtain a return on their money and borrowers can use the money to finance their purchases or projects through loans.

INTERNET INSURER

An insurer that sells exclusively via the Internet.

INTERNET LIABILITY INSURANCE

Coverage designed to protect businesses from liabilities that arise from the conducting of business over the Internet, including copyright infringement, defamation and violation of privacy.

INVESTMENT ANNUITY

See Deferred annuity.

INVESTMENT INCOME

Income generated by the investment of assets. Insurers have two sources of income, underwriting (premiums less claims and expenses) and investment income. The latter can offset underwriting operations, which are frequently unprofitable.

*IRREVOCABLE BENEFICIARY

A life insurance policy beneficiary who has a vested interest in the policy proceeds even during the insured's lifetime because the policy owner has the right to change the beneficiary designation only after obtaining the beneficiary's consent. Contrast with Revocable beneficiary.

J

JOINT AND SURVIVOR ANNUITY

An annuity with two annuitants, usually spouses. Payments continue until the death of the longest living of the two.

JOINT UNDERWRITING ASSOCIATION/JUA

Insurers that join together to provide coverage for a particular type of risk or size of exposure, when there are difficulties in obtaining coverage in the regular market, and which share in the profits and losses associated with the program. JUAs may be set up to provide auto and homeowners in-surance and various commercial coverages, such as medical malpractice. (See Assigned risk plans; Residual market)

JUNK BONDS

Corporate bonds with credit ratings of BB or less. They pay a higher yield than investment grade bonds because issuers have a higher perceived risk of default. Such bonds involve market risk that could force investors, including insurers, to sell the bonds when their value is low. Most states place limits on insurers' investments in these bonds. In general, because property/casualty insurers can be called upon to provide huge sums of money immediately after a disaster, their investments must be liquid. Less than 2 percent are in real estate and a similarly small percent are in junk bonds.

JOINT AND SURVIVOR ANNUITY

An annuity with two annuitants, usually spouses. Payments continue until the death of the longest living of the two.

K

KEY PERSON INSURANCE

Insurance on the life or health of a key individual whose services are essential to the continuing success of a business and whose death or disability could cause the firm a substantial financial loss.

KIDNAP/RANSOM INSURANCE

Coverage up to specific limits for the cost of ransom or extortion payments and related expenses. Often bought by international corporations to cover employees. Most policies have large deductibles and may exclude certain geographic areas. Some policies require that the policyholder not reveal the existence of the coverage.

L

L-SHARE VARIABLE ANNUITIES

A form of variable annuity contract usually with short surrender periods and higher mortality and expense risk charges.

LADDERING

A technique that consists of staggering the maturity dates and the mix of different types of bonds.

*LAPSE

The termination of an insurance policy because a renewal premium is not paid by the end of the grace period.

LAW OF LARGE NUMBERS

The theory of probability on which the business of insurance is based. Simply put, this mathematical premise says that the larger the group of units insured, such as sport-utility vehicles, the more accurate the predictions of loss will be.

*LEVEL PREMIUM POLICIES

Premiums paid for a life insurance policy or for a deferred annuity that remain the same each year that the contract is in force. *Contrast with* Modified premium policies and Single premium policies.

LIABILITY INSURANCE

Insurance for what the policyholder is legally obligated to pay because of bodily injury or property damage caused to another person.

*LIFE ANNUITY

A type of annuity contract that guarantees periodic income payments throughout the lifetime of a named individual—the annuitant. If a life annuity provides no further benefits after the death of the annuitant, the annuity is known as a straight life annuity. However, some life annuities provide that income payments will be paid either for the life of the annuitant or for a guaranteed period—life income with period certain—or at least until a guaranteed amount has been paid—life income with refund annuity. (*See* Life annuity with period certain; Life income with refund annuity; Straight life annuity)

*LIFE ANNUITY WITH PERIOD CERTAIN

A type of annuity contract that guarantees periodic income payments throughout the lifetime of a named individual—the annuitant—and guarantees that the payments will continue for at least a specified period. If the annuitant dies before the end of that specified period, the payments will continue to be paid until the end of the period to a beneficiary designated by the annuitant. (*See* Life annuity)

*LIFE INCOME WITH REFUND ANNUITY

A type of annuity contract that guarantees specified periodic income payments throughout the lifetime of a named individual—the annuitant—and guarantees that a refund will be made if the annuitant dies before the total of the periodic payments made equals the amount paid for the annuity. Also known as refund annuity. (*See* Life annuity)

LIFE INSURANCE

Protection against the death of a policyholder in the form of a payment to a beneficiary. (*See* Ordinary life insurance; Term insurance; Variable life insurance; Whole life insurance)

LIMITED PAYMENT LIFE INSURANCE

Life insurance policy with premiums that are fully paid up within a stated period of time, such as 20 years.

LIMITS
Maximum amount of insurance that can be paid for a covered loss.

LINE
Type or kind of insurance.

LIQUIDATION
Enables the state insurance department as liquidator or its appointed deputy to wind up the insurance company's affairs by selling its assets and settling claims upon those assets. After receiving the liquidation order, the liquidator notifies insurance departments in other states and state guaranty funds of the liquidation proceedings. Such insurance company liquidations are not subject to the Federal Bankruptcy Code but to each state's liquidation statutes.

LIQUIDITY
The ability and speed with which a security can be converted into cash.

LIQUOR LIABILITY
Coverage for bodily injury or property damage caused by an intoxicated person who was served liquor by the policyholder.

LIVING BENEFIT RIDER
An addition to a policy that enables early payout of anticipated death benefits. The rider affords terminally ill policyholders an additional source of funds to pay medical bills and maintain their lifestyle.

LLOYD'S OF LONDON
A marketplace where underwriting syndicates, or mini-insurers, gather to sell insurance policies and reinsurance. Each syndicate is managed by an underwriter who decides whether or not to accept the risk. The Lloyd's market is a major player in the international reinsurance market as well as a primary market for marine insurance and large risks. Originally, Lloyd's was a London coffee house in the 1600s patronized by shipowners who insured each other's hulls and cargoes. As Lloyd's developed, wealthy individuals, called "Names," placed their personal assets behind insurance risks as a business venture. Increasingly since the 1990s, most of the capital comes from corporations.

LLOYDS
Corporation formed to market services of a group of underwriters. Does not issue insurance policies or provide insurance protection. Insurance is written by individual underwriters, with each assuming a part of every risk. Has no connection to Lloyd's of London, and is found primarily in Texas.

LONG-TERM CARE INSURANCE
Long-term care (LTC) insurance pays for services to help individuals who are unable to perform certain activities of daily living without assistance, or require supervision due to a cognitive impairment such as Alzheimer's disease. LTC is available as individual insurance or through an employer-sponsored or association plan.

*LONG-TERM DISABILITY INCOME INSURANCE
A type of disability income insurance that provides disability income benefits after short-term disability income benefits terminate and continues until the earlier of the date when the insured person returns to work, dies, or becomes eligible for pension benefits. *Contrast with* Short-term disability income insurance.

LOSS
A reduction in the quality or value of a property, or a legal liability.

LOSS ADJUSTMENT EXPENSES
The sum insurers pay for investigating and settling insurance claims, including the cost of defending a lawsuit in court.

LOSS COSTS
The portion of an insurance rate used to cover claims and the costs of adjusting claims. Insurance companies typically determine their rates by estimating their future loss costs and adding a provision for expenses, profit and contingencies.

LOSS OF USE
A provision in homeowners and renters insurance policies that reimburses policyholders for any extra living expenses due to having to live elsewhere while their home is being restored following a disaster.

LOSS RATIO
Percentage of each premium dollar an insurer spends on claims.

LOSS RESERVES
The company's best estimate of what it will pay for claims, which is periodically readjusted. They represent a liability on the insurer's balance sheet.

M

MALPRACTICE INSURANCE
Professional liability coverage for physicians, lawyers, and other specialists against suits alleging negligence or errors and omissions that have harmed clients.

MANAGED CARE
Arrangement between an employer or insurer and selected providers to provide comprehensive health care at a discount to members of the insured group and coordinate the financing and delivery of health care. Managed care uses medical protocols and procedures agreed on by the medical profession to be cost effective, also known as medical practice guidelines.

MANUAL
A book published by an insurance or bonding company or a rating association or bureau that gives rates, classifications and underwriting rules.

MARINE INSURANCE
Coverage for goods in transit, and for the commercial vehicles that transport them, on water and over land. The term may apply to inland marine but more generally applies to ocean marine insurance. Covers damage or destruction of a ship's hull and cargo and perils include collision, sinking, capsizing, being stranded, fire, piracy and jettisoning cargo to save other property. Wear and tear, dampness, mold, and war are not included. (See Inland marine; Ocean marine)

*MATURITY DATE
(1) For endowment in insurance, the date on which an insurer will pay the face amount of an endowment policy to the policy owner if the insured is still living. (2) In investing, the date on which a bond issuer must repay to the bondholder the amount originally borrowed. (3) For an annuity, the date on which the insurer begins to make annuity payments. Also known as income date.

McCARRAN-FERGUSON ACT
Federal law signed in 1945 in which Congress declared that states would continue to regulate the insurance business. Grants insurers a limited exemption from federal antitrust legislation.

MEDIATION
Nonbinding procedure in which a third party attempts to resolve a conflict between two other parties.

MEDICAID
A federal/state public assistance program created in 1965 and administered by

the states for people whose income and resources are insufficient to pay for health care.

*MEDICAL INFORMATION BUREAU
See MIB, Inc.

MEDICAL MALPRACTICE INSURANCE
See Malpractice insurance.

MEDICAL PAYMENTS INSURANCE
A coverage in which the insurer agrees to reimburse the insured and others up to a certain limit for medical or funeral expenses as a result of bodily injury or death by accident. Payments are without regard to fault.

MEDICAL UTILIZATION REVIEW
The practice used by insurance companies to review claims for medical treatment.

MEDICARE
Federal program for people 65 or older that pays part of the costs associated with hospitalization, surgery, doctors' bills, home health care and skilled nursing care.

MEDIGAP/MEDSUP
Policies that supplement federal insurance benefits particularly for those covered under Medicare.

*MIB, INC.
A nonprofit organization established to provide information to insurers about impairments that applicants have admitted to, or that other insurers have detected, in connection with previous applications for insurance. Formerly known as Medical Information Bureau.

MINE SUBSIDENCE COVERAGE
An endorsement to a homeowners insurance policy, available in some states, for losses to a home caused by the land under a house sinking into a mine shaft. Excluded

from standard homeowners policies, as are other forms of earth movement.

*MISREPRESENTATION
A false or misleading statement. (1) In insurance sales, a false or misleading statement made by a sales agent to induce a customer to purchase insurance is a prohibited sales practice. (2) In insurance underwriting, a false or misleading statement by an insurance applicant may provide a basis for the insurer to avoid the policy.

*MISSTATEMENT OF AGE OR SEX PROVISION
A life insurance, health insurance, and annuity policy provision that describes how policy benefits will be adjusted if the age or sex of the insured has been misstated in the insurance application. Typically, the benefits payable will be those that the premiums paid would have purchased for the correct age or sex.

*MODIFIED PREMIUM POLICIES
An insurance policy for which the policy owner first pays a lower premium than she would for a similar level premium policy for a specified initial period and then pays a higher premium than she would for a similar level premium policy. Contrast with Level premium policies and Single premium policies.

MONEY SUPPLY
Total supply of money in the economy, composed of currency in circulation and deposits in savings and checking accounts. By changing the interest rates the Federal Reserve seeks to adjust the money supply to maintain a strong economy.

*MORAL HAZARD
The possibility that a person may act dishonestly in an insurance transaction.

*MORBIDITY RATE

The rate at which sickness and injury occur within a defined group of people. Insurers base health insurance premiums in part on the morbidity rate for a proposed insured's age group. *Contrast with* Mortality rate.

MORTALITY AND EXPENSE (M&E) RISK CHARGE

A fee that covers such annuity contract guarantees as death benefits.

*MORTALITY RATE

A percentage rate at which death occurs among a defined group of people of a specified age and sometimes of a specified gender. Insurers base the premiums for life insurance in part on the mortality rate for a proposed insured's age group. *Contrast with* Morbidity rate.

MORTGAGE GUARANTEE INSURANCE

Coverage for the mortgagee (usually a financial institution) in the event that a mortgage holder defaults on a loan. Also called private mortgage insurance (PMI).

MORTGAGE INSURANCE

A form of decreasing term insurance that covers the life of a person taking out a mortgage. Death benefits provide for payment of the outstanding balance of the loan. Coverage is in decreasing term insurance, so the amount of coverage decreases as the debt decreases. A variant, mortgage unemployment insurance pays the mortgage of a policyholder who becomes involuntarily unemployed. (*See* Term insurance)

MORTGAGE-BACKED SECURITIES

Investment grade securities backed by a pool of mortgages. The issuer uses the cash flow from mortgages to pay interest on the bonds.

MULTIPLE PERIL POLICY

A package policy, such as a homeowners or business insurance policy, that provides coverage against several different perils. It also refers to the combination of property and liability coverage in one policy. In the early days of insurance, coverages for property damage and liability were purchased separately.

MUNICIPAL BOND INSURANCE

Coverage that guarantees bondholders timely payment of interest and principal even if the issuer of the bonds defaults. Offered by insurance companies with high credit ratings, the coverage raises the credit rating of a municipality offering the bond to that of the insurance company. It allows a municipality to raise money at lower interest rates. A form of financial guarantee insurance. (*See* Financial guarantee insurance)

MUNICIPAL LIABILITY INSURANCE

Liability insurance for governments and government agencies. Coverages range from general liability to public officials errors and omissions to environment liability.

MUTUAL HOLDING COMPANY

An organizational structure that provides mutual companies with the organizational and capital raising advantages of stock insurers, while retaining the policyholder ownership of the mutual.

MUTUAL INSURANCE COMPANY

A company owned by its policyholders that returns part of its profits to the policyholders as dividends. The insurer uses the rest as a surplus cushion in case of large and unexpected losses.

N

NAMED PERIL
Peril specifically mentioned as covered in an insurance policy.

NATIONAL FLOOD INSURANCE PROGRAM
Federal government-sponsored program under which flood insurance is sold to homeowners and businesses. (*See* Adverse selection; Flood insurance)

NEGLIGENCE
A failure to exercise the legally required degree of care of others, resulting in harm or damage.

*NET ANNUITY COST
A monetary amount equal to the present value of future periodic payments under an annuity contract, calculated on a net basis, without any specific provision for expense loading. *Contrast with* Gross annuity cost. (*See* Annuity cost)

*NET PAYMENT COST COMPARISON INDEX
A cost comparison index used to compare life insurance policies that takes into account the time value of money and that measures the cost of a policy over a 10- or 20-year period assuming the policy owner pays premiums over the entire period. *Contrast with* Surrender cost comparison index.

NET PREMIUMS WRITTEN
See Premiums written.

NO-FAULT
Auto insurance coverage that pays for each driver's own injuries, regardless of who caused the accident. No-fault varies from state to state. It also refers to an auto liability insurance system that restricts lawsuits to serious cases. Such policies are designed to promote faster reimbursement and to reduce litigation.

NO-FAULT MEDICAL
A type of accident coverage in homeowners policies.

NO-PAY, NO-PLAY
The idea that people who don't buy coverage should not receive benefits. Prohibits uninsured drivers from collecting damages from insured drivers. In most states with this law, uninsured drivers may not sue for noneconomic damages such as pain and suffering. In other states, uninsured drivers are required to pay the equivalent of a large deductible ($10,000) before they can sue for property damages and another large deductible before they can sue for bodily harm.

NONADMITTED ASSETS
Assets that are not included on the balance sheet of an insurance company, including furniture, fixtures, past-due accounts receivable, and agents' debt balances. (*See* Assets)

NONADMITTED INSURER
Insurers licensed in some states, but not others. States where an insurer is not licensed call that insurer nonadmitted. They sell coverage that is unavailable from licensed insurers within the state.

*NONCANCELLABLE AND GUARANTEED RENEWABLE POLICY
An individual health insurance policy, which stipulates that, until the insured reaches a specified age (usually age 65), the insurer will not cancel the coverage, increase the premiums, or change the policy provisions as long as the premiums are paid when due. Also known as noncancellable policy. *Contrast with* Guaranteed renewable policy.

*NONFORFEITURE OPTIONS
The various ways in which a contract owner may apply the cash surrender value

of an insurance or an annuity contract if the contract lapses. In the United States, the typical nonforfeiture options for life insurance are the cash payment option, the extended term insurance option and the reduced paid-up insurance option. (*See* Cash payment option; Cash surrender value; Extended term insurance option; Reduced paid-up insurance option)

NONFORFEITURE VALUES

The benefits, as printed in a life insurance policy, that the insurance guarantees to the insured if the insured stops paying premiums.

NOTICE OF LOSS

A written notice required by insurance companies immediately after an accident or other loss. Part of the standard provisions defining a policyholder's responsibilities after a loss.

NUCLEAR INSURANCE

Covers operators of nuclear reactors and other facilities for liability and property damage in the case of a nuclear accident and involves both private insurers and the federal government.

NURSING HOME INSURANCE

A form of long-term care policy that covers a policyholder's stay in a nursing facility.

O

OCCUPATIONAL DISEASE

Abnormal condition or illness caused by factors associated with the workplace. Like occupational injuries, this is covered by workers compensation policies. (*See* Workers compensation)

OCCURRENCE POLICY

Insurance that pays claims arising out of incidents that occur during the policy term,

even if they are filed many years later. (*See* Claims made policy)

OCEAN MARINE INSURANCE

Coverage of all types of vessels and watercraft, for property damage to the vessel and cargo, including such risks as piracy and the jettisoning of cargo to save other property. Coverage for marine-related liabilities. War is excluded from basic policies, but can be bought back.

OPEN COMPETITION STATES

States where insurance companies can set new rates without prior approval, although the state's commissioner can disallow them if they are not reasonable and adequate or are discriminatory.

OPERATING EXPENSES

The cost of maintaining a business's property, includes insurance, property taxes, utilities and rent, but excludes income tax, depreciation and other financing expenses.

OPTIONS

Contracts that allow, but do not oblige, the buying or selling of property or assets at a certain date at a set price.

ORDINANCE OR LAW COVERAGE

Endorsement to a property policy, including homeowners, that pays for the extra expense of rebuilding to comply with ordinances or laws, often building codes, that did not exist when the building was originally built. For example, a building severely damaged in a hurricane may have to be elevated above the flood line when it is rebuilt. This endorsement would cover part of the additional cost.

ORDINARY LIFE INSURANCE

A life insurance policy that remains in force for the policyholder's lifetime.

ORIGINAL EQUIPMENT MANUFACTURER PARTS/OEM

Sheet metal auto parts made by the manu-facturer of the vehicle. (*See* Generic auto parts)

OVER-THE-COUNTER/OTC

Security that is not listed or traded on an exchange such as the New York Stock Exchange. Business in over-the-counter se-curities is conducted through dealers using electronic networks.

P

PACKAGE POLICY

A single insurance policy that combines several coverages previously sold separately. Examples include homeowners insurance and commercial multiple peril insurance.

*PAID-UP ADDITIONAL INSURANCE OPTION

An option, available to the owners of participating life insurance policies, that allows the policy owner to use policy dividends to purchase additional insurance on the insured's life; the paid-up additional insurance is issued on the same plan as the basic policy and in whatever face amount the dividend can provide at the insured's attained age. (*See* Dividend; Participating policy; Policy dividend options)

*PAID-UP POLICY

An insurance policy that requires no fur-ther premium payments but continues to provide coverage.

*PARTIAL DISABILITY

See Residual disability.

*PARTICIPATING POLICY

A type of insurance policy that allows policy owners to receive policy dividends. Also known as par policy. (*See* Dividend)

PAY-AT-THE-PUMP

A system proposed in the 1990s in which auto insurance premiums would be paid to state governments through a per-gallon surcharge on gasoline.

PAY-AS-YOU-DRIVE (PAYD)

An auto insurance product whose pricing takes into account the number of miles driven by the policyholder.

*PAYOUT OPTIONS

The methods available to an annuity contract owner for the distribution of the annuity's accumulated value. (1) The lump sum distribution method allows the contract owner to receive the balance of his account in a single payment. (2) The fixed period option provides that the annuity's accumulated value will be paid out over a specified period of time. (3) The fixed-amount option provides that the annuity's accumulated value will be paid out in a pre-selected payment amount until the ac-cumulated value is exhausted. (4) A life an-nuity option provides that periodic income payments will be tied in some manner to the life expectancy of a named individual. (*See* Life annuity)

PENSION BENEFIT GUARANTY CORPORATION

An independent federal government agency that administers the Pension Plan Termi-nation Insurance program to ensure that vested benefits of employees whose pen-sion plans are being terminated are paid when they come due. Only defined benefit plans are covered. Benefits are paid up to certain limits.

PENSIONS

Programs to provide employees with retire-ment income after they meet minimum age and service requirements. Life insur-ers hold some of these funds. Since the

1970s responsibility for funding retirement has increasingly shifted from employers (defined benefit plans that promise workers a specific retirement income) to employees (defined contribution plans financed by employees that may or may not be matched by employer contributions). (*See* Defined benefit plan; Defined contribution plan)

*PER CAPITA BENEFICIARY DESIGNATION

A type of life insurance policy beneficiary designation in which the life insurance benefits are divided equally among the designated beneficiaries who survive the insured. For example, if the policy specifies two beneficiaries, but only one is surviving at the time of the insured's death, then the remaining beneficiary receives the entire policy benefit. *Contrast with* Per stirpes beneficiary designation.

*PER STIRPES BENEFICIARY DESIGNATION

A type of life insurance policy beneficiary designation in which the life insurance benefits are divided among a class of beneficiaries; for example, children of the insured. The living members of the class and the descendants of any deceased members of the class share in the benefits equally. *Contrast with* Per capita beneficiary designation.

PERIL

A specific risk or cause of loss covered by an insurance policy, such as a fire, windstorm, flood, or theft. A named-peril policy covers the policyholder only for the risks named in the policy in contrast to an all-risk policy, which covers all causes of loss except those specifically excluded.

*PERIOD CERTAIN

The stated period over which an insurer makes periodic benefit payments under an annuity certain. (*See* Annuity certain)

PERSONAL ARTICLES FLOATER

A policy or an addition to a policy used to cover personal valuables, like jewelry or furs.

PERSONAL INJURY PROTECTION COVERAGE/PIP

Portion of an auto insurance policy that covers the treatment of injuries to the driver and passengers of the policyholder's car.

PERSONAL LINES

Property/casualty insurance products that are designed for and bought by individuals, including homeowners and automobile policies. (*See* Commercial lines)

POINT-OF-SERVICE PLAN

Health insurance policy that allows the employee to choose between in-network and out-of-network care each time medical treatment is needed.

POLICY

A written contract for insurance between an insurance company and a policyholder stating details of coverage.

*POLICY DIVIDEND OPTIONS

Ways in which the owner of a participating insurance policy may receive policy dividends. (*See* Additional term insurance option; Cash dividend option; Dividend accumulations option; Paid-up additional insurance option; Premium reduction option)

POLICYHOLDERS' SURPLUS

The amount of money remaining after an insurer's liabilities are subtracted from its assets. It acts as a financial cushion above and beyond reserves, protecting policy-holders against an unexpected or cata-strophic situation.

POLITICAL RISK INSURANCE

Coverage for businesses operating abroad against loss due to political upheaval such as war, revolution, or confiscation of property.

POLLUTION INSURANCE

Policies that cover property loss and liabil-ity arising from pollution-related damages, for sites that have been inspected and found uncontaminated. It is usually writ-ten on a claims-made basis so policies pay only claims presented during the term of the policy or within a specified time frame after the policy expires. (*See* Claims made policy)

POOL

See Insurance pool.

*PRE-EXISTING CONDITION

(1) According to most group health insur-ance policies, a condition for which an individual received medical care during the three months immediately prior to the effective date of her coverage. (2) Accord-ing to most individual health insurance policies, an injury that occurred or a sick-ness that first appeared or manifested itself within a specified period—usually two years—before the policy was issued and that was not disclosed on the application for insurance.

PREFERRED PROVIDER ORGANIZATION

Network of medical providers which charge on a fee-for-service basis, but are paid on a negotiated, discounted fee schedule.

*PREFERRED RISK CLASS

In insurance underwriting, the group of proposed insureds who represent a signifi-cantly lower than average likelihood of loss within the context of the insurer's under-writing practices. *Contrast with* Declined risk class, Standard risk class and Substan-dard risk class.

PREMISES

The particular location of the property or a portion of it as designated in an insurance policy.

PREMIUM

The price of an insurance policy, typically charged annually or semiannually. (*See* Di-rect premiums; Earned premium; Unearned premium)

*PREMIUM REDUCTION OPTION

An option, available to the owners of participating insurance policies, that al-lows the insurer to apply policy dividends toward the payment of renewal premiums. (*See* Dividend; Policy dividend options)

PREMIUM TAX

A state tax on premiums paid by its residents and businesses and collected by insurers.

PREMIUMS IN FORCE

The sum of the face amounts, plus divi-dend additions, of life insurance policies outstanding at a given time.

PREMIUMS WRITTEN

The total premiums on all policies written by an insurer during a specified period of time, regardless of what portions have been earned. Net premiums written are premi-ums written after reinsurance transactions.

*PRIMARY BENEFICIARY

The party designated to receive the pro-ceeds of a life insurance policy following the death of the insured. Also known as first beneficiary. (*See* Contingent benefi-ciary)

PRIMARY COMPANY

In a reinsurance transaction, the insurance company that is reinsured.

PRIMARY MARKET

Market for new issue securities where the proceeds go directly to the issuer.

PRIME RATE

Interest rate that banks charge to their most creditworthy customers. Banks set this rate according to their cost of funds and market forces.

PRIOR APPROVAL STATES

States where insurance companies must file proposed rate changes with state regulators, and gain approval before they can go into effect.

PRIVATE MORTGAGE INSURANCE

See Mortgage guarantee insurance.

PRIVATE PLACEMENT

Securities that are not registered with the Securities and Exchange Commission and are sold directly to investors.

PRODUCT LIABILITY

A section of tort law that determines who may sue and who may be sued for damages when a defective product injures someone. No uniform federal laws guide manufacturer's liability, but under strict liability, the injured party can hold the manufacturer responsible for damages without the need to prove negligence or fault.

PRODUCT LIABILITY INSURANCE

Protects manufacturers' and distributors' exposure to lawsuits by people who have sustained bodily injury or property damage through the use of the product.

PROFESSIONAL LIABILITY INSURANCE

Covers professionals for negligence and errors or omissions that injure their clients.

PROOF OF LOSS

Documents showing the insurance company that a loss occurred.

PROPERTY/CASUALTY INSURANCE

Covers damage to or loss of policyholders' property and legal liability for damages caused to other people or their property. Property/casualty insurance, which includes auto, homeowners and commercial insurance, is one segment of the insurance industry. The other sector is life/health. Outside the United States, property/casualty insurance is referred to as nonlife or general insurance.

PROPERTY/CASUALTY INSURANCE CYCLE

Industry business cycle with recurrent periods of hard and soft market conditions. In the 1950s and 1960s, cycles were regular with three year periods each of hard and soft market conditions in almost all lines of property/casualty insurance. Since then they have been less regular and less frequent.

PROPOSITION 103

A November 1988 California ballot initiative that called for a statewide auto insurance rate rollback and for rates to be based more on driving records and less on geographical location. The initiative changed many aspects of the state's insurance system and was the subject of lawsuits for more than a decade.

PURCHASING GROUP

An entity that offers insurance to groups of similar businesses with similar exposures to risk.

PURE ENDOWMENT

A life insurance contract that pays a periodic income benefit for the life of the owner of the annuity. The payment can be monthly, quarterly, semiannually or annually.

PURE LIFE ANNUITY

A form of annuity that ends payments when the annuitant dies. Payments may be fixed or variable.

Q

QUALIFIED ANNUITY

A form of annuity purchased with pretax dollars as part of a retirement plan that benefits from special tax treatment, such as a 401(k) plan.

R

RATE

The cost of a unit of insurance, usually per $1,000. Rates are based on historical loss experience for similar risks and may be regulated by state insurance offices.

RATE REGULATION

The process by which states monitor insurance companies' rate changes, done either through prior approval or open competition models. (See Open competition states; Prior approval states)

*RATED POLICY

An insurance policy that is classified as having a greater-than-average likelihood of loss, usually issued with special exclusions, a premium rate that is higher than the rate for a standard policy, a reduced face amount, or any combination of these.

RATING AGENCIES

There are several major credit agencies that determine insurers' financial strength and viability to meet claims obligations. They include A.M. Best Co.; Fitch, Inc.; Moody's Investors Services; Standard & Poor's Corp.; and Weiss Ratings, Inc. Factors considered include company earnings, capital adequacy, operating leverage, liquidity, investment performance, reinsurance programs, and management ability, integrity and experience.

RATING BUREAU

The insurance business is based on the spread of risk. The more widely risk is spread, the more accurately loss can be estimated. An insurance company can more accurately estimate the probability of loss on 100,000 homes than on ten. Years ago, insurers were required to use standardized forms and rates developed by rating agencies. Today, large insurers use their own statistical loss data to develop rates. But small insurers, or insurers focusing on special lines of business, with insufficiently broad loss data to make them actuarially reliable depend on pooled industry data collected by such organizations as ISO, which provides information to help develop rates such as estimates of future losses and loss adjustment expenses like legal defense costs.

REAL ESTATE INVESTMENTS

Investments generally owned by life insurers that include commercial mortgage loans and real property.

RECEIVABLES

Amounts owed to a business for goods or services provided.

REDLINING

Literally means to draw a red line on a map around areas to receive special treatment. Refusal to issue insurance based solely on where applicants live is illegal in all states. Denial of insurance must be risk-based.

*REDUCED PAID-UP INSURANCE OPTION

One of several nonforfeiture options included in life insurance policies that allows the owner of a policy with cash values to discontinue premium payments and to use the policy's net cash value to purchase paid-up insurance of the same plan as the original policy. (*See* Nonforfeiture options)

*REGISTERED PRINCIPAL

An officer or manager of a National Association of Securities Dealers (NASD) member, who is involved in the day-to-day operation of the securities business, has qualified as a registered representative, and has an NASD Series 24 or 26 registration.

*REGISTERED REPRESENTATIVE

A sales representative or other person who has registered with the National Association of Securities Dealers (NASD), disclosed the required background information, and passed one or more NASD examination. A registered representative engages in the securities business on behalf of a NASD member by soliciting the sale of securities or training securities salespeople.

*REINSTATEMENT

The process by which an insurer puts back into force an insurance policy that has either been terminated for nonpayment of premiums or continued as extended term or reduced paid-up coverage.

REINSURANCE

Insurance bought by insurers. A reinsurer assumes part of the risk and part of the premium originally taken by the insurer, known as the primary company. Reinsurance effectively increases an insurer's capital and therefore its capacity to sell more coverage. The business is global and some of the largest reinsurers are based abroad. Reinsurers have their own reinsurers, called retrocessionaires. Reinsurers don't pay policyholder claims. Instead, they reimburse insurers for claims paid. (*See* Treaty reinsurance; Facultative reinsurance)

RELATION OF EARNINGS TO INSURANCE CLAUSE

A clause included in some individual disability policies that limits the amount of benefits that an insurer will pay when the total amount of disability benefits from all insurers exceeds the individual's usual earnings.

*RENEWABLE TERM INSURANCE POLICY

A term life insurance policy that gives the policy owner the option to continue the coverage at the end of the specified term without presenting evidence of insurability, although typically at a higher premium based on the insured's attained age.

RENTERS INSURANCE

A form of insurance that covers a policyholder's belongings against perils such as fire, theft, windstorm, hail, explosion, vandalism, riots, and others. It also provides personal liability coverage for damage the policyholder or dependents cause to third parties. It also provides additional living expenses, known as loss-of-use coverage, if a policyholder must move while his or her dwelling is repaired. It also can include coverage for property improvements. Possessions can be covered for their replacement cost or for their actual cash value, which includes depreciation.

REPLACEMENT COST

Insurance that pays the dollar amount needed to replace damaged personal property or dwelling property without deducting for depreciation but limited by the maximum dollar amount shown on the declarations page of the policy.

REPURCHASE AGREEMENT/'REPO'

Agreement between a buyer and seller where the seller agrees to repurchase the securities at an agreed upon time and price. Repurchase agreements involving U.S. government securities are utilized by the Federal Reserve to control the money supply.

RESERVES

A company's best estimate of what it will pay for claims.

*RESIDUAL DISABILITY

In disability income insurance, a condition in which the insured is not totally disabled, but is still unable to function as before the sickness or injury, and therefore suffers a reduction in income of at least the percentage—typically 20 percent to 25 percent—specified in the disability income plan. Also known as partial disability.

*RESIDUAL DISABILITY INSURANCE

See Income protection insurance.

RESIDUAL MARKET

Facilities, such as assigned risk plans and FAIR Plans, that exist to provide coverage for those who cannot get it in the regular market. Insurers doing business in a given state generally must participate in these pools. For this reason the residual market is also known as the shared market.

RETENTION

The amount of risk retained by an insurance company that is not reinsured.

RETROCESSION

The reinsurance bought by reinsurers to protect their financial stability.

RETROSPECTIVE RATING

A method of permitting the final premium for a risk to be adjusted, subject to an agreed upon maximum and minimum limit based on actual loss experience. It is available to large commercial insurance buyers.

RETURN ON EQUITY

Net income divided by total equity. Measures profitability by showing how efficiently invested capital is being used.

*REVOCABLE BENEFICIARY

A life insurance policy beneficiary whose right to the policy's proceeds can be cancelled or reduced by the policy owner at any time before the insured's death. Contrast with Irrevocable beneficiary.

RIDER

An attachment to an insurance policy that alters the policy's coverage or terms.

RISK

The chance of loss or the person or entity that is insured.

RISK MANAGEMENT

Management of the varied risks to which a business firm or association might be subject. It includes analyzing all exposures to gauge the likelihood of loss and choosing options to better manage or minimize loss. These options typically include reducing and eliminating the risk with safety measures, buying insurance, and self-insurance.

RISK-RETENTION GROUPS

Businesses that band together to self-insure and form an organization, which is chartered and licensed as an insurer in at least one state, to handle liability insurance.

RISK-BASED CAPITAL

The need for insurance companies to be capitalized according to the inherent riskiness of the type of insurance they sell. Higher risk types of insurance, liability as opposed to property business, generally necessitate higher levels of capital.

*ROLLOVER

A direct transfer of retirement funds from one qualified plan to another plan of the same type or to an individual retirement arrangement (IRA) that does not pass through the hands of the owner and thus does not incur any tax liability for the owner. Also known as direct rollover and direct transfer.

S

SALVAGE
Damaged property an insurer takes over to reduce its loss after paying a claim. Insurers receive salvage rights over property on which they have paid claims, such as badly damaged cars. Insurers that paid claims on cargoes lost at sea now have the right to recover sunken treasures. Salvage charges are the costs associated with recovering that property.

SCHEDULE
A list of individual items or groups of items that are covered under one policy or a listing of specific benefits, charges, credits, assets or other defined items.

SECOND-TO-DIE LIFE INSURANCE
See Survivorship Life insurance.

SECONDARY MARKET
Market for previously issued and outstanding securities.

*SECTION 1035 EXCHANGE
In the United States, a taxfree replacement of an insurance policy for another insurance contract covering the same person that is performed in accordance with the conditions of Section 1035 of the Internal Revenue Code.

SECTION 415
A section of the Internal Revenue Code that provides for dollar limitations on benefits and contributions under qualified retirement plans. Section 415 also requires that the Internal Revenue Service annually adjust these limits for cost-of-living increases.

SECURITIES AND EXCHANGE COMMISSION/SEC
The organization that oversees publicly held insurance companies. Those companies make periodic financial disclosures to the SEC, including an annual financial statement (or 10K) and a quarterly financial statement (or 10-Q). Companies must also disclose any material events and other information about their stock.

SECURITIES OUTSTANDING
Stock held by shareholders.

SECURITIZATION OF INSURANCE RISK
Using the capital markets to expand and diversify the assumption of insurance risk. The issuance of bonds or notes to third-party investors directly or indirectly by an insurance or reinsurance company or a pooling entity as a means of raising money to cover risks. (*See* Catastrophe bonds)

*SEGREGATED ACCOUNT
In Canada, an investment account that insurers maintain separately from a general account to help manage the funds placed in variable insurance products such as variable annuities. (*See* Separate account)

SELF-INSURANCE
The concept of assuming a financial risk oneself, instead of paying an insurance company to take it on. Every policyholder is a self-insurer in terms of paying a deductible and co-payments. Large firms often self-insure frequent, small losses such as damage to their fleet of vehicles or minor workplace injuries. However, to protect injured employees state laws set out requirements for the assumption of workers compensation programs. Self-insurance also refers to employers who assume all or

part of the responsibility for paying the health insurance claims of their employees. Firms that self insure for health claims are exempt from state insurance laws mandating the illnesses that group health insurers must cover.

*SEPARATE ACCOUNT
In the United States, an investment account maintained separately from an insurer's general account to help manage the funds placed in variable insurance products such as variable annuities. *Contrast with* General account. (*See* Segregated account)

*SETTLEMENT OPTIONS
Choices given to the owner or beneficiary of a life insurance policy regarding the method by which the insurer will pay the policy's proceeds when the policy owner does not receive the benefits in one single payment. Typically, the owner can elect (1) to leave the proceeds with the insurer and earn a specified interest rate, (2) to have the proceeds paid in a series of installments for a pre-selected period, (3) to have the proceeds paid in a pre-selected sum in a series of installments for as long as the proceeds last, or (4) to have the insurer tie payment of the proceeds to the life expectancy of a named individual through a life annuity. Also known as optional modes of settlement. (*See* Life annuity)

SEVERITY
Size of a loss. One of the criteria used in calculating premiums rates.

SEWER BACKUP COVERAGE
An optional part of homeowners insurance that covers sewers.

SHARED MARKET
See Residual market.

*SHORT-TERM DISABILITY INCOME INSURANCE
A type of disability income coverage that provides disability income benefits for a maximum benefit period of from one to five years. *Contrast with* Long-term disability income insurance.

*SINGLE PREMIUM POLICIES
A type of life insurance or annuity contract that is purchased by the payment of one lump sum. (1) A single-premium deferred annuity (SPDA) is an annuity contract purchased with a single premium payment whose periodic income payments generally do not begin until several years in the future. (2) A single premium immediate annuity (SPIA) contract is an annuity contract that is purchased with a single premium payment and that will begin making periodic income payments one annuity period after the contract's issue date.

SOFT MARKET
An environment where insurance is plentiful and sold at a lower cost, also known as a buyers' market. (*See* Property/casualty insurance cycle)

SOLVENCY
Insurance companies' ability to pay the claims of policyholders. Regulations to promote solvency include minimum capital and surplus requirements, statutory accounting conventions, limits to insurance company investment and corporate activities, financial ratio tests and financial data disclosure.

SOLVENCY II
A collection of regulatory requirements for insurance firms that operate in the European Union, scheduled to take effect in 2012.

*SPECIFIED DISEASE COVERAGE
A type of health insurance coverage that provides benefits for the diagnosis and treatment of a specifically named disease or diseases, such as cancer. Also known as dread disease coverage. *Contrast with* Critical illness (CI) insurance.

SPENDTHRIFT TRUST CLAUSE
Life insurance provision that protects policy payouts from the beneficiary's creditors.

*SPLIT-DOLLAR LIFE INSURANCE PLAN
An agreement under which a business provides individual life insurance policies for certain employees, who share in paying the cost of the policies.

SPREAD OF RISK
The selling of insurance in multiple areas to multiple policyholders to minimize the danger that all policyholders will have losses at the same time. Companies are more likely to insure perils that offer a good spread of risk. Flood insurance is an example of a poor spread of risk because the people most likely to buy it are the people close to rivers and other bodies of water that flood. (*See* Adverse selection)

STACKING
Practice that increases the money available to pay auto liability claims. In states where this practice is permitted by law, courts may allow policyholders who have several cars insured under a single policy, or multiple vehicles insured under different policies, to add up the limit of liability available for each vehicle.

*STANDARD RISK CLASS
In insurance underwriting, the group of proposed insureds who represent average risk within the context of the insurer's underwriting practices and therefore pay average premiums in relation to others of similar insurability. *Contrast with* Declined risk class, Preferred risk class and Substandard risk class.

STATUTORY ACCOUNTING PRINCIPLES/SAP
More conservative standards than under GAAP accounting rules, they are imposed by state laws that emphasize the present solvency of insurance companies. SAP helps ensure that the company will have sufficient funds readily available to meet all anticipated insurance obligations by recognizing liabilities earlier or at a higher value than GAAP and assets later or at a lower value. For example, SAP requires that selling expenses be recorded immediately rather than amortized over the life of the policy. (*See* Admitted assets; GAAP accounting)

STOCK INSURANCE COMPANY
An insurance company owned by its stockholders who share in profits through earnings distributions and increases in stock value.

*STRAIGHT LIFE ANNUITY
A type of life annuity contract that provides periodic income payments for as long as the annuitant lives but provides no benefit payments after the annuitant's death. (*See* Life annuity)

STRUCTURED SETTLEMENT
Legal agreement to pay a designated person, usually someone who has been injured, a specified sum of money in periodic payments, usually for his or her lifetime, instead of in a single lump sum payment. (*See* Annuity)

SUBROGATION
The legal process by which an insurance company, after paying a loss, seeks to re-

cover the amount of the loss from another party who is legally liable for it.

*SUBSTANDARD PREMIUM RATES

The premium rates charged insureds who are classified as substandard risks. Also known as special class rates.

*SUBSTANDARD RISK CLASS

In insurance underwriting, the group of proposed insureds who represent a significantly greater-than-average likelihood of loss within the context of the insurer's underwriting practices. Also known as special class risk. *Contrast with* Declined risk class, Preferred risk class and Standard risk class.

*SUICIDE EXCLUSION PROVISION

A life insurance policy provision stating that policy proceeds will not be paid if the insured dies as the result of suicide as defined within the policy within a specified period following the date of policy issue.

SUPERFUND

A federal law enacted in 1980 to initiate cleanup of the nation's abandoned hazardous waste dump sites and to respond to accidents that release hazardous substances into the environment. The law is officially called the Comprehensive Environmental Response, Compensation, and Liability Act.

*SUPPLEMENTAL COVERAGE

An amount of coverage that adds to the amount of coverage specified in a basic insurance policy.

SURETY BOND

A contract guaranteeing the performance of a specific obligation. Simply put, it is a three-party agreement under which one party, the surety company, answers to a second party, the owner, creditor or "obligee," for a third party's debts, default or nonperformance. Contractors are often required to purchase surety bonds if they are working

on public projects. The surety company becomes responsible for carrying out the work or paying for the loss up to the bond "penalty" if the contractor fails to perform.

SURPLUS

The remainder after an insurer's liabilities are subtracted from its assets. The financial cushion that protects policyholders in case of unexpectedly high claims. (*See* Capital; Risk-based capital)

SURPLUS LINES

Property/casualty insurance coverage that isn't available from insurers licensed in the state, called admitted companies, and must be purchased from a nonadmitted carrier. Examples include risks of an unusual nature that require greater flexibility in policy terms and conditions than exist in standard forms or where the highest rates allowed by state regulators are considered inadequate by admitted companies. Laws governing surplus lines vary by state.

SURRENDER CHARGE

A charge for withdrawals from an annuity contract before a designated surrender charge period, usually from five to seven years.

*SURRENDER COST COMPARISON INDEX

A cost comparison index, used to compare insurance policies, which takes into account the time value of money and measures the cost of a policy over a 10- or 20-year period assuming the policy owner surrenders the policy for its cash value at the end of the period. *Contrast with* Net payment cost comparison index.

SURVIVORSHIP LIFE INSURANCE

A form of insurance that covers more than one person and pays a benefit after all of the insureds die. It can be used to help pay estate taxes after the deaths of a husband

and wife or as a form of business continuation insurance. Also known as second-to-die life insurance.

SWAPS
The simultaneous buying, selling or exchange of one security for another among investors to change maturities in a bond portfolio, for example, or because investment goals have changed.

T

*TAX-DEFERRED BASIS
Accumulation of investment income on which income taxes are not payable until money is withdrawn from the investment vehicle.

*TAX SHELTERED ANNUITY (TSA)
In the United States, a retirement annuity sold only to organizations offering qualified retirement plans under section 403(b) of the U.S. Internal Revenue Code. (*See* 403(b) plan)

*TEN-DAY FREE LOOK PROVISION
See Free-look period.

TERM CERTAIN ANNUITY
A form of annuity that pays out over a fixed period rather than when the annuitant dies.

TERM INSURANCE
A form of life insurance that covers the insured person for a certain period of time, the "term" that is specified in the policy. It pays a benefit to a designated beneficiary only when the insured dies within that specified period which can be one, five, 10 or even 20 years. Term life policies are renewable but premiums increase with age.

TERRITORIAL RATING
A method of classifying risks by geographic location to set a fair price for coverage.

The location of the insured may have a considerable impact on the cost of losses. The chance of an accident or theft is much higher in an urban area than in a rural one, for example.

TERRORISM INSURANCE
Included as a part of the package in standard commercial insurance policies before September 11 virtually free of charge. Terrorism coverage is now generally offered separately at a price that more adequately reflects the risk. The Terrorism Risk Insurance Act (TRIA) was created by Congress in 2002, and renewed for two years in December 2005, to provide a temporary backstop for incurred losses resulting from certain acts of terrorism.

THIRD-PARTY ADMINISTRATOR
Outside group that performs clerical functions for an insurance company.

THIRD-PARTY COVERAGE
Liability coverage purchased by the policyholder as a protection against possible lawsuits filed by a third party. The insured and the insurer are the first and second parties to the insurance contract. (*See* First-party coverage)

TIME DEPOSIT
Funds that are held in a savings account for a predetermined period of time at a set interest rate. Banks can refuse to allow withdrawals from these accounts until the period has expired or assess a penalty for early withdrawals.

*TIME LIMIT ON CERTAIN DEFENSES PROVISION
An individual health insurance policy provision that limits the time during which the insurer may contest the validity of the contract on the ground of misrepresentation in the application or may reduce or deny a claim on the ground it results from

a preexisting condition. (*See* Incontestability provision)

TITLE INSURANCE
Insurance that indemnifies the owner of real estate in the event that his or her clear ownership of property is challenged by the discovery of faults in the title.

TORT
A legal term denoting a wrongful act resulting in injury or damage on which a civil court action, or legal proceeding, may be based.

TORT LAW
The body of law governing negligence, intentional interference, and other wrongful acts for which civil action can be brought, except for breach of contract, which is covered by contract law.

TORT REFORM
Refers to legislation designed to reduce liability costs through limits on various kinds of damages and through modification of liability rules.

*TOTAL DISABILITY
For disability insurance purposes, an insured's disability that meets the requirements of the definition of total disability included in the disability insurance policy or policy rider and that qualifies for payment of the specified disability benefits. When a disability begins, total disability is usually the complete and continuous inability of an insured to perform the essential duties of his regular occupation. After a disability has existed for a specified period, total disability usually exists only if the insured is prevented from working at any occupation for which he is reasonably fitted by education, training or experience. (*See* Disability; Residual disability)

TOTAL LOSS
The condition of an automobile or other property when damage is so extensive that repair costs would exceed the value of the vehicle or property.

TRANSPARENCY
A term used to explain the way information on financial matters, such as financial reports and actions of companies or markets, are communicated so that they are easily understood and frank.

TRAVEL INSURANCE
Insurance to cover problems associated with traveling, generally including trip cancellation due to illness, lost luggage and other incidents.

TREASURY SECURITIES
Interest-bearing obligations of the U.S. government issued by the Treasury as a means of borrowing money to meet government expenditures not covered by tax revenues. Marketable Treasury securities fall into three categories—bills, notes and bonds. Marketable Treasury obligations are currently issued in book entry form only; that is, the purchaser receives a statement, rather than an engraved certificate.

TREATY REINSURANCE
A standing agreement between insurers and reinsurers. Under a treaty each party automatically accepts specific percentages of the insurer's business.

*TWISTING
An illegal insurance sales practice, in which a sales agent misrepresents the features of a contract in order to induce the contract owner to replace his current contract, often to the disadvantage of the contract owner. (*See* Misrepresentation)

U

UMBRELLA POLICY
Coverage for losses above the limit of an underlying policy or policies such as homeowners and auto insurance. While it applies to losses over the dollar amount in the underlying policies, terms of coverage are sometimes broader than those of underlying policies.

UNBUNDLED CONTRACTS
A form of annuity contract that gives purchasers the freedom to choose among certain optional features in their contract.

UNCLAIMED LIFE INSURANCE BENEFITS
Life insurance benefits that are unclaimed and unpaid because the beneficiaries aren't aware that the policies exist or can't locate the policies because they don't know which insurance company wrote them. If an insurance company knows that an insured died and cannot find the beneficiary, the money is transferred to the state where the insured bought the policy.

UNDERINSURANCE
The result of the policyholder's failure to buy sufficient insurance. An underinsured policyholder may only receive part of the cost of replacing or repairing damaged items covered in the policy.

UNDERWRITING
Examining, accepting, or rejecting insurance risks and classifying the ones that are accepted, in order to charge appropriate premiums.

UNDERWRITING INCOME
The insurer's profit on the insurance sale after all expenses and losses have been paid. When premiums aren't sufficient to cover claims and expenses, the result is an underwriting loss. Underwriting losses are typically offset by investment income.

UNEARNED PREMIUM
The portion of a premium already received by the insurer under which protection has not yet been provided. The entire premium is not earned until the policy period expires, even though premiums are typically paid in advance.

UNINSURABLE RISK
Risks that do not meet the criteria of an insurable risk. (*See* Insurable risk)

UNINSURED MOTORISTS COVERAGE
Portion of an auto insurance policy that protects a policyholder from uninsured and hit-and-run drivers.

UNIVERSAL LIFE INSURANCE
A flexible premium policy that combines protection against premature death with a type of savings vehicle, known as a cash value account, that typically earns a money market rate of interest. Death benefits can be changed during the life of the policy within limits, generally subject to a medical examination. Once funds accumulate in the cash value account, the premium can be paid at any time but the policy will lapse if there isn't enough money to cover annual mortality charges and administrative costs.

UTILIZATION REVIEW
See Medical utilization review.

V

VALUED POLICY
A policy under which the insurer pays a specified amount of money to or on behalf of the insured upon the occurrence of a defined loss. The money amount is not related to the extent of the loss. Life insurance policies are an example.

VANDALISM

The malicious and often random destruction or spoilage of another person's property.

VARIABLE ANNUITY

An annuity whose contract value or income payments vary according to the performance of the stocks, bonds and other investments selected by the contract owner.

VARIABLE LIFE INSURANCE

A policy that combines protection against premature death with a savings account that can be invested in stocks, bonds and money market mutual funds at the policyholder's discretion.

*VARIABLE PREMIUM LIFE INSURANCE POLICY

See Indeterminate premium life insurance policy.

VIATICAL SETTLEMENT COMPANIES

Insurance firms that buy life insurance policies at a steep discount from policyholders who are often terminally ill and need the payment for medications or treatments. The companies provide early payouts to the policyholder, assume the premium payments, and collect the face value of the policy upon the policyholder's death.

*VARIABLE UNIVERSAL LIFE (VUL) INSURANCE

A form of permanent life insurance that combines the premium and death benefit flexibility of universal life insurance with the investment flexibility and risk of variable life insurance. With this type of policy, the death benefit and the cash value fluctuate according to the contract's investment performance. Also known as universal life II.

VOID

A policy contract that for some reason specified in the policy becomes free of all legal effect. One example under which a policy could be voided is when information a policyholder provided is proven untrue.

VOLATILITY

A measure of the degree of fluctuation in a stock's price. Volatility is exemplified by large, frequent price swings up and down.

VOLCANO COVERAGE

Most homeowners policies cover damage from a volcanic eruption.

VOLUME

Number of shares a stock trades either per day or per week.

W

*WAITING PERIOD

For a health insurance policy, the period of time that must pass from the date of policy issue before benefits are payable to an insured. Also known as elimination period and probationary period.

WAIVER

The surrender of a right or privilege. In life insurance, a provision that sets certain conditions, such as disablement, which allow coverage to remain in force without payment of premiums.

*WAIVER OF PREMIUM FOR DISABILITY (WP) BENEFIT

A supplementary life insurance policy or annuity contract benefit under which the insurer promises to give up its right to collect premiums that become due while the insured is disabled according to the policy or rider's definition of disability.

WARRANTY INSURANCE

Coverage that compensates consumers for the cost of repairing or replacing defective products past the normal warranty period provided by manufacturers.

WAR RISK

Special coverage on cargo in overseas ships against the risk of being confiscated by a government in wartime. It is excluded from standard ocean marine insurance and can be purchased separately. It often excludes cargo awaiting shipment on a wharf or on ships after 15 days of arrival in port.

WATER-DAMAGE INSURANCE COVERAGE

Protection provided in most homeowners insurance policies against sudden and accidental water damage, from burst pipes for example. Does not cover damage from problems resulting from a lack of proper maintenance such as dripping air conditioners. Water damage from floods is covered under separate flood insurance policies issued by the federal government.

WEATHER DERIVATIVE

An insurance or securities product used as a hedge by energy-related businesses and others whose sales tend to fluctuate depending on the weather.

WEATHER INSURANCE

A type of business income insurance that compensates for financial losses caused by adverse weather conditions, such as constant rain on the day scheduled for a major outdoor concert.

WHOLE LIFE INSURANCE

The oldest kind of cash value life insurance that combines protection against premature death with a savings account. Premiums are fixed and guaranteed and remain level throughout the policy's lifetime.

WORKERS COMPENSATION

Insurance that pays for medical care and physical rehabilitation of injured workers and helps to replace lost wages while they are unable to work. State laws, which vary significantly, govern the amount of benefits paid and other compensation provisions.

WRAP-UP INSURANCE

Broad policy coordinated to cover liability exposures for a large group of businesses that have something in common. Might be used to insure all businesses working on a large construction project, such as an apartment complex.

WRITE

To insure, underwrite, or accept an application for insurance.

WRITTEN PREMIUMS

See Premiums written.

X

XXX Regulation

The National Association of Insurance Commissioner's current model valuation law for life insurance policies, adopted in March 1999. The law tells insurance companies how much they should hold as a reserve for each term life insurance policy. The model has been adopted by most of the states.

Y

*YEARLY RENEWABLE TERM (YRT) INSURANCE

One-year term life insurance that is renewable at the end of the policy term. Also known as annually renewable term (ART) insurance. (*See* Term life insurance)

Directories

Property/Casualty Insurance Industry Organizations

AMERICAN INSURANCE ASSOCIATION (AIA) – NATIONAL OFFICE
2101 L Street, NW, Suite 400
Washington, DC 20037
Tel: 202-828-7100
Fax: 202-293-1219
Web: www.aiadc.org
Trade and service organization for property/casualty insurance companies. Provides a forum for the discussion of problems as well as safety, promotional and legislative services.

AMERICAN INSURANCE ASSOCIATION (AIA) – MID-ATLANTIC REGION
2101 L Street, NW, Suite 400
Washington, DC 20037
Tel: 202-828-7139
Fax: 202-293-1219
Web: www.aiadc.org

AMERICAN INSURANCE ASSOCIATION (AIA) – MIDWEST REGION
150 North Wacker Drive, Suite 2525
Chicago, IL 60606
Tel: 312-782-7720
Fax: 312-782-7718
Web: www.aiadc.org

AMERICAN INSURANCE ASSOCIATION (AIA) – NORTHEAST REGION (ALBANY)
95 Columbia Street
Albany, NY 12210
Tel: 518-462-1695
Fax: 518-465-6023
Web: www.aiadc.org

AMERICAN INSURANCE ASSOCIATION (AIA) – NORTHEAST REGION (BOSTON)
1 Walnut Street
Boston, MA 02108
Tel: 617-305-4155
Fax: 617-305-4154
Web: www.aiadc.org

AMERICAN INSURANCE ASSOCIATION (AIA) – SOUTHEAST REGION

5605 Glenridge Drive, Suite 845
Atlanta, GA 30342
Tel: 404-261-8834
Fax: 404-231-5780
Web: www.aiadc.org

AMERICAN INSURANCE ASSOCIATION (AIA) – SOUTHWEST REGION

500 West 13th Street
Austin, TX 78701
Tel: 512-322-3111
Fax: 512-322-3112
Web: www.aiadc.org

AMERICAN INSURANCE ASSOCIATION (AIA) – WESTERN REGION

915 L Street, Suite 1480
Sacramento, CA 95814
Tel: 916-442-7617
Fax: 916-422-8178
Web: www.aiadc.org

INDEPENDENT INSURANCE AGENTS & BROKERS OF AMERICA, INC.

127 S. Peyton Street
Alexandria, VA 22314
Tel: 800-221-7917
Fax: 703-683-7556
Web: www.iiaba.org
Trade association of independent insurance agents and brokers.

INSTITUTE FOR BUSINESS & HOME SAFETY

4775 E. Fowler Avenue
Tampa, FL 33617
Tel: 813-286-3400
Fax: 813-286-9960
Web: www.ibhs.org
An insurance industry-sponsored nonprofit organization dedicated to reducing losses, deaths, injuries and property damage resulting from natural hazards.

INSURANCE INFORMATION INSTITUTE (I.I.I.)

110 William Street
New York, NY 10038
Tel: 212-346-5500
Fax: 212-732-1916
Web: www.iii.org
A primary source for information, analysis and reference on insurance subjects.

INSURANCE INFORMATION INSTITUTE (I.I.I.)

Florida Representative Lynne McChristian
4775 E. Fowler Avenue
Tampa, Florida 33617
Tel: 813-480-6446
Fax: 813-915-3463
Web: www.InsuringFlorida.org

INSURANCE INFORMATION NETWORK OF CALIFORNIA (IINC)

3530 Wilshire Blvd., Suite 1610
Los Angeles, CA 90010
Tel: 213-624-4462
Web: www.iinc.org

INSURANCE RESEARCH COUNCIL (A DIVISION OF THE AMERICAN INSTITUTE FOR CPCU)

718 Providence Road, PO Box 3025
Malvern, PA 19355-0725
Tel: 610-644-2212
Fax: 610-640-5388
Web: www.ircweb.org
A division of the American Institute for CPCU. Provides the public and the insurance industry with timely research information relevant to public policy issues affecting risk and insurance.

ISO
545 Washington Blvd.
Jersey City, NJ 07310-1686
Tel: 800-888-4476
Fax: 201-748-1472
Web: www.iso.com
Provider of products and services that help measure, manage and reduce risk. Provides data, analytics and decision-support solutions to professionals in many fields, including insurance, finance, real estate, health services, government and human resources.

NATIONAL ASSOCIATION OF INSURANCE AND FINANCIAL ADVISORS
2901 Telestar Court, PO Box 12012
Falls Church, VA 22042-1205
Tel: 703-770-8100
Web: www.naifa.org
Professional association representing health and life insurance agents.

NATIONAL ASSOCIATION OF MUTUAL INSURANCE COMPANIES (NAMIC)
3601 Vincennes Rd., PO Box 68700
Indianapolis , IN 46268
Tel: 317-875-5250
Fax: 317-879-8408
Web: www.namic.org
Trade association of property/casualty mutual insurance companies.

NAMIC – WASHINGTON, DC OFFICE
122 C Street, NW, Suite 540
Washington, DC 20001
Tel: 202-628-1558
Fax: 202-628-1601
Web: www.namic.org

NATIONAL ASSOCIATION OF PROFESSIONAL INSURANCE AGENTS
400 N. Washington Street Alexandria, Virginia 22314-2353
Tel: 703-836-9340
Fax: 703-836-1279
Web: www.pianet.com

NATIONAL ASSOCIATION OF PROFESSIONAL SURPLUS LINES OFFICES, LTD.
200 N.E. 54th Street, Suite 200
Kansas City, MO 64118
Tel: 816-741-3910
Fax: 816-741-5409
Web: www.napslo.org
Professional association of wholesale brokers, excess and surplus lines companies, affiliates and supporting members.

NATIONAL INSURANCE CRIME BUREAU
1111 East Touhy, Suite 400
Des Plaines, IL 60018
Tel: 847-544-7085
Fax: 847-544-7101
Web: www.nicb.org
Not-for-profit organization dedicated to combating crime and vehicle theft.

NCCI HOLDINGS, INC.
901 Peninsula Corporate Circle
Boca Raton, FL 33487
Tel: 561-893-1000
Fax: 561-893-1500
Web: www.ncci.com
Develops and administers rating plans and systems for workers compensation insurance.

NCCI, INC. – REGULATORY SERVICES DIVISION
111 River Street, Suite 1202
Hoboken, NJ 07030
Tel: 201-222-0500
Fax: 201-222-8880
Web: www.ncci.com

PROPERTY CASUALTY INSURERS ASSOCIATION OF AMERICA (PCI)
2600 South River Road
Des Plaines, IL 60018-3286
Tel: 847-297-7800
Fax: 847-297-5064
Web: www.pciaa.net
Serves as a voice on public policy issues and advocates positions that foster a competitive market place for property/casualty insurers and insurance consumers.

PCI – CALIFORNIA (Western Region)
1415 L Street, Suite 670
Sacramento, CA 95814
Tel: 916-449-1370
Fax: 916-449-1378
Web: www.pciaa.net

PCI – COLORADO
1535 Grant Street, Suite 225
Denver, CO 80203
Tel: 303-830-6772
Fax: 303-830-6775
Web: www.pciaa.net

PCI – FLORIDA
215 S. Monroe Street, Suite 830
Tallahassee, FL 32302
Tel: 850-681-2615
Fax: 850-681-2614
Web: www.pciaa.net

PCI – GEORGIA
6636 Church Street, Suite 300
Douglasville, GA 30134
Tel: 770-949-1776
Fax: 770-949-0889
Web: www.pciaa.net

PCI – MASSACHUSETTS (New England Region)
One State Street, Suite 1500
Boston, MA 02109
Tel: 617-723-1976
Fax: 617-227-3590
Web: www.pciaa.net

PCI – NEW JERSEY (Northeastern Region)
28 West State Street, Suite 719
Trenton, NJ 08608
Tel: 609-396-9601
Fax: 609-396-9603
Web: www.pciaa.net

PCI – NEW YORK
90 South Swan Street
Albany, NY 12210
Tel: 518-443-2220
Fax: 518-443-2237
Web: www.pciaa.net

PCI – PENNSYLVANIA
116 Pine Street, Suite 205
Harrisburg, PA 17101
Tel: 717-232-0991
Fax: 717-232-0992
Web: www.pciaa.net

PCI – TEXAS (Southwestern Region)
700 Lavaca Street, Suite 1400
Austin, TX 78701
Tel: 512-334-6638
Fax: 847-759-4346
Web: www.pciaa.net

PCI – WASHINGTON (Northwestern Region)
1500 Water Street SW, Suite 2
Olympia, WA 98501
Tel: 360-915-6268
Fax: 360-357-5343
Web: www.pciaa.net

PCI – WASHINGTON, DC
444 North Capitol Street NW, Suite 801
Washington, DC 20001
Tel: 202-639-0490
Fax: 202-639-0494
Web: www.pciaa.net

REINSURANCE ASSOCIATION OF AMERICA
1301 Pennsylvania Avenue, NW, Suite 900
Washington, DC 20004
Tel: 202-638-3690
Fax: 202-638-0936
Web: www.reinsurance.org
Trade association of property/casualty reinsurers; provides legislative services for members.

SURETY & FIDELITY ASSOCIATION OF AMERICA (SFAA)
1101 Connecticut Avenue, NW, Suite 800
Washington, DC 20036
Tel: 202-463-0600
Fax: 202-463-0606
Web: www.surety.org
Statistical, rating, development and advisory organization for surety companies.

SURETY INFORMATION OFFICE
1828 L Street, NW, Suite 720
Washington, DC 20036-5104
Tel: 202-686-7463
Fax: 202-686-3656
Web: www.sio.org
Statistical, rating, development and advisory organization for surety companies. Membership includes insurance companies licensed to write fidelity or surety insurance in one or more states and foreign affiliates.

Life/Health Insurance Industry Organizations

AMERICA'S HEALTH INSURANCE PLANS (AHIP)
601 Pennsylvania Avenue NW, South Building, Suite 500
Washington, DC 20004
Tel: 202-778-3200
Fax: 202-778-8486
Web: www.ahip.org
National trade association representing health insurance plans providing medical, long-term care, disability income, dental supplemental, stop-gap and reinsurance coverage.

AMERICAN COUNCIL OF LIFE INSURERS (ACLI)
101 Constitution Avenue NW, Suite 700
Washington, DC 20001-2133
Tel: 202-624-2000
Fax: 202-572-4745
Web: www.acli.com
Trade association responsible for the public affairs, government, legislative and research aspects of the life insurance business.

THE LIFE AND HEALTH INSURANCE FOUNDATION FOR EDUCATION
1655 North Fort Myer Drive, Suite 610
Arlington, VA 22209
Tel: 888-LIFE-777
Fax: 202-464-5011
Web: http://lifehappens.org
Nonprofit organization dedicated to addressing the public's growing need for information and education about life, health, disability and long-term care insurance.

LIFE INSURANCE SETTLEMENT ASSOCIATION
1011 East Colonial Drive, Suite 500
Orlando, FL 32803
Tel: 407-894-3797
Fax: 407-897-1325
Web: www.thevoiceoftheindustry.org
Promotes the development, integrity and reputation of the life settlement industry and a competitive market for the people it serves.

LIMRA INTERNATIONAL
300 Day Hill Road
Windsor, CT 06095
Tel: 860-285-7787
Fax: 860-298-9555
Web: www.limra.com
Worldwide association providing research, consulting and other services to insurance and financial services companies in more than 60 countries. LIMRA helps its member companies maximize their marketing effectiveness.

LOMA (LIFE OFFICE MANAGEMENT ASSOCIATION)
2300 Windy Ridge Parkway, Suite 600
Atlanta, GA 30339-8443
Tel: 770-951-1770
Fax: 770-984-0441
Web: www.loma.org
Worldwide association of insurance companies specializing in research and education, with a primary focus on home office management.

MIB, INC.
50 Braintree Hill Park, Suite 400
Braintree, MA 02184-8734
Tel: 781-751-6000
Web: www.mib.com/html/lost-life-insurance.html
Database of individual life insurance applications processed since 1995.

NATIONAL ALLIANCE OF LIFE COMPANIES (NALC)
PO Box 50053
Sarasota, FL 34232
Tel: 941-379-6100
Fax: 941-379-6112
Web: www.nalc.net

NATIONAL ASSOCIATION OF HEALTH UNDERWRITERS
2000 North 14th Street, Suite 450
Arlington, VA 22201
Tel: 703-276-0220
Fax: 703-841-7797
Web: www.nahu.org
Professional association of people who sell and service disability income, and hospitalization and major medical health insurance companies.

NATIONAL ORGANIZATION OF LIFE AND HEALTH INSURANCE GUARANTY ASSOCIATIONS (NOLHGA)
13873 Park Center Road, Suite 329
Herndon, VA 20171
Tel: 703-481-5206
Fax: 703-481-5209
Web: www.nolhga.com
A voluntary association composed of the life and health insurance guaranty associations of all 50 states, the District of Columbia and Puerto Rico. When insolvency involves multiple states, NOLHGA assists its state guaranty association members in fulfilling their statutory obligations to policyholders.

Financial Services Industry Organizations

ADVANTAGE GROUP ASSOCIATES, INC.
215 SE Wildflower Court
Pleasant Hill, IA 50327
Tel: 515-262-2623
Web: www.annuityspecs.com
A third-party market research firm that tracks indexed annuity and indexed life products, carriers and sales.

AMERICAN BANKERS ASSOCIATION
1120 Connecticut Avenue NW
Washington, DC 20036
Tel: 800-BANKERS
Fax: 202-828-4540
Web: www.aba.com
Represents banks of all sizes on issues of national importance for financial institutions and their customers. Brings together all categories of banking institutions, including community, regional and money center banks and holding companies, as well as savings associations, trust companies and savings banks.

AMERICAN BANKERS INSURANCE ASSOCIATION
1120 Connecticut Avenue, NW
Washington, DC 20036
Tel: 202-663-5163
Fax: 202-828-4546
Web: www.theabia.com
 A separately chartered affiliate of the American Bankers Association. A full service association for bank insurance interests dedicated to furthering the policy and business objectives of banks in insurance.

AMERICAN FINANCIAL SERVICES ASSOCIATION
115 S. LaSalle Street, Suite 3300
Chicago, IL 60603-3801
Tel: 800-224-0900
Fax: 312-683-2373
Web: www.americanfinsvcs.com
The national trade association for market funded providers of financial services to consumers and small businesses.

BANK ADMINISTRATION INSTITUTE
One North Franklin, Suite 1000
Chicago, IL 60606-3421
Tel: 888-284-4078
Fax: 800-375-5543
Web: www.bai.org
A professional organization devoted exclusively to improving the performance of financial services companies through strategic research and information, education and training.

BANK FOR INTERNATIONAL SETTLEMENTS
CH-4002, Basel, Centralbahnplatz 2
Basel, Switzerland
Tel: 41-61-280-8080
Fax: 41-61-280-9100
Web: www.bis.org
An international organization which fosters cooperation among central banks and other agencies in pursuit of monetary and financial stability.

BANK INSURANCE & SECURITIES ASSOCIATION

303 West Lancaster Avenue, Suite 2D
Wayne, PA 19087
Tel: 610-989-9047
Fax: 610-989-9102
Web: www.bisanet.org
Fosters the full integration of securities and insurance businesses with depository institutions' traditional banking businesses. Participants include executives from the securities, insurance, investment advisory, trust, private banking, retail, capital markets and commercial divisions of depository institutions.

BANK INSURANCE MARKET RESEARCH GROUP

154 East Boston Post Road
Mamaroneck, NY 10543
Tel: 914-381-7475
Web: www.singerpubs.com
Provides market research and investment sales data to the bank and insurance industries based on in-depth surveys of depository and insurance entities augmented by analysis of government data.

BANKINSURANCE. COM NEWSLETTER

823 King of Prussia Road
Radnor, PA 19087
Tel: 610-254-0440
Fax: 610-254-5044
Web: www.bankinsurance.com
A monthly electronic publication that distills the important news stories in the bank insurance and investment marketplace with information, impact and analytic benchmarking not found elsewhere.

CERTIFIED FINANCIAL PLANNER BOARD OF STANDARDS, INC.

1425 K Street NW, Suite 500
Washington, DC 20005
Tel: 202-379-2200
Fax: 202-379-2299
Web: www.cfp.net
Group whose mission is to create awareness of the importance of financial planning and the value of the financial planning process and to help underserved populations have access to competent and ethical financial planning.

COLLEGE SAVINGS PLANS NETWORK

PO Box 11910
Lexington, KY 40578-1910
Tel: 859-244-8175
Web: www.collegesavings.org
The College Savings Plans Network is an affiliate to the National Association of State Treasurers. It is intended to make higher education more attainable. The Network serves as a clearinghouse for information on existing college savings programs.

THE COMMITTEE OF ANNUITY INSURERS

c/o Davis & Harman LLP
1455 Pennsylvania Avenue NW, Suite 1200
Tel: 202-347-2230
Fax: 202-393-3310
Web: www.annuity-insurers.org
Group whose goal is to address federal legislative and regulatory issues relevant to the annuity industry and to participate in the development of federal tax and securities policies regarding annuities.

COMMODITY FUTURES TRADING COMMISSION

Three Lafayette Centre
1155 21st Street NW
Washington, DC 20581
Tel: 202-418-5000
Fax: 202-418-5521
Web: www.cftc.gov
Independent agency created by Congress to protect market participants against manipulation, abusive trade practices and fraud.

CONFERENCE OF STATE BANK SUPERVISORS

1155 Connecticut Avenue NW, 5th Floor
Washington, DC 20036-4306
Tel: 202-296-2840
Fax: 202-296-1928
Web: www.csbs.org
National organization that advocates on behalf of the nation's state banking system.

CONSUMERS BANKERS ASSOCIATION

1000 Wilson Boulevard, Suite 2500
Arlington, VA 22209-3912
Tel: 703-276-1750
Fax: 703-528-1290
Web: www.cbanet.org
This group is the recognized voice on retail banking issues in the nation's capital.

DMA FINANCIAL SERVICES COUNCIL

1120 Avenue of the Americas
New York, NY 10036-6700
Tel: 212-768-7277
Fax: 212-302-6714
Web: www.the-dma.org
Integrates the direct marketing concept, its tactics and its practices with mainstream insurance and financial services marketing to create a strategic business synergism, a division of the Direct Marketing Association.

EASTBRIDGE CONSULTING GROUP, INC.

50 Avon Meadow Lane
Avon, CT 06001
Tel: 860-676-9633
Web: www.eastbridge.com
Provides consulting, marketing, training and research services to financial services firms, including those involved in worksite marketing and the distribution of individual and employee benefits products.

EMPLOYEE BENEFIT RESEARCH INSTITUTE

1100 13th Street NW, Suite 878
Washington, DC 20037-1896
Tel: 202-659-0670
Fax: 202-775-6312
Web: www.ebri.org
The Institute's mission is to advance the public's, the media's and policymakers' knowledge and understanding of employee benefits and their importance to the U.S. economy.

FEDERAL DEPOSIT INSURANCE CORPORATION (FDIC)

550 17th Street NW
Washington, DC 20429-9990
Tel: 877-275-3342
Web: www.fdic.gov
The FDIC's mission is to maintain the stability of and public confidence in the nation's financial system. To achieve this goal, the FDIC has insured deposits and promoted safe and sound banking practices since 1933.

FEDERAL FINANCIAL INSTITUTIONS EXAMINATION COUNCIL
3501 Fairfax Drive
Arlington, VA 22201-2305
Tel: 703-516-5487
Fax: 703-516-5588
Web: www.ffiec.gov
A formal interagency body empowered to prescribe uniform principles, standards, and report forms for the federal examination of financial institutions by the Board of Governors of the Federal Reserve System.

FEDERAL RESERVE
20th Street and Constitution Avenue NW
Washington, DC 20551
Tel: 202-452-3000
Web: www.federalreserve.gov
Central bank of the United States, founded by Congress in 1913 to provide the nation with a safer, more flexible and more stable monetary and financial system.

FINANCIAL INDUSTRY REGULATORY AUTHORITY (FINRA)
1735 K Street, NW
Washington, DC 20006
Tel: 301-590-6500
Fax: 240-386-4838
Web: www.finra.org
Largest non-governmental regulator for all securities firms doing business in the United States. Created in July 2007 through the consolidation of NASD and the member regulation, enforcement and arbitration functions of the New York Stock Exchange.

THE FINANCIAL PLANNING ASSOCIATION
4100 East Mississippi Avenue, Suite 400
Denver, CO 80246-3053
Tel: 800-322-4237
Fax: 303-759-0749
Web: www.fpanet.org
Group whose primary aim is to foster the value of financial planning and advance the financial planning profession.

FINANCIAL SERVICES FORUM
601 13th Street NW, Suite 750 South
Washington, DC 20005
Tel: 202-457-8765
Fax: 202-457-8769
Web: www.financialservicesforum.org
An organization of 20 chief executive officers of major U.S. financial services firms dedicated to the execution and coordination of activities designed to promote the development of an open and competitive financial services industry.

THE FINANCIAL SERVICES ROUNDTABLE
1001 Pennsylvania Avenue NW, Suite 500 South
Washington, DC 20004
Tel: 202-289-4322
Fax: 202-628-2507
Web: www.fsround.org
A forum for U.S. financial industry leaders working together to determine and influence the most critical public policy concerns related to the integration of the financial services.

FUTURES INDUSTRY ASSOCIATION
2001 Pennsylvania Avenue NW, Suite 600
Washington, DC 20006
Tel: 202-466-5460
Fax: 202-296-3184
Web: www.futuresindustry.org
Association representative of all organizations that have an interest in the futures market.

GLOBAL ASSOCIATION OF RISK PROFESSIONALS
111 Town Square Place, Suite 1215
Jersey City, NJ 07310
Tel: 201-719-7210
Fax: 201-222-5022
Web: www.garp.com
International group whose aim is to encourage and enhance communications between risk professionals, practitioners and regulators worldwide.

THE HEDGE FUND ASSOCIATION
2875 Northeast 191st Street, Suite 900
Aventura, FL 33180
Tel: 202-478-2000
Fax: 202-478-1999
Web: www.thehfa.org
An international not-for-profit association of hedge fund managers, service providers and investors formed to unite the hedge fund industry and add to the increasing awareness of the advantages and opportunities in hedge funds.

INSURANCE MARKETPLACE STANDARDS ASSOCIATION
4550 Montgomery Avenue, Suite 700N
Bethesda, MD 20814
Tel: 240-744-3030
Fax: 240-744-3031
Web: www.imsaethics.org
A nonprofit, independent organization created to strengthen consumer trust and confidence in the marketplace for individually sold life insurance, long-term care insurance and annuities.

INSURED RETIREMENT INSTITUTE
1331 L St, NW Ste. 310
Washington, DC 20005
Tel: 202-469-3000
Fax: 202-898-5786
Web: www.irionline.org
Source of knowledge pertaining to annuities, insured retirement products and retirement planning; provides educational and informational resources. Formerly the National Association for Variable Annuities (NAVA).

INTERNATIONAL SWAPS AND DERIVATIVES ASSOCIATION
360 Madison Avenue, 16th Floor
New York, NY 10017
Tel: 212-901-6000
Fax: 212-901-6001
Web: www.isda.org
The association's primary purpose is to encourage the prudent and efficient development of the privately negotiated derivatives business.

INVESTMENT COMPANY INSTITUTE
1401 H Street NW
Washington, DC 20005
Tel: 202-326-5800
Web: www.ici.org
The national association of the American investment company industry.

KEHRER-LIMRA
300 Day Hill Road
Windsor, CT 06095-4761
Tel: 978-448-0198
Fax: 860-298-9555
Web: www.kehrerlimra.com
Consultant focusing on the financial services marketplace. Conducts studies of sales penetration, profitability, compensation and compliance.

MICHAEL WHITE ASSOCIATES
823 King of Prussia Road
Radnor, PA 19087
Tel: 610-254-0440
Fax: 610-254-5044
Web: www.bankinsurance.com
Consulting firm that helps clients plan, develop and implement bank insurance sales programs. Conducts research on and benchmarks performance of bank insurance and investment fee income activities.

MORTGAGE BANKERS ASSOCIATION OF AMERICA

1331 L Street NW
Washington, DC 20006-3404
Tel: 202-557-2700
Web: www.mbaa.org
Represents the real estate finance industry.

MORTGAGE INSURANCE COMPANIES OF AMERICA (MICA)

1425 K Street, Suite 210
Washington, DC 20005
Tel: 202-682-2683
Fax: 202-842-9252
Web: www.privatemi.com
Represents the private mortgage insurance industry. MICA provides information on related legislative and regulatory issues, and strives to enhance understanding of the vital role private mortgage insurance plays in housing Americans.

MUSEUM OF AMERICAN FINANCE

48 Wall Street
New York, NY 10005
Tel: 212-908-4110
Fax: 212-908-4601
Web: www.financialhistory.org
An affiliate of the Smithsonian Institution, the museum is the nation's only independent public museum dedicated to celebrating the spirit of entrepreneurship and the democratic free market tradition.

NATIONAL ASSOCIATION FOR FIXED ANNUITIES

2300 East Kensington Boulevard
Milwaukee, WI 53211
Tel: 414-332-9306
Fax: 415-946-3532
Web: www.nafa.us
Promotes the growth, acceptance and understanding of annuity and life products; provides educational and informational resources.

NATIONAL ASSOCIATION OF FEDERAL CREDIT UNIONS

3138 10th Street North
Arlington, VA 22201-2149
Tel: 800-336-4644
Fax: 703-524-1082
Web: www.nafcunet.org
Trade association that exclusively represents the interests of federal credit unions before the federal government and the public.

NATIONAL ASSOCIATION OF INSURANCE AND FINANCIAL ADVISORS

2901 Telestar Court, PO Box 12012
Falls Church, VA 22042-1205
Tel: 703-770-8100; 877-866-2432
Fax: 703-770-8224
Web: www.naifa.org
Professional association representing health and life insurance agents.

NATIONAL ASSOCIATION OF INVESTMENT PROFESSIONALS

Tel: 952-322-4322
Web: www.naip.com/
Promotes the interests and the image of its financial professionals members, and encourages and facilitates higher levels of competency in members so that they may better serve the investing public.

THE NATIONAL ASSOCIATION OF PERSONAL FINANCIAL ADVISORS

3250 North Arlington Heights Road
Suite 109
Arlington Heights, IL 60004
Tel: 847-483-5400
Fax: 847-483-5415
Web: www.napfa.org
Organization of fee-only financial planning professionals serving individuals and institutions.

NATIONAL ASSOCIATION OF PROFESSIONAL INSURANCE AGENTS

400 North Washington Street
Alexandria, VA 22314-2353
Tel: 703-836-9340
Fax: 703-836-1279
Web: www.pianet.com
Trade association of independent insurance agents.

NATIONAL CREDIT UNION ADMINISTRATION

1775 Duke Street
Alexandria, VA 22314-3428
Tel: 703-518-6300
Fax: 703-518-6660
Web: www.ncua.gov
An independent agency in the executive branch of the federal government responsible for chartering, insuring, supervising and examining federal credit unions.

NATIONAL FUTURES ASSOCIATION

300 South Riverside Plaza, #1800
Chicago, IL 60606-6615
Tel: 312-781-1300
Fax: 312-781-1467
Web: www.nfa.futures.org
Industrywide self-regulatory organization for the commodity futures industry.

NATIONAL REVERSE MORTGAGE LENDERS ASSOCIATION

1400 16th Street NW, Suite 420
Washington, DC 20036
Tel: 202-939-1760
Fax: 202-265-4435
Web: www.nrmlaonline.org
The group educates consumers about the opportunity to utilize reverse mortgages and trains lenders to be sensitive to the needs of older Americans.

OFFICE OF THRIFT SUPERVISION

1700 G Street NW
Washington, DC 20552
Tel: 202-906-6000
Web: www.ots.treas.gov
The primary regulator of all federal and many state-chartered thrift institutions, which include savings banks and savings and loan associations.

OPTIONS INDUSTRY COUNCIL

One North Wacker Drive, Suite 500
Chicago, IL 60606
Tel: 800-678-4667
Web: www.optionscentral.com
Nonprofit association created to educate the investing public and brokers about the benefits and risks of exchange-traded options.

PENSION RESEARCH COUNCIL

The Wharton School of the University of Pennsylvania, 3620 Locust Walk, 3000 Steinberg Hall - Dietrich Hall
Philadelphia, PA 19104-6302
Tel: 215-898-7620
Fax: 215-573-3418
Web: www.pensionresearchcouncil.org/about
Organization committed to generating debate on key policy issues affecting pensions and other employee benefits.

RETIREMENT INCOME INDUSTRY ASSOCIATION

101 Federal Street, Suite 1900
Boston, MA 02110
Tel: 617-342-7390
Fax: 617-342-7080
Web: www.riia-usa.org
Financial services industry association focusing on the financial and public policy issues related to the income needs of retirees. Members include insurance companies, banks, securities firms and others.

SECURITIES AND EXCHANGE COMMISSION
100 F Street NE
Washington, DC 20549
Tel: 202-942-8088
Web: www.sec.gov
Primary mission is to protect investors and maintain the integrity of the securities markets.

SECURITIES INDUSTRY AND FINANCIAL MARKETS ASSOCIATION (SIFMA)
120 Broadway, 35th Floor
New York, NY 10271-0080
Tel: 212-313-1200
Fax: 212-313-1301
Web: www.sifma.org
Association bringing together the shared interests of securities firms to accomplish common goals.

SOCIETY OF FINANCIAL SERVICES PROFESSIONALS
17 Campus Boulevard, Suite 201
Newtown Square, PA 19073-3230
Tel: 610-526-2500
Fax: 610-527-1499
Web: www.financialpro.org
Advances the professionalism of credentialed members with state-of-the-art resources to serve their clients' financial needs.

TOWERGROUP
Two Charles River Place, 63 Kendrick Street
Needham, MA 02494-2708
Tel: 781-292-5200
Fax: 781-449-6982
Web: www.towergroup.com
Research and advisory firm focused exclusively on the global financial services industry.

VARDS/MORNINGSTAR, INC.
225 West Wacker Drive
Chicago, IL 60606
Tel: 312-696-6000
Web: http://corporate.morningstar.com
Software technology and research data firm that helps annuity manufacturers, distributors, and financial advisors implement new technology and business practices in the sale and servicing of annuities.

Agents And Brokers
(See also state organizations section)

AGENTS FOR CHANGE
1001 Pennsylvania Avenue, NW
Suite 500 South
Washington, D.C. 20004
Tel: 202 589-1929
Fax: 202 628-2507
Web: www.agents4change.net
A trade association of insurance agents and brokers from across all lines of insurance working together to enact a national insurance charter to allow producers and insurers the option of being regulated at either the federal or state level.

AMERICAN ASSOCIATION OF MANAGING GENERAL AGENTS
150 South Warner Road, Suite 156
King of Prussia, PA 19406
Tel: 610-225-1999
Fax: 610-225-1996
Web: http://www.aamga.org
Membership association of managing general agents of insurers.

THE COUNCIL OF INSURANCE AGENTS AND BROKERS

701 Pennsylvania Avenue NW, Suite 750
Washington, DC 20004-2608
Tel: 202-783-4400
Fax: 202-783-4410
Web: http://www.ciab.com
A trade organization representing leading commercial insurance agencies and brokerage firms.

INDEPENDENT INSURANCE AGENTS & BROKERS OF AMERICA, INC.

127 S. Peyton Street
Alexandria, VA 22314
Tel: 800-221-7917
Fax: 703-683-7556
Web: www.iiaba.org
Trade association of independent insurance agents and brokers.

LATIN AMERICAN AGENTS ASSOCIATION

11819 Valley Boulevard
El Monte, CA 91732
Tel: 626-444-0999
Fax: 626-444-2999
Web: www.latinagents.com
An independent group of Hispanic agents and brokers, whose goal is to educate, influence and inform the insurance community about the specific needs of the Latino community in the United States.

LATIN AMERICAN ASSOCIATION OF INSURANCE AGENCIES

2550 Northwest 72nd Avenue, Suite 318
Miami, FL 33122
Tel: 305-477-1442
Fax: 305-477-5298
Web: www.laaia.com
An association of insurance professionals whose purpose is to protect the rights of its members, benefit the consumer through education, provide information and networking services, and promote active participation in the political environment and community service.

NATIONAL ASSOCIATION OF PROFESSIONAL INSURANCE AGENTS

400 N. Washington Street
Alexandria, VA 22314-2353
Tel: 703-836-9340
Fax: 703-836-1279
Web: www.pianet.com
Trade association of independent insurance agents.

NATIONAL ASSOCIATION OF INSURANCE AND FINANCIAL ADVISORS

2901 Telestar Court, PO Box 12012
Falls Church, VA 22042-1205
Tel: 703-770-8100
Web: www.naifa.org
Professional association representing health and life insurance agents.

Regulatory/ Legislative Organizations

NATIONAL ASSOCIATION OF INSURANCE COMMISSIONERS

2301 McGee Street, Suite 800
Kansas City, MO 64108-2662
Tel: 816-842-3600
Fax: 816-783-8175
Web: www.naic.org
Organization of state insurance commissioners to promote uniformity in state supervision of insurance matters and to recommend legislation in state legislatures.

NATIONAL CONFERENCE OF INSURANCE GUARANTY FUNDS

300 North Meridian Street, Suite 1020
Indianapolis, IN 46204
Tel: 317-464-8199
Fax: 317-464-8180
Web: www.ncigf.org
Advisory organization to the state guaranty fund boards; gathers and disseminates information regarding insurer insolvencies.

NATIONAL CONFERENCE OF INSURANCE LEGISLATORS

385 Jordan Road
Troy, NY 12180
Tel: 518-687-0178
Fax: 518-687-0401
Web: www.ncoil.org
Organization of state legislators whose main area of public policy concern is insurance and insurance regulation.

Educational Organizations

THE AMERICAN COLLEGE

270 South Bryn Mawr Avenue
Bryn Mawr, PA 19010
Tel: 610-526-1000
Fax: 610-526-1465
Web: www.theamericancollege.edu
An independent, accredited nonprofit institution, originally The American College of Life Underwriters. Provides graduate and professional education in insurance and other financial services.

AMERICAN INSTITUTE FOR CHARTERED PROPERTY CASUALTY UNDERWRITERS

720 Providence Road, Suite 100
Malvern, PA 19355-0716
Tel: 800-644-2101
Fax: 610-640-9576
Web: www.aicpcu.org
An independent, nonprofit educational organization that confers the Chartered Property Casualty Underwriter (CPCU) professional designation on those individuals who meet its education, experience and ethics requirements.

CFA INSTITUTE

560 Ray C. Hunt Drive
Charlottesville, VA 22903-2981
Tel: 800-247-8132
Fax: 434-951-5262
Web: www.cfainstitute.org
Global membership organization that awards the CFA designation, the institute leads the investment industry by setting the highest standards of ethics and professional excellence and vigorously advocating fair and transparent capital markets.

CPCU (CHARTERED PROPERTY CASUALTY UNDERWRITERS) SOCIETY

720 Providence Road
Malvern, PA 19355-0709
Tel: 800-932-2728
Fax: 610-251-2780
Web: www.cpcusociety.org
Professional society established to foster the higher education of those engaged in insurance and risk management; encourages and conducts research.

GRIFFITH INSURANCE EDUCATION FOUNDATION

623 High Street
Worthington, OH 43085
Tel: 614-880-9870
Fax: 614-880-9872
Web: www.griffithfoundation.org
The foundation promotes the teaching and study of risk management and insurance at colleges and universities nationwide and provides education programs for public policymakers on the basic principles of risk management and insurance.

INSURANCE INSTITUTE OF AMERICA, INC.

720 Providence Road, Suite 100
Malvern, PA 19355-0716
Tel: 800-644-2101
Fax: 610-640-9576
Web: www.aicpcu.org
Provides educational programs and professional certification to people in property and liability insurance. Offerings range from entry-level to advanced, specialized programs. Certification is determined through the administration of national exams.

INSURANCE LIBRARY ASSOCIATION OF BOSTON

156 State Street
Boston, MA 02109
Tel: 617-227-2087
Fax: 617-723-8524
Web: www.insurancelibrary.org
The Insurance Library Association of Boston founded in 1887, is a nonprofit insurance association that has an extensive insurance library on all lines of insurance.

SCHOOL OF RISK MANAGEMENT, INSURANCE AND ACTUARIAL SCIENCE OF THE TOBIN COLLEGE OF BUSINESS AT STREET JOHN'S UNIVERSITY

101 Murray Street
New York, NY 10007
Tel: 212-277-5193
Fax: 212-277-5189
Web: www.stjohns.edu/academics/graduate/tobin/srm
Insurance industry-supported college providing a curriculum leading to bachelor's and master's degrees in business administration, financial management of risk, insurance finance and actuarial science. The Kathryn and Shelby Cullom Davis Library (212-217-5135) provides services, products and resources to its members.

SOCIETY OF CERTIFIED INSurance COUNSELORS

The National Alliance for Insurance Education & Research, PO Box 27027
Austin, TX 78755-2027
Tel: 800-633-2165
Fax: 512-349-6194
Web: www.scic.com
National education program in property, liability and life insurance, with a continuing education requirement upon designation.

SOCIETY OF FINANCIAL EXAMINERS

174 Grace Boulevard
Altamonte Springs, FL 32714
Tel: 407-682-4930
Fax: 407-682-3175
Web: www.sofe.org
Professional society for examiners of insurance companies, banks, savings and loans, and credit unions.

SOCIETY OF INSURANCE TRAINERS AND EDUCATORS
6635 West Happy Valley Road
Suite A104-#444
Glendale, AZ 85310
Tel: 623-547-6401
Fax: 623-547-6814
Web: www.insurancetrainers.org
Professional organization of trainers and educators in insurance.

Specialty Organizations

Actuarial/Accounting

THE ACTUARIAL FOUNDATION
475 North Martingale Road, Suite 600
Schaumburg, IL 60173-2226
Tel: 847-706-3535
Fax: 847-706-3599
Web: www.actuarialfoundation.org
Develops, funds and executes education and research programs that serve the public by harnessing the talents of actuaries.

AMERICAN ACADEMY OF ACTUARIES
1100 17th Street NW, 7th Floor
Washington, DC 20036
Tel: 202-223-8196
Fax: 202-872-1948
Web: www.actuary.org
Professional association for actuaries. Issues standards of conduct and provides government liaison and advisory opinions.

CASUALTY ACTUARIAL SOCIETY
4350 North Fairfax Drive, Suite 250
Arlington, VA 22203
Tel: 703-276-3100
Fax: 703-276-3108
Web: www.casact.org
Promotes actuarial and statistical science in property/casualty insurance fields.

GROUP OF NORTH AMERICAN INSURANCE ENTERPRISES
40 Exchange Place, Suite 1707
New York, NY 10005
Tel: 212-480-0808
Fax: 212-480-9090
Web: www.gnaie.net
International group whose goals are to influence international accounting standards to ensure that they result in high quality accounting standards for insurance companies and, to that end, to increase communication between insurers doing business in North America and the International Accounting Standards Board and the U.S. Financial Accounting Standards Board.

INSURANCE ACCOUNTING AND SYSTEMS ASSOCIATION, INC.
3511 Shannon Road, Suite 160
Durham, NC 27707
Tel: 919-489-0991
Fax: 919-489-1994
Web: www.iasa.org
An international organization to promote the study, research and development of modern techniques in insurance accounting and systems.

SOCIETY OF ACTUARIES
475 North Martingale Road, Suite 600
Schaumburg, IL 60173
Tel: 847-706-3500
Fax: 847-706-3599
Web: www.soa.org
An educational, research and professional organization dedicated to serving the public and its members. The Society's vision is for actuaries to be recognized as the leading professionals in the modeling and management of financial risk and contingent events.

Adjusters

NATIONAL ASSOCIATION OF INDEPENDENT INSURANCE ADJUSTERS

825 West State Street, Suite 117-C&B
Geneva, IL 60134
Tel: 630-397-5012
Fax: 630-397-5013
Web: www.naiia.com
Association of claims adjusters and firms operating independently on a fee basis for all insurance companies.

NATIONAL ASSOCIATION OF PUBLIC INSURANCE ADJUSTERS

21165 Whitefield Place #105
Potamac Falls, VA 20165
Tel: 703-433-9217
Web: www.napia.com
Association of adjusters who are employed by policyholders.

Alternative Markets

CAPTIVE INSURANCE COMPANIES ASSOCIATION

4248 Park Glen Rd.
Minneapolis, MN 55416
Tel: 952-928-4655
Fax: 952-929-1318
Web: www.cicaworld.com
Organization that disseminates information useful to firms that utilize the captive insurance company concept to solve corporate insurance problems.

NATIONAL RISK RETENTION ASSOCIATION

4248 Park Glen Road
Minneapolis, MN 55416
Tel: 952-928-4656
Fax: 952-929-1318
Web: www.nrra-usa.org
The voice of risk retention group and purchasing group liability insurance programs, organized pursuant to the Federal Liability Risk Retention Act.

SELF-INSURANCE INSTITUTE OF AMERICA

PO Box 1237
Simpsonville, SC 29681
Tel: 800-851-7789
Fax: 864-962-2483
Web: www.siia.org
Organization that fosters and promotes alternative methods of risk protection.

Auto/Auto Insurance

AUTOMOBILE INSURANCE PLANS SERVICE OFFICE

302 Central Avenue
Johnston, RI 02919
Tel: 401-946-2600
Fax: 401-528-1409
Web: www.aipso.com
Develops and files rates and provides other services for state-mandated automobile insurance plans.

CERTIFIED AUTOMOTIVE PARTS ASSOCIATION

1518 K Street NW, Suite 306
Washington, DC 20005
Tel: 202-737-2212
Fax: 202-737-2214
Web: www.capacertified.org
Nonprofit organization formed to develop and oversee a test program guaranteeing the suitability and quality of automotive parts.

Automation and Claims Services

ACORD
Two Blue Hill Plaza, 3rd Floor, PO Box 1529,
Pearl River, NY 10965-8529
Tel: 845-620-1700
Fax: 845-620-3600
Web: www.acord.com
An industry-sponsored institute serving as the focal point for improving the computer processing of insurance transactions through the insurance agency system.

IVANS (INSURANCE VALUE ADDED NETWORK SERVICES)
100 First Stamford Place
Stamford, CT 06902
Tel: 800-288-4826
Fax: 203-698-7299
Web: www.ivans.com
An industry-sponsored organization offering a data communications network linking agencies, companies and providers of data to the insurance industry.

Aviation

GLOBAL AEROSPACE, INC.
51 John F. Kennedy Parkway
Short Hills, NJ 07078
Tel: 973-379-0800
Fax: 973-379-8602
Web: www.aau.com
A pool of property/casualty companies engaged in writing all classes of aviation insurance.

U.S. AVIATION UNDERWRITERS, INC.
One Seaport Plaza, 199 Water Street
New York, NY 10038-3526
Tel: 212-952-0100
Web: www.usau.com
Underwriting managers for Aircraft Insurance Group.

Community Development

INSURANCE INDUSTRY CHARITABLE FOUNDATION
1990 North California Boulevard, Suite 230
Walnut Creek, CA 94596
Tel: 925-280-8009
Fax: 925-280-8059
Web: www.iicf.org
The Insurance Industry Charitable Foundation seeks to help communities and enrich lives by combining the collective strengths of the industry to provide grants, volunteer service and leadership.

NEIGHBORWORKS AMERICA
1325 G Street NW, Suite 800
Washington, DC 20005-3100
Tel: 202-220-2300
Fax: 202-376-2600
Web: www.nw.org/network/neighborworksprogs/insurance/default.asp
The goal of this group is to develop partnerships between the insurance industry and NeighborWorks organizations to better market the products and services of both, for the benefit of the customers and communities they serve.

Crime/Fraud

COALITION AGAINST INSURANCE FRAUD
1012 14th Street NW, Suite 200
Washington, DC 20005
Tel: 202-393-7330
Fax: 202-393-7329
Web: www.insurancefraud.org
An alliance of consumer, law enforcement, and insurance industry groups dedicated to reducing all forms of insurance fraud through public advocacy and education.

INSURANCE COMMITTEE FOR ARSON CONTROL

3601 Vincennes Road
Indianapolis, IN 46268
Tel: 317-876-6226
Fax: 317-879-8408
Web: www.arsoncontrol.org
All-industry coalition that serves as a catalyst for insurers' anti-arson efforts and a liaison with government agencies and other groups devoted to arson control.

INTERNATIONAL ASSOCIATION OF INSURANCE FRAUD AGENCIES, INC.

PO Box 10018
Kansas City, MO 64171
Tel: 816-756-5285
Fax: 816-756-5287
Web: www.iaifa.org
An international association opening the doors of communication, cooperation and exchange of information in the fight against sophisticated global insurance and related financial insurance fraud.

INTERNATIONAL ASSOCIATION OF SPECIAL INVESTIGATION UNITS

8015 Corporate Drive, Suite A
Baltimore, MD 21236
Tel: 410-931-3332
Fax: 410-931-2060
Web: www.iasiu.com
Group whose goals are to promote a coordinated effort within the industry to combat insurance fraud and to provide education and training for insurance investigators.

NATIONAL INSURANCE CRIME BUREAU (NICB)

1111 East Touhy Avenue, Suite 400
Des Plaines, IL 60018
Tel: 847-544-7000
Web: www.nicb.org
Not-for-profit organization dedicated to combating crime and vehicle theft.

NATIONAL INSURANCE CRIME BUREAU (NICB) - WASHINGTON MEDIA RELATIONS

12701 Fair Lakes Circle, Suite 380
Fairfax, VA 22033
Tel: 703-222-6250; 888-241-7159
Fax: 703-469-2206
Web: www.nicb.org

NEW YORK ALLIANCE AGAINST INSURANCE FRAUD

c/o New York Insurance Association, Inc.,
130 Washington Ave
Albany, NY 12210
Tel: 518-432-3576
Fax: 518-432-4220
Web: www.fraudny.com
A cooperative effort of insurance companies in New York State to educate the industry about the costs of insurance fraud, the many forms is can take and what can be done to fight it.

Crop Insurance

AMERICAN ASSOCIATION OF CROP INSURERS

1 Massachusetts Avenue NW, Suite 800
Washington, DC 20001-1401
Tel: 202-789-4100
Fax: 202-408-7763
Web: www.cropinsurers.com/
Trade association of insurance companies to promote crop insurance.

CROP INSURANCE RESEARCH BUREAU

10800 Farley, Suite 330
Overland Park, KS 66210
Tel: 913-338-0470; 888-274-2472
Fax: 913-339-9336
Web: www.cropinsurance.org
Crop insurance trade organization.

NATIONAL CROP INSURANCE SERVICES, INC.
8900 Indian Creek Parkway, Suite 600
Overland Park, KS 66210-1567
Tel: 913-685-2767
Fax: 913-685-3080
Web: www.ag-risk.org
National trade association of insurance companies writing hail insurance, fire insurance and insurance against other weather perils to growing crops, with rating and research services for crop-hail and rain insurers.

Flood Insurance

FEDERAL INSURANCE ADMINISTRATION
500 C Street SW
Washington, DC 20472
Tel: 800-621-3362
Fax: 800-827-8112
Web: www.fema.gov
Administers the federal flood insurance program.

International

ASSOCIATION OF SUPERINTENDENTS OF INSURANCE OF LATIN AMERICA
c/o Superintendencia de Valores y Seguros
Chile
Av. Libertador Bernardo O'Higgins 1449, Piso 11
Tel: 56-2-473-4000
Fax: 56-2-473-4101
Web: www.assalweb.org
International body that brings together the highest regulatory authorities in the Latin American insurance field. Comprised of 20 Latin American countries in addition to two associate members, Spain and Portugal.

AXCO INSURANCE INFORMATION SERVICES
39 Cornhill
London, United Kingdom
Tel: 44-20-7623-9828
Fax: 44-20-7623-9003
Web: www.axcoinfo.com
Research firm providing detailed insurance, healthcare and pensions market information on 160 countries.

GENEVA ASSOCIATION
53 Route de Malagnou
Geneva, CH-1208
Tel: 41-22-707-66-00
Fax: 41-22-736-75-36
Web: www.genevaassociation.org/
World organization formed by some 80 chief executive officers of leading insurance companies in Europe, North America, South America, Asia, Africa and Australia. Its main goal is to research the growing economic importance of worldwide insurance activities in the major sectors of the economy. Produces The Geneva Papers and other publications.

GROUP OF NORTH AMERICAN INSURANCE ENTERPRISES
40 Exchange Place, Suite 1707
New York, NY 10005
Tel: 212-480-0808
Fax: 212-480-9090
Web: www.gnaie.net
International group whose goals are to influence international accounting standards to ensure that they result in high quality accounting standards for insurance companies and, to that end, to increase communication between insurers doing business in North America and the International Accounting Standards Board and the U.S. Financial Accounting Standards Board.

INSURANCE SERVICES NETWORK

PO Box 455
Lake Forest, IL 60045
Tel: 847-234-4762
Fax: 847-295-2608
Web: www.isn-inc.com
Independent insurance information company offering international industry news and analyses of the regulatory climate in dozens of countries. Publishes Insurance Research Letter.

INTERNATIONAL ASSOCIATION OF INSURANCE SUPERVISORS

c/o Bank For International Settlements
Basel, Switzerland CH-4002
Tel: 41-61-225-7300
Fax: 41-61-280-9151
Web: www.iaisweb.org
Represents insurance supervisory authorities of some 100 jurisdictions. Promotes cooperation among members and sets international standards for insurance supervision.

INTERNATIONAL FEDERATION OF RISK AND INSURANCE MANAGEMENT ASSOCIATIONS, INC.

c/o RIMS
1065 Avenue of the Americas, 13th Floor
Tel: 212-286-9292
Fax: 212-655-5931
Web: www.rims.org/ifrima
Worldwide umbrella organization dedicated to the advancement of risk management and its practice through education and interaction.

INTERNATIONAL INSURANCE SOCIETY, INC.

101 Murray Street
New York, NY 10007
Tel: 212-815-9291
Fax: 212-815-9297
Web: www.iisonline.org
A nonprofit membership organization whose mission is to facilitate international understandings, the transfer of ideas and innovations, and the development of personal networks across insurance markets through a joint effort of leading executives and academics throughout the world.

INTERNATIONAL SOCIAL SECURITY ASSOCIATION

Institute for OSH, Rue Gachardstraat 88 b 4
Brussels, Belgium 1050
Tel: 32-2-643-44-92
Fax: 32-2-643-44-40
Web: http://information.prevention.issa.int
Nonprofit international organization consisting of institutions and administrative bodies dealing with diverse aspects of social security in countries around the world.

INTERNATIONAL TRADE ADMINISTRATION

U.S. Department of Commerce, 1401 Constitution Avenue
Washington, DC 20230
Tel: 202-482-3809
Fax: 202-482-5819
Web: www.ita.doc.gov
Division of the U.S. Department of Commerce that helps U.S. businesses participate in the growing global marketplace.

ORGANISATION FOR ECONOMIC CO-OPERATION AND DEVELOPMENT (OECD)
2, rue André Pascal
75775 Paris Cedex, France 16
Tel: 33-1-45-24-82-00
Fax: 33-1-45-24-85-00
Web: www.oecd.org
International organization of industrialized, market-economy countries. The OECD publishes numerous reports, including the Insurance Statistics Yearbook.

ORGANISATION FOR ECONOMIC CO-OPERATION AND DEVELOPMENT (OECD), WASHINGTON CENTER
2001 L Street NW, Suite 650
Washington, DC 20036-4922
Tel: 202-785-6323
Fax: 202-785-0350
Web: www.oecdwash.org
Markets the publications of the OECD in the and serves as an information center for the U.S. market. The Center is engaged in public outreach activities and acts as a liaison office to the U.S. legislative and executive branches.

OVERSEAS PRIVATE INVESTMENT CORPORATION
1100 New York Avenue NW
Washington, DC 20527
Tel: 202-336-8400
Fax: 202-336-7949
Web: www.opic.gov
Self-sustaining U.S. government agency providing political risk insurance and finance services for U.S. investment in developing countries.

SIGMA
c/o Swiss Re
Mythenquai 50/60, PO Box
Tel: 41-43-285-2121
Fax: 41-43-285-2999
Web: www.swissre.com
The sigma publication series provides comprehensive information on international insurance markets and in-depth analyses of economic trends and strategic issues in insurance, reinsurance and financial services.

TOPICS
c/o Munich Re
Munich, Germany 80802
Tel: 49-89-38-91-0
Web: www.munichre.com
This annual publication presents a detailed account of the natural catastrophes that occurred in the past year and also examines long-term trends.

WORLD FACT BOOK
c/o Central Intelligence Agency (CIA)
Washington, DC 20505
Tel: 703-482-0623
Fax: 703-482-1739
Web: www.cia.gov/cia/publications/factbook/index.html
Produced by the CIA's Directorate of Intelligence, the fact book is a comprehensive resource of facts and statistics on more than 250 countries and other entities.

Legal Issues and Services

AMERICAN PREPAID LEGAL SERVICES INSTITUTE
321 North Clark Street
Chicago, IL 60610
Tel: 312-988-5751
Fax: 312-988-5710
Web: www.aplsi.org
National membership organization providing information and technical assistance to lawyers, insurance companies, administrators, marketers and consumers regarding group and prepaid legal service plans.

AMERICAN TORT REFORM ASSOCIATION
1101 Connecticut Avenue NW, Suite 400
Washington, DC 20036
Tel: 202-682-1163
Fax: 202-682-1022
Web: www.atra.org
A broad based, bipartisan coalition of more than 300 businesses, corporations, municipalities, associations and professional firms that support civil justice reform.

ARBITRATION FORUMS, INC.
3350 Buschwood Park Drive, Building 3, Suite 295
Tampa, FL 33618-1500
Tel: 888-272-3453
Fax: 813-931-4618
Web: www.arbfile.org
Nonprofit provider of interinsurance dispute resolution services for self-insureds, insurers and claim service organizations.

DEFENSE RESEARCH INSTITUTE
150 North Michigan Avenue, Suite 300
Chicago, IL 60601
Tel: 312-795-1101
Fax: 312-795-0747
Web: www.dri.org
A national and international membership association of lawyers and others concerned with the defense of civil actions.

NATIONAL ARBITRATION FORUM
PO Box 50191
Minneapolis, MN 55405-0191
Tel: 800-474-2371
Fax: 952-345-1160
Web: www.arbitration-forum.com
A leading neutral administrator of arbitration, mediation and other forms of alternative dispute resolution worldwide.

NATIONAL STRUCTURED SETTLEMENTS TRADE ASSOCIATION
2025 M Street NW, Suite 800
Washington, DC 20036
Tel: 202-367-1159
Fax: 202-367-2159
Web: www.nssta.com
Trade association representing consultants, insurers and others who are interested in the resolution and financing of tort claims through periodic payments.

Marine and Ground Transportation

AMERICAN INSTITUTE OF MARINE UNDERWRITERS
14 Wall Street, 8th Floor
New York, NY 10005
Tel: 212-233-0550
Fax: 212-227-5102
Web: www.aimu.org
Provides information of concern to marine underwriters and promotes their interests.

INLAND MARINE UNDERWRITERS ASSOCIATION

14 Wall Street, 8th Floor
New York, NY 10005
Tel: 212-233-0550
Fax: 212-227-5102
Web: www.imua.org
Forum for discussion of problems of common concern to inland marine insurers.

Medical Malpractice/ Professional Liability

PHYSICIAN INSURERS ASSOCIATION OF AMERICA

2275 Research Boulevard, Suite 250
Rockville, MD 20850
Tel: 301-947-9000
Fax: 301-947-9090
Web: www.thepiaa.org
Trade association representing physician-owned mutual insurance companies that provide medical malpractice insurance.

PROFESSIONAL LIABILITY UNDERWRITING SOCIETY (PLUS)

5353 Wayzata Boulevard, Suite 600
Minneapolis, MN 55416
Tel: 952-746-2580; 800-845-0788
Fax: 952-746-2599
Web: www.plusweb.org
An international, nonprofit association that provides educational opportunities and programs to enhance the professionalism of its members.

Nuclear Insurance

AMERICAN NUCLEAR INSURERS

95 Glastonbury Boulevard, Suite 300
Glastonbury, CT 06033
Tel: 860-682-1301
Fax: 860-659-0002
Web: www.amnucins.com
A nonprofit unincorporated association through which liability insurance protection is provided against hazards arising out of nuclear reactor installations and their operations.

Professional

APIW: A PROFESSIONAL ASSOCIATION OF WOMEN IN INSURANCE

555 Fifth Avenue, 8th Floor
New York, NY 10017
Tel: 212-867-0228
Fax: 212-867-2544
Web: www.apiw.org
A professional association of women in the insurance and reinsurance industry and related fields. Provides professional education, networking and support services to encourage the development of professional leadership among its members.

INSURANCE DATA MANAGEMENT ASSOCIATION, INC. (IDMA)

545 Washington Boulevard
Jersey City, NJ 07310-1686
Tel: 201-469-3069
Fax: 201-748-1690
Web: www.idma.org
An independent, nonprofit, professional, learned association dedicated to increasing the level of professionalism, knowledge and visibility of insurance data management. To achieve that goal, IDMA focuses on courses and certification, forums and seminars, and data management publications and periodicals.

INSURANCE REGULATORY EXAMINERS SOCIETY

12710 South Pflumm Road, Suite 200
Olathe, KS 66062
Tel: 913-768-4700
Fax: 913-768-4900
Web: www.go-ires.org
Nonprofit professional and educational association for examiners and other professionals working in insurance industry.

NAIW

9343 East 95th Court South
Tulsa, OK 74133
Tel: 800-766-6249
Fax: 918-743-1968
Web: www.naiw.org
Fosters educational programs for members. Promotes public safety and service programs.

NATIONAL AFRICAN-AMERICAN INSURANCE ASSOCIATION

1718 M Street NW, PO Box 1110
Washington, DC 20036
Tel: 866-56-NAAIA
Web: www.naaia.org
NAAIA fosters the nationwide presence, participation and long-term financial success of African-American insurance professionals within the greater insurance community and provides its members and the insurance industry a forum for sharing information and ideas that enhance business and professional development.

NATIONAL ASSOCIATION OF INSURANCE AND FINANCIAL ADVISORS

2901 Telestar Court, PO Box 12012
Falls Church, VA 22042-1205
Tel: 703-770-8100; 877-866-2432
Fax: 703-770-8224
Web: www.naifa.org
Professional association representing health and life insurance agents.

Property Insurance Plans

PROPERTY INSURANCE PLANS SERVICE OFFICE

27 School Street, Suite 302
Boston, MA 02108
Tel: 617-371-4175
Fax: 617-371-4177
Web: www.pipso.com
Provides technical and administrative services to state property insurance plans.

Reinsurance

INTERMEDIARIES AND REINSURANCE UNDERWRITERS ASSOCIATION, INC.

971 Route 202 North
Branchburg, NJ 08876
Tel: 908-203-0211
Fax: 908-203-0213
Web: www.irua.com
Educational association to encourage the exchange of ideas among reinsurers worldwide writing principally treaty reinsurance.

REINSURANCE ASSOCIATION OF AMERICA

1301 Pennsylvania Avenue NW, Suite 900
Washington, DC 20004
Tel: 202-638-3690
Fax: 202-638-0936
Web: www.reinsurance.org
Trade association of property/casualty reinsurers; provides legislative services for members.

Risk Management

LOSS EXECUTIVES ASSOCIATION

PO Box 37
Tenafly, NJ 07670
Tel: 732-388-5700
Fax: 732-388-0171
Web: www.lossexecutives.com
A professional association of property loss executives providing education to the industry.

NONPROFIT RISK MANAGEMENT CENTER

15 North King Street, Suite 203
Leesburg, VA 20176
Tel: 202-785-3891
Fax: 202-296-0349
Web: www.nonprofitrisk.org
Conducts research and education on risk management and insurance issues of special concern to nonprofit organizations.

PUBLIC RISK MANAGEMENT ASSOCIATION

500 Montgomery Street, Suite 750
Alexandria, VA 22314
Tel: 703-528-7701
Fax: 703-739-0200
Web: www.primacentral.org
Membership organization representing risk managers in state and local public entities.

RISK AND INSURANCE MANAGEMENT SOCIETY, INC.

1065 Avenue of the Americas, 13th Floor
New York, NY 10018
Tel: 212-286-9292
Web: www.rims.org
Organization of corporate buyers of insurance, which makes known to insurers the insurance needs of business and industry, supports loss prevention and provides a forum for the discussion.

SOCIETY OF RISK MANAGEMENT CONSULTANTS

330 S. Executive Dr., Suite 301
Brookfield, WI 53005-4275
Tel: 800-765-SRMC
Web: www.srmcsociety.org
International organization of professionals engaged in risk management, insurance and employee benefits consulting.

Safety/Disaster Mitigation

ADVOCATES FOR HIGHWAY AND AUTO SAFETY

750 First Street NE, Suite 901
Washington, DC 20002
Tel: 202-408-1711
Fax: 202-408-1699
Web: www.saferoads.org
An alliance of consumer, safety and insurance organizations dedicated to highway and auto safety.

HIGHWAY LOSS DATA INSTITUTE

1005 North Glebe Road, Suite 800
Arlington, VA 22201
Tel: 703-247-1600
Fax: 703-247-1595
Web: www.hwysafety.org
Nonprofit organization to gather, process and provide the public with insurance data concerned with human and economic losses resulting from highway accidents.

INSTITUTE FOR BUSINESS & HOME SAFETY (IBHS)

4775 East Fowler Avenue
Tampa, FL 33617
Tel: 813-286-3400
Fax: 813-286-9960
Web: www.disastersafety.org
The Institute for Business & Home Safety works to reduce the social and economic effects of natural disasters and other property losses by conducting research and advocating improved construction, maintenance and preparation practices.

INSURANCE INSTITUTE FOR HIGHWAY SAFETY (IIHS)

1005 North Glebe Road, Suite 800
Arlington, VA 22201
Tel: 703-247-1500
Fax: 703-247-1588
Web: www.highwaysafety.org
Research and education organization
dedicated to reducing loss, death, injury,
and property damage on the highways.
Fully funded by property/casualty insurers.

LIGHTNING PROTECTION INSTITUTE

PO Box 99
Maryville, MO 64468
Tel: 800-488-6864
Web: www.lightning.org
Not-for-profit organization dedicated
to ensuring that its members' lightning
protection systems are the best possible
quality in design, materials and
installation.

NATIONAL FIRE PROTECTION ASSOCIATION

One Batterymarch Park
Quincy, MA 02169-7471
Tel: 617-770-3000
Fax: 617-770-0700
Web: www.nfpa.org
Independent, nonprofit source of
information on fire protection, prevention
and suppression. Develops and publishes
consensus fire safety standards; sponsors
national Learn Not to Burn campaign.

NATIONAL HIGHWAY TRAFFIC SAFETY ADMINISTRATION (NHTSA)

1200 New Jersey Avenue SE, West Building
Washington, DC 20590
Tel: 888-327-4236
Fax: 202-366-2106
Web: www.nhtsa.dot.gov
Carries out programs and studies aimed at
reducing economic losses in motor vehicle
crashes and repairs.

NATIONAL INSTITUTE OF BUILDING SCIENCES

1090 Vermont Avenue NW, Suite 700
Washington, DC 20005-4905
Tel: 202-289-7800
Fax: 202-289-1092
Web: www.nibs.org/pubsbetec.html
A nonprofit, nongovernmental
organization bringing together
representatives of government, the
professions, industry, labor and consumer
interests to focus on the identification
and resolution of problems and potential
problems that hamper the construction
of safe, affordable structures for housing,
commerce and industry throughout the
United States.

NATIONAL SAFETY COUNCIL

1121 Spring Lake Drive
Itasca, IL 60143-3201
Tel: 630-285-1121 or 800-621-7619
Fax: 630-285-1315
Web: www.nsc.org
Provides national support and leadership in
the field of safety, publishes safety material
and conducts public information and
publicity programs.
fire insurance claims.

UNDERWRITERS' LABORATORIES, INC.

333 Pfingsten Road
Northbrook, IL 60062-2096
Tel: 847-272-8800
Fax: 847-272-8129
Web: www.ul.com
Investigates and tests electrical materials
and other products to determine that fire
prevention and protection standards are
being met.

Surety, Financial Guaranty and Mortgage

ASSOCIATION OF FINANCIAL GUARANTY INSURORS

Mackin & Company,139 Lancaster Street
Albany, NY 12210
Tel: 518-449-4698
Fax: 518-432-5651
Web: www.afgi.org
Trade association of the insurers and reinsurers of municipal bonds and asset-backed securities.

MORTGAGE INSURANCE COMPANIES OF AMERICA (MICA)

1425 K Street, Suite 210
Washington, DC 20005
Tel: 202-682-2683
Fax: 202-842-9252
Web: www.privatemi.com
Represents the private mortgage insurance industry. MICA provides information on related legislative and regulatory issues, and strives to enhance understanding of the vital role private mortgage insurance plays in housing Americans.

NATIONAL ASSOCIATION OF SURETY BOND PRODUCERS (NASBP)

1828 L Street NW, Suite 720
Washington, DC 20036-5104
Tel: 202-686-3700
Fax: 202-686-3656
Web: www.nasbp.org
NASBP members are professionals who specialize in providing surety bonds for construction and other commercial purposes to companies and individuals needing the assurance offered by surety bonds. Its members have broad knowledge of the surety marketplace and the business strategies and underwriting differences among surety companies.

SURETY ASSOCIATION OF AMERICA

1101 Connecticut Avenue NW, Suite 800
Washington, DC 20036
Tel: 202-463-0600
Fax: 202-463-0606
Web: www.surety.org
Statistical, rating, development and advisory organization for surety companies.

SURETY INFORMATION OFFICE

1828 L Street NW, Suite 720
Washington, DC 20036-5104
Tel: 202-686-7463
Fax: 202-686-3656
Web: www.sio.org
Statistical, rating, development and advisory organization for surety companies. Membership includes insurance companies licensed to write fidelity or surety insurance in one or more states and foreign affiliates.
Surplus Lines Organizations

NATIONAL ASSOCIATION OF PROFESSIONAL SURPLUS LINES OFFICES, LTD.

200 Northeast 54th Street, Suite 200
Kansas City, MO 64118
Tel: 816-741-3910
Fax: 816-741-5409
Web: www.napslo.org
Professional association of wholesale brokers, excess and surplus lines companies, affiliates and supporting members.

Surplus Lines
(See state organizations section)

Title Insurance

AMERICAN LAND TITLE ASSOCIATION
1828 L Street NW, Suite 705
Washington, DC 20036
Tel: 800-787-ALTA
Fax: 888-787-ALTA
Web: www.alta.org
Trade organization for title insurers, abstractors and agents. Performs statistical research and lobbying services.

Weather

WEATHER RISK MANAGEMENT ASSOCIATION (WRMA)
750 National Press Building, 529 14th Street, NW
Washington, DC 20045
Tel: 202-289-3800
Fax: 202-223-9741
Web: www.wrma.org
The goal of the WRMA is to serve the weather risk management industry by providing forums for discussion and interaction with others associated with financial weather products.

Workers Compensation

INTEGRATED BENEFITS INSTITUTE
595 Market Street, Suite 810
San Francisco, CA 94105
Tel: 415-222-7280
Fax: 415-222-7281
Web: www.ibiweb.org
A private, nonprofit organization that provides research, discussion and analysis, data services and legislative review to measure and improve integrated benefits programs, enhance efficiency in delivery of all employee-based benefits and promote effective return-to-work.

NATIONAL ACADEMY OF SOCIAL INSURANCE
1776 Massachusetts Avenue NW, Suite 615
Washington, DC 20036
Tel: 202-452-8097
Fax: 202-452-8111
Web: www.nasi.org/info-url_nocat2708/info-url_nocat.htm
A nonprofit, nonpartisan organization made up of the nation's leading experts on social insurance. Its mission is to promote understanding and informed policymaking on social insurance and related programs through research, public education, training and the open exchange of ideas.

NCCI HOLDINGS, INC.
901 Peninsula Corporate Circle
Boca Raton, FL 33487
Tel: 561-893-1000
Fax: 561-893-1191
Web: www.ncci.com
Develops and administers rating plans and systems for workers compensation insurance.

WORKERS COMPENSATION RESEARCH INSTITUTE
955 Massachusetts Avenue
Cambridge, MA 02139
Tel: 617-661-9274
Web: www.wcrinet.org
A nonpartisan, not-for-profit membership organization conducting public policy research on workers' compensation, health care and disability issues. Members include employers, insurers, insurance regulators and state regulatory agencies, as well as several state labor organizations.

Research and Ratings Organizations

A.M. BEST COMPANY INC.
Ambest Road
Oldwick, NJ 08858
Tel: 908-439-2200
Web: www.ambeStreetcom
Rating organization and publisher of reference books and periodicals relating to the insurance industry.

AIR WORLDWIDE CORPORATION
131 Dartmouth Street
Boston, MA 02116
Tel: 617-267-6645
Fax: 617-267-8284
Web: www.air-worldwide.com
Risk modeling and technology firm that develops models of global natural hazards, enabling companies to identify, quantify and plan for the financial consequences of catastrophic events.

AMERICAN ASSOCIATION OF INSURANCE SERVICES
1745 South Naperville Road
Wheaton, IL 60189-8132
Tel: 630-681-8347; 800-564-AAIS
Fax: 630-681-8356
Web: www.aaisonline.com
Rating, statistical and advisory organization, made up principally of small and medium-sized property/casualty companies.

CONNING RESEARCH AND CONSULTING, INC.
One Financial Plaza
Hartford, CT 06103-2627
Tel: 860-299-2000
Web: www.conningresearch.com
Research and consulting firm that offers a growing array of specialty information products, insights and analyses of key issues confronting the insurance industry.

EQECAT
475 14th Street, 5th Floor, Suite 550
Oakland, CA 94612-1900
Tel: 510-817-3100
Web: www.eqecat.com
Provider of products and services for managing natural and man-made risks. Provides innovative catastrophe management solutions for property and casualty insurance underwriting, accumulation management and transfer of natural hazard and terrorism risk.

FITCH CREDIT RATING COMPANY
One State Street Plaza
New York, NY 10004
Tel: 212-908-0500
Fax: 212-480-4435
Web: www.fitchratings.com
Assigns claims-paying ability ratings to insurance companies.

HIGHLINE DATA LLC
One Alewife Center, Suite 460
Cambridge, MA 02140
Tel: 877-299-9424
Fax: 617-864-2396
Web: www.highlinedata.com
An information and data services company comprised of two principal product lines: National Underwriter Insurance Data Services and Highline Banking Data Services.

INSURANCE ADVISORY BOARD C/O THE CORPORATE EXECUTIVE BOARD

1919 North Lynn Street
Arlington, VA 22209
Tel: 571-303-3000
Fax: 571-303-3100
Web: www.insuranceadvisoryboard.com
Membership organization of senior executives committed to sharing insights and strategies for addressing common challenges in the life and property/casualty (general) insurance markets.

INSURANCE RESEARCH COUNCIL (A DIVISION OF THE AMERICAN INSTITUTE FOR CPCU)

718 Providence Road, PO Box 3025
Malvern, PA 19355-0725
Tel: 610-644-2212
Fax: 610-640-5388
Web: www.ircweb.org
Provides the public and the insurance industry with timely research information relevant to public policy issues affecting risk and insurance.

ISO

545 Washington Boulevard
Jersey City, NJ 07310-1686
Tel: 800-888-4476
Fax: 201-748-1472
Web: www.iso.com
Provider of products and services that help measure, manage and reduce risk. Provides data, analytics and decision-support solutions to professionals in many fields, including insurance, finance, real estate, health services, government and human resources.

MOODY'S INVESTORS SERVICE

7 World Trade Center at 250 Greenwich Street
New York, NY 10007
Tel: 212-553-1653
Fax: 212-553-0882
Web: www.moodys.com
Global credit analysis and financial information firm.

MSB

2885 South Calhoun Road
New Berlin, WI 53151
Tel: 262-780-2800; 800-809-0016
Fax: 262-780-0306
Web: www.msbinfo.com
Building cost research company providing data and estimating technologies to the property insurance industry.

NATIONAL INDEPENDENT STATISTICAL SERVICE

3601 Vincennes Road, PO Box 68950
Indianapolis, IN 46268
Tel: 317-876-6200
Fax: 317-876-6210
Web: www.niss-stat.org
National statistical agent and advisory organization for all lines of insurance, except workers compensation.

RAND INSTITUTE FOR CIVIL JUSTICE

1776 Main Street, PO Box 2138
Santa Monica, CA 90407-2138
Tel: 310-393-0411
Fax: 310-451-6979
Web: www.rand.org/centers/icj
Organization formed within The Rand Corporation to perform independent, objective research and analysis concerning the civil justice system.

RISK MANAGEMENT SOLUTIONS, INC.
7015 Gateway Boulevard
Newark, CA 94560
Tel: 510-505-2500
Fax: 510-505-2501
Web: www.rms.com
Provides products and services for the quantification and management of catastrophe risk associated with natural perils as well as products for weather derivatives and enterprise risk management for the property/casualty insurance industry.

SNL FINANCIAL LC
One SNL Plaza, PO Box 2124
Charlottesville, VA 22902
Tel: 434-977-1600
Fax: 434-977-4466
Web: www.snl.com
Research firm that collects, standardizes and disseminates all relevant corporate, financial, market and M&A data as well as news and analytics for the industries it covers: banking, specialized financial services, insurance, real estate and energy.

SOCIETY OF INSURANCE RESEARCH
631 Eastpointe Drive
Shelbyville, IN 46176
Tel: 317-398-3684
Fax: 317-642-0535
Web: www.sirnet.org
Stimulates insurance research and fosters exchanges among society members on research methodology.

STANDARD & POOR'S RATING GROUP
55 Water Street
New York, NY 10041
Tel: 212-438-1000
Web: www.standardandpoors.com

Monitors the credit quality of bonds and other financial instruments of corporations, governments and supranational entities.

THE STREET.COM
14 Wall Street, 15th floor
New York, NY 10005
Web: www.thestreet.com/
Evaluates the strength of insurance and financial services firms.

WARD GROUP
11500 Northlake Drive, Suite 305
Cincinnati, OH 45249-1662
Tel: 513-791-0303
Fax: 513-985-3442
Web: www.wardinc.com
Management consulting firm specializing in the insurance industry.

State Organizations

Alabama

State Associations

NAIFA — Alabama
2820 Fairlane Drive, Suite A-1
Montgomery, Alabama 36116-1637
Tel: 334-271-4900
Fax: 334-271-4960
Web: www.naifa-alabama.com

Agent Associations

**Alabama Independent
Agents Association, Inc.**
141 London Parkway
Birmingham, Alabama 35211
Tel: 205-326-4129
Fax: 205-326-3086
Web: www.aiia.org

**Professional Insurance
Agents of Alabama**
3805 Crestwood Parkway, Suite 140
Duluth, Georgia 30096
Tel: 770-921-7585; 800-233-4902
Fax: 770-921-7590
Web: www.piaal.com

Alaska

No State Associations

Agent Associations

**Alaska Independent Insurance
Agents & Brokers, Inc.**
701 W. 41st Avenue, Suite 103
Anchorage, Alaska 99503
Tel: 907-349-2500
Fax: 907-349-1300
Web: www.aiiab.org

**Professional Insurance
Agents of Alaska**
See PIA of Western Alliance
(under Washington)

Arizona

State Associations

Arizona Insurance Council
PO Box 27006
Scottsdale, Arizona 85255
Tel: 602-996-7009
Fax: 602-996-7016
Web: www.azinsurance.org

**National Association of
Insurance and Financial
Advisors (NAIFA — Arizona)**
PO Box 4728
Scottsdale, Arizona 85261-4728
Tel: 480-661-6393
Fax: 480-661-6743
Web: www.naifa-az.org

Agent Associations

**Independent Insurance Agents
& Brokers of Arizona, Inc.**
333 E. Flower Street
Phoenix, Arizona 85012
Tel: 602-956-1851
Fax: 602-468-1392
Web: www.iiabaz.com

**Professional Insurance
Agents of Arizona**
See PIA Western Alliance
(under Washington)
Western Insurance Agents
Association (WIAA)
See Western Insurance Agents
Association (under California)

Other Organizations

The Surplus Line Association of Arizona

15849 N. 71st St., Suite 100
Scottsdale, Arizona 85254
Tel: 602-279-6344
Fax: 602-222-9332
Web: www.sla-az.org

Arkansas

State Associations

The National Association of Insurance and

Financial Advisors (NAIFA – Arkansas)
650 Edgewood Drive, Suite 201
Maumelle, Arkansas 72113
Tel: 501-851-6617
Fax: 501-851-1126
Web: http://arkansas.naifa.org

Agent Associations

Independent Insurance Agents of Arkansas

5000 North Shore Drive
North Little Rock, Arkansas 72118
Tel: 501-221-2444
Fax: 501-221-0364
Web: www.iiaar.org

Professional Insurance Agents of Arkansas

10 Corporate Hill, Suite 130
Little Rock, Arkansas 72205
Tel: 501-225-1645
Fax: 501-225-2550
Web: www.piaar.com

California

State Associations

Association of California Insurance Companies

1415 L Street, Suite 670
Sacramento, California 95814-3972
Tel: 916-449-1370
Fax: 916-449-1378
Web: www.acicnet.org

Association of California Life and Health Insurance Companies

1201 K Street, Suite 1820
Sacramento, California 95814
Tel: 916-442-3648
Fax: 916-442-1730
Web: www.aclhic.com

Insurance Information Network of California (IINC)

900 Wilshire Blvd., Suite 1414
Los Angeles, California 90017
Tel: 213-624-IINC
Fax: 213-624-4432
Web: www.iinc.org

National Association of Insurance and Financial Advisors — California (NAIFA – California)

1451 River Park Drive, Suite 175
Sacramento, California 95815-4520
Tel: 916-646-8600
Fax: 916-646-8130
Web: www.naifacalifornia.org

Pacific Association of Domestic Insurance Companies (PADIC)
1940 Burlin Way
Auburn, California 95603
Tel: 530-888-6045
Fax: 530-888-6435

Personal Insurance Federation of California
1201 K Street, Suite 1220
Sacramento, California 95814
Tel: 916-442-6646
Fax: 916-446-9548
Web: www.pifc.org

Agent Associations

Professional Insurance Agents of California
See PIA Western Alliance
(under Washington)

Western Insurance Agents Association (WIAA)
(Serving Arizona, California, Colorado, Nevada and New Mexico)
11190 Sun Center Drive, Suite 100
Rancho Cordova, California 95670
Tel: 916-443-4221; 800-553-4221
Fax: 916-443-5559
Web: www.wiaagroup.org

Other Organizations

Insurance Brokers & Agents of The West (IBA West)
7041 Koll Center Parkway, Suite 290
Pleasanton, California 94566
Tel: 800-772-8998 or 925-426-3300
Fax: 925-484-6014
Web: www.ibawest.com

Surplus Line Association of California
(Stamping Office)
50 California Street, 18th Fl.
San Francisco, California 94111
Tel: 415-434-4900
Fax: 415-434-3716
Web: www.slacal.org

Colorado

State Associations

NAIFA — Colorado
Lundy Enterprises
PO Box 271273
Louisville, Colorado 80027
Tel: 303-283-6001
Fax: 303-362-5809
Web: www.naifa-colorado.org

Rocky Mountain Insurance Information Association — CO, NM, UT and WY
7951 E. Maplewood Avenue, Suite 130
Greenwood Village, Colorado 80111
Tel: 303-790-0216/800-355-9524
Fax: 303-790-0433
Web: www.rmiia.org

Agent Associations

Professional Independent Insurance Agents of Colorado & Agents Service Corporation
1660 Tower, 1660 S. Albion St., Suite 518
Denver, Colorado 80222
Tel: 303-512-0627
Fax: 303-512-0575
Web: www.piiac.com

Other Organizations

Surplus Line Association of Colorado
PO Box 1500
Denver, Colorado 80201
Tel: 303-331-9399
Fax: 303-331-9006
Web: www.colosla.org

Connecticut

State Associations

Insurance Association of Connecticut
21 Oak Street #607
Hartford, Connecticut 06106-8003
Tel: 860-547-0610
Fax: 860-547-0615

NAIFA of Connecticut, Inc.
15 Chipmunk Lane
Norwalk, Connecticut 06850
Tel: 203-866-4700
Fax: 203-866-1788
Web: www.naifa-ct.org

Agent Associations

Independent Insurance Agents of Connecticut, Inc.
30 Jordan Lane
Wethersfield, Connecticut 06109
Tel: 860-563-1950
Fax: 860-563-6730
Web: www.iiact.org

Professional Insurance Agents of Connecticut
See PIA (under New York)

Delaware

State Associations

NAIFA — Delaware
646 Plaza Drive
Newark, Delaware 19702
Tel: 302-283-1880
Fax: 302-283-1885
Web: www.naifanet.com/delaware

Agent Associations

Independent Insurance Agents of Delaware
See Insurance Agents & Brokers
(under Pennsylvania)

District Of Columbia

State Associations

District of Columbia Insurance Federation
PO Box 34757
Washington, D.C. 20043
Tel: 202-797-0757
Fax: 202-797-0758
Web: www.dcif.org

Agent Associations

Professional Insurance Agents of D.C.
See PIA (under Virginia)

Florida

State Associations

Florida Insurance Council
2888 Remington Green Lane, Suite A
Tallahassee, Florida 32308
Tel: 850-386-6668
Fax: 850-386-7371
Web: www.flains.org

NAIFA—Florida
1836 Hermitage Blvd., #200
Tallahassee, Florida 32308-7706
Tel: 850-422-1701
Fax: 850-422-2762
Web: www.faifa.org

Agent Associations

Florida Association of Insurance Agents (FAIA)
3159 Shamrock South
PO Box 12129
Tallahassee, Florida 32317-2129
Tel: 850-893-4155
Fax: 850-668-2852
Web: www.faia.com

Professional Insurance Agents of Florida, Inc.
1390 Timberlane Road
Tallahassee, Florida 32312
Tel: 850-893-8245
Fax: 850-893-8316
Web: www.piafl.org

Other Organizations

Florida Surplus Lines Association
PO Box 331444
Atlantic Beach, Florida 32233-1444
Tel: 904-631-1322
Fax: 904-270-1198
Web: www.FloridaSurplusLinesAssociation.com

Georgia

State Associations

Georgia Association of Insurance and Financial Advisors (NAIFA – Georgia)
677 Main Street
Suwanee, Georgia 30024
Tel: 770-455-4459; 800-422-0773
Fax: 770-455-4469
Web: www.naifageorgia.org

Georgia Association of Property/ Casualty Insurance Companies
PO Box 1
Gainesville, Georgia 30503
Tel: 770-535-4001
Fax: 770-532-7361

Georgia Insurance Information Service
1225 Johnson Ferry Rd., Suite 330
Marietta, Georgia 30068
Tel: 770-565-3806; 770-317-5749
Web: www.giis.org

Agent Associations

Independent Insurance Agents of Georgia, Inc.
3186 Chestnut Drive Connector
Doraville, Georgia 30340
Tel: 770-458-0093
Fax: 770-458-8007
Web: www.iiag.org

Professional Insurance Agents of Georgia
3805 Crestwood Parkway, Suite 140
Duluth, Georgia 30096
Tel: 770-921-2578; 800-233-4902
Fax: 770-921-7590
Web: www.piaga.com

Hawaii

State Associations

Hawaii Insurers Council
1003 Bishop Street
Suite 2010 Pauahi Tower
Honolulu, Hawaii 96813
Tel: 808-525-5877
Fax: 808-525-5879
Web: www.hawaiiinsurerscouncil.org

NAIFA Hawaii
516 Kawaihae Street, #E
Honolulu, Hawaii 96825
Tel: 808-394-3451

Agent Associations

Hawaii Independent Insurance Agents Association
84 N. King Street, 2nd Floor
Honolulu, Hawaii 96817
Tel: 808-531-3125
Fax: 808-531-9995

Other Organizations

Hawaii Insurance Bureau, Inc.
715 South King Street, Suite 320
Honolulu, Hawaii 96813
Tel: 808-531-2771
Fax: 808-536-3516
Web: www.hibinc.com

Idaho

State Associations

Idaho Insurance Council
1408 Brooklawn Dr.
Boise, Idaho 83709-2049
Tel: 208-850-2342
Web: www.iiabi.org

NAIFA — Idaho
7684 Remuda Drive
Boise, Idaho 83709
Tel: 208-362-4953; 208-287-4433
Fax: 208-362-3580
Web: www.naifanet.com/idaho

NW Insurance Council
(Serving Idaho, Oregon and Washington)
101 Elliott Avenue West, Suite 520
Seattle, Washington 98119
Tel: 206-624-3330; Helpline: 800-664-4942
Fax: 206-624-1975
Web: www.nwinsurance.org

Agent Associations

Independent Insurance Agents & Brokers of Idaho, Inc.
595 South 14th
Boise, Idaho 83702
Tel: 208-342-9326
Fax: 208-336-2901
Web: www.iiabi.org

Professional Insurance Agents of Idaho
See PIA Western Alliance
(under Washington)

Other Organizations

Idaho Surveying & Rating Bureau, Inc.
1871 South Cobalt Point Way
Meridian, Idaho 83642
Tel: 208-343-5483
Fax: 208-895-8059
Web: www.isrb.com

Surplus Line Association of Idaho, Inc.
(Stamping Office)
595 South 14th Street
Boise, Idaho 83702
Tel: 208-336-2901
Fax: 208-336-2901
Web: www.idahosurplusline.org

Illinois

State Associations

NAIFA — Illinois
60 Adloff Lane
Springfield, Illinois 62703
Tel: 217-529-0126; 800-543-9961
Fax: 217-529-0977
Web: www.naifa-il.com

Illinois Association of Mutual Insurance Companies
PO Box 116
Ohlman, Illinois 62076
Tel: 217-563-8300
Fax: 888-403-0935
Web: www.iamic.org

Illinois Insurance Association
Illinois Insurance Hotline
217 East Monroe Street, Suite 110
Springfield, Illinois 62701
Tel: 217-789-1010
Fax: 217-789-6559
Web: www.illinoisinsurance.org

Illinois Life Insurance Council
600 South Second, Suite 401
Springfield, Illinois 62704
Tel: 217-544-1637
Fax: 217-544-6604

Agent Associations

Independent Insurance Agents of Illinois (IIA of IL)
4360 Wabash Avenue
Springfield, Illinois 62711
Tel: 217-793-6660; 800-628-6436
Fax: 217-793-6744
Web: www.iiaofillinois.org

Other Organizations

Surplus Line Association of Illinois
100 S. Wacker Drive, Ste. 350
Chicago, Illinois 60606
Tel: 312-263-1993
Fax: 312-263-1996
Web: www.slai.org

Indiana

State Associations

Indiana Association of Insurance and Financial Advisors (INAIFA)
3009 East 96th Street
Indianapolis, Indiana 46240
Tel: 317-844-6268
Fax: 317-844-7659
Web: www.naifa-indiana.org

Insurance Institute of Indiana, Inc.
201 N. Illinois Street, Suite 1410
Indianapolis, Indiana 46204
Tel: 317-464-2450
Fax: 317-464-2460
Web: www.insuranceinstitute.org

Agent Associations

Independent Insurance Agents of Indiana, Inc.
3435 West 96th Street
Indianapolis, Indiana 46268
Tel: 317-824-3780; 800-438-4424
Fax: 317-824-3786
Web: www.bigi.org

Iowa

State Associations

Iowa Insurance Institute
215 10th St., Suite 1300
Des Moines, Iowa 50309
Tel: 515-288-2500
Fax: 515-43-0654
Web: http://iowains.com

Federation of Iowa Insurers
700 Walnut, Suite 1600
Des Moines, Iowa 50309
Tel: 515-283-8023
Fax: 515-283-3108
Web: www.federationofiowainsurers.com

National Association of Insurance and Financial Advisors (IOWA)
409 Washington Street, Suite A
Cedar Falls, Iowa 50613
Tel: 866-632-1491
Fax: 703-342-0386
Web: www.naifaiowa.org

Agent Associations

Independent Insurance Agents of Iowa
4000 Westown Parkway
West Des Moines, Iowa 50266
Tel: 515-223-6060
Fax: 515-222-0610
Web: www.iiaiowa.org

Kansas

State Associations

National Association of Insurance and
Financial Advisors of Kansas 825
S. Kansas, Suite 500Topeka, Kansas
66612Tel: 785-354-7770
Fax: 785-233-2206
Web: www.kansasaifa.org

Kansas Association of Property &Casualty Insurance Companies
800 SW Jackson, Suite 900
Topeka, Kansas 66612-1259
Tel: 785-232-0545
Fax: 785-232-0005

Kansas Life Insurance Association
800 SW Jackson, Suite 900
Topeka, Kansas 66612-1259
Tel: 785-232-0545
Fax: 785-232-0005

Agent Associations

Kansas Association of Insurance Agents
815 S.W. Topeka Blvd.
Topeka, Kansas 66612
Tel: 785-232-0561
Fax: 785-232-6817
Web: www.kaia.com

Kentucky

State Associations

Insurance Institute of Kentucky
PO Box 54542
Lexington, Kentucky 40555-
4542Tel: 859-543-9759
Fax: 859-263-0497
Web: www.iiky.org

NAIFA – Kentucky
12808 Townepark Way, Suite 200
Louisville, Kentucky 40243
Tel: 502-244-0150
Fax: 502-244-3111
Web: www.naifakentucky.org

Kentucky Insurance Council
c/o Independent Insurance
Agents of Kentucky, Inc.
13265 O'Bannon Station Way
Louisville, Kentucky 40223
Tel: 502-245-5432; 866-426-4425
Fax: 502-245-5750
Web: www.iiak.org

Agent Associations

Independent Insurance
Agents of Kentucky, Inc.
13265 O'Bannon Station Way
Louisville, Kentucky 40223
Tel: 502-245-5432; 866-426-4425
Fax: 502-245-5750
Web: www.iiak.org

Professional Insurance
Agents of Kentucky
107 Consumer Lane
Frankfort, Kentucky 40601
Tel: 502-875-3888
Fax: 502-227-0839
Web: www.piaky.org

Other Organizations

Kentucky Surplus Lines Association
c/o Risk Placement Services, Inc.
PO Box 14032
Lexington, Kentucky 40512-4032
Tel: 859-245-2500
Fax: 859-272-9622
Web: www.rpslex.com

Louisiana

State Associations

Louisiana Insurers Conference
450 Laurel Street, Suite 1400
Baton Rouge, Louisiana 70801
Tel: 225-343-2776
Fax: 225-344-1132
Web: www.lainsconf.org

NAIFA — Louisiana
5526 Galeria Drive
Baton Rouge, Louisiana 70816
Tel: 225-293-5258
Fax: 225-292-3394
Web: www.naifalouisiana.org

Agent Associations

Independent Insurance Agents
and Brokers of Louisiana, Inc.
9818 Bluebonnet Boulevard
Baton Rouge, Louisiana 70810
Tel: 225-819-8007
Fax: 225-819-8027

Professional Insurance
Agents of Louisiana, Inc.
8064 Summa Avenue, Suite C
Baton Rouge, Louisiana 70809
Tel: 225-766-7770; 800-349-3434
Fax: 225-766-1601
Web: www.piaoflouisiana.com

Other Organizations

Louisiana Surplus Line Association
PO Box 446
Mandeville, Louisiana 70470-0446
Tel: 985-792-4798
Fax: 985-792-4796
Web: www.lsla.bizland.com

Property Insurance Association of Louisiana (Independent Rating Bureau)
433 Metairie Road, Suite 203
Metairie, Louisiana 70005
Tel: 504-836-7980
Fax: 504-831-3444
Web: www.pial.org

Maine

State Associations

National Association of Insurance and Financial Advisors (NAIFA – Maine)
PO Box 2695 Bangor, Maine 04402-2695
Tel: 207-945-4766
Fax: 207-941-0241
Web: www.naifa-me.org

Agent Associations

Maine Insurance Agents Association
432 Western Avenue
Augusta, Maine 04330
Tel: 207-623-1875
Fax: 207-626-0275
Web: www.maineagents.com

Maryland

State Associations

League of Life & Health Insurers of Maryland
200 Duke of Gloucester Street
Annapolis, Maryland 21401
Tel: 410-269-1554
Fax: 410-268-0612

Agent Associations

Independent Insurance Agents of Maryland, Inc.
2408 Peppermill Drive, Suite A
Glen Burnie, Maryland 21061-3257
Tel: 410-766-0600; 800-544-3368
Fax: 410-766-0993
Web: www.iiamd.org

NAIFA — Maryland
9 State Circle, Suite 303
Annapolis, Maryland 21401
Tel: 877-304-9934
Fax: 443-458-0444
Web: www.naifa-maryland.org

Massachusetts

State Associations

Life Insurance Association of Massachusetts
501 Boylston Street
Boston, Massachusetts 02116
Tel: 617-375-9200
Fax: 617-375-1029

Massachusetts Insurance Federation, Inc.
Two Center Plaza, 8th Floor
Boston, Massachusetts 02108
Tel: 617-557-5538
Fax: 617-557-5675
Web: www.massinsurance.org

Agent Associations

Massachusetts Association of Insurance Agents
91 Cedar Street
Milford, Massachusetts 01757
Tel: 508-634-2900; 800-972-9312
Fax: 508-634-2929
Web: www.massagent.com

Association Headquarters — NAIFA Massachusetts & New Hampshire
PO Box 500
Hingham, Massachusetts 02043
Tel: 617-266-1919; 800-480-8719 (In state)
Fax: 617-266-6849
Web: www.naifamass.org

Michigan

State Associations

Insurance Institute of Michigan
334 Townsend Street
Lansing, Michigan 48933
Tel: 517-371-2880
Fax: 517-371-2882
Web: www.iiminfo.org

Life Insurance Association of Michigan
334 Townsend Street
Lansing, Michigan 48933
Tel: 517-482-7058
Fax: 517-482-5405

NAIFA — Michigan
240 S. Bridge Street, Suite 210
DeWitt, Michigan 48820
Tel: 517-668-3960
Fax: 517-668-3961
Web: www.naifanet.com/michigan

Agent Associations

Michigan Association of Insurance Agents
1141 Centennial Way (48917)
PO Box 80620
Lansing, Michigan 48908-0620
Tel: 517-323-9473
Fax: 517-323-1629
Web: www.michagent.org

Other Organizations

Michigan Surplus Lines Association
215 Lakeview
Grosse Pointe Farms, Michigan 48236
Tel: 313-446-9636
Fax: 313-446-9706
Web: www.gossllc.com

Minnesota

State Associations

Insurance Federation of Minnesota
15490-101st Ave.
North Maple Grove, Minnesota 55369
Tel: 651-292-1099
Fax: 763-322-8831
Web: www.insurancefederation.org

Minnesota Association of Farm Mutual Insurance Companies Inc. (MAFMIC)
601 Elm Street East
PO Box 880
St. Joseph, Minnesota 56374
Tel: 320-271-0909
Fax: 320-277-0912
Web: www.mafmic.org

The National Association of Insurance andFinancial Advisors (NAIFA – Minnesota)
1405 North Lilac Drive, Suite 121
Golden Valley, Minnesota 55422
Tel: 763-544-8087
Fax: 763-544-1631
Web: www.naifa-mn.org

Agent Associations

**Minnesota Independent
Insurance Agents & Brokers**
7500 Flying Cloud Drive, Suite 900
Eden Prairie, Minnesota 55344
Tel: 800-864-3846 or 952-835-4180
Fax: 952-835-4774
Web: www.miia.org

Mississippi

State Associations

**National Association of
Insurance and Financial Advisors
– Mississippi (NAIFA)**
5475 Executive Place
Jackson, Mississippi 39206
Tel: 601-981-1522
Fax: 601-981-2745
Web: www.naifams.org

Mississippi Life Companies Association
PO Box 78
Jackson, Mississippi 39205
Tel: 601-981-5332 x1461
Fax: 601-321-2931

Agent Associations

**Independent Insurance Agents
of Mississippi (IIAM)**
124 Riverview Drive
Flowood, Mississippi 39232-8908
Tel: 601-939-9909; 800-898-0821
Fax: 601-939-9553
Web: www.msagent.org

**Professional Insurance Agents
Association of Mississippi**
4 River Bend Place, Suite 115
Jackson, Mississippi 39232
Tel: 601-936-6474; 800-898-0136
Fax: 601-936-6477
Web: www.piams.com

Other Organizations

Mississippi State Rating Bureau
2685 Crane Ridge Drive
PO Box 5231
Jackson, Mississippi 39296-5231
Tel: 601-981-2915
Fax: 601-981-2924
Web: www.msratingbureau.com

Missouri

State Associations

NAIFA – Missouri
722 E. Capitol Avenue
Jefferson City, Missouri 65101
Tel: 888-634-5202
Fax: 573-634-5954
Web: www.naifamo.org

Missouri Insurance Coalition
220 Madison Street, 3rd Floor
Jefferson City, Missouri 65101
Tel: 573-893-4241
Fax: 573-893-4996
Web: www.moinsurancecoalition.com

Agent Associations

**Missouri Association of
Insurance Agents**
2701 Industrial Drive
PO Box 1785
Jefferson City, Missouri 65102-1785
Tel: 573-893-4301; 800-617-3658
Fax: 573-893-3708
Web: www.missouriagent.org

Montana

State Associations

NAIFA Montana
PO Box 2950
Bigfork, Montana 59911
Tel: 406-837-7254
Fax: 406-837-7255
Web: www.naifamt.org

Agent Associations

Independent Insurance Agents Association of Montana, Inc.
3131 Dredge Drive
Helena, Montana 59602
Tel: 406-442-9555
Fax: 406-442-8263
Web: www.iiamt.org
Professional Insurance Agents of Montana
See PIA of Western Alliance
(under Washington)

Other Organizations

Montana Surplus Lines Agents Association
3131 Dredge Drive
Helena, Montana 59602
Tel: 406-443-7324
Fax: 406-442-8263
Web: www.mslaa.org

Nebraska

State Associations

National Association of Insurance and Financial Advisors – Nebraska (NAIFA – Nebraska)
1633 Normandy Court, Suite A
Lincoln, Nebraska 68512
Tel: 402-474-7723
Fax: 402-476-6547
Web: www.naifa-ne.org

Nebraska Insurance Information Service
PO Box 81529
1220 Lincoln MallLincoln, Nebraska 68501
Tel: 402-434-8364
Fax: 402-434-8302
Web: www.nebins.com

Agent Associations

Independent Insurance Agents of Nebraska
8321 Northwoods Drive, Suite B
Lincoln, Nebraska 68505
Tel: 402-476-2951; 800-377-3985
Fax: 402-476-1586
Web: www.iian.org

Professional Insurance Agents Association of Nebraska & Iowa
920 S. 107th Avenue, Suite 305
Omaha, Nebraska 68114
Tel: 402-392-1611; 877-717-2074
Fax: 402-392-2228
Web: www.pianebraska.com

Nevada

State Associations

Nevada Insurance Council
PO Box 30367
Las Vegas, Nevada 89173-0367
Tel: 702-355-9007
Fax: 702-541-8615
Web: www.Nevadainsurancecouncil.com

NAIFA — Nevada
1122 Alta Vista Ct.
Sparks, Nevada 89434
Tel: 775-358-9058
Fax: 775-358-9187
Web: www.naifanv.org

Agent Associations

**Nevada Independent
Insurance Agents**
310 North Stewart Street (89701)
PO Box 645
Carson City, Nevada 89702
Tel: 775-882-1366
Fax: 775-883-0524
Web: www.niia.org

**Professional Insurance
Agents of Nevada**
See PIA Western Alliance
(under Washington)

**Western Insurance Agents
Association (WIAA)**
See Western Insurance Agents
Association (under California)

New Hampshire

State Associations

**Association Headquarters —
NAIFA — Mass. & NH**
PO Box 500
Hingham, Massachusetts 02043

Tel: 617-266-1919; 800-480-8719 (In state)
Fax: 617-266-6849
Web: www.naifanh.org

**New Hampshire Association
of Domestic Insurance
Companies (NHADIC)**
Peerless Insurance Company
62 Maple Avenue
Keene, New Hampshire 03431
Tel: 603-357-9558
Fax: 603-358-4616

Agent Associations

**Independent Insurance Agents
& Brokers of New Hampshire**
125 Airport Road
Concord, New Hampshire 03301
Tel: 603-224-3965
Fax: 603-224-0550
Web: www.iianh.com

New Jersey

State Associations

Insurance Council of New Jersey
820 Bear Tavern Road, Suite 303
Ewing, New Jersey 08628-1021
Tel: 609-882-4400
Fax: 609-538-1849
Web: www.icnj.org

**New Jersey Association of Insurance
and Financial Advisors (NJAIFA)**
1 Distribution Way, Suite 202

Monmouth Junction, New Jersey 08852
Tel: 732-422-0748
Fax: 732-422-0842
Web: www.naifanj.com

Agent Associations

Independent Insurance Agents & Brokers of New Jersey Inc.
2211 Whitehorse - Mercerville Road
PO Box 3230
Trenton, New Jersey 08619
Tel: 609-587-4333
Fax: 609-587-4515
Web: www.iiabnj.org

Professional Insurance Agents of New Jersey
See PIA (under New York)

New Mexico

State Associations

National Association of Insurance and

Financial Advisors (NAIFA — New Mexico)
7815 Eagle Rock Avenue NE
Albuquerque, New Mexico 87122
Tel: 505-797-9007
Fax: 505-797-9007
Web: www.naifa.org

Rocky Mountain Insurance Information Association – NM
See RMIIA of CO, NM, UT and WY (under Colorado)

Agent Associations

Independent Insurance Agents of New Mexico, Inc.
1511 University Boulevard, N.E.
Albuquerque, New Mexico 87102
Tel: 505-843-7231; 800-621-3978
Fax: 505-243-3367
Web: www.iianm.org

Professional Insurance Agents of New Mexico
See PIA Western Alliance
(under Washington)

Western Insurance Agents Association (WIAA)
See Western Insurance Agents Association (under California)

New York

State Associations

Life Insurance Council of New York, Inc.
551 Fifth Avenue, Floor 29New York, New York 10176-0001
Tel: 212-986-6181
Fax: 212-986-6549
Web: www.licony.org

New York Insurance Association, Inc.
130 Washington AvenueAlbany, New York 12210
Tel: 518-432-4227
Fax: 518-432-4220
Web: www.nyia.org

The New York Alliance Against Insurance Fraud, Inc.
c/o New York Insurance Association, Inc.
130 Washington Avenue
Albany, New York 12210
Tel: 518-432-3576
Fax: 518-432-4220
Web: www.fraudny.org

NAIFA – New York State
38 Sheridan Avenue
Albany, New York 12210-2714
Tel: 518-462-5567
Fax: 518-462-5569
Web: www.naifanys.org

Agent Associations

**Independent Insurance Agents
& Brokers of New York, Inc.**
5784 Widewaters Parkway, 1st Floor
Dewitt, New York 13214
Tel: 800-962-7950; 315-432-9111
Fax: 888-432-0510
Web: www.iiabny.org

**Professional Insurance
Agents of NY, NJ, CT, NH**
25 Chamberlain Street
PO Box 997
Glenmont, New York 12077-0997
Tel: 800-424-4244
Fax: 888-225-6935
Web: www.pia.org

Other Organizations

Excess Line Association of New York
(Stamping Office)
One Exchange Plaza
55 Broadway, 29th Floor
New York, New York 10006-3728
Tel: 646-292-5500
Web: www.elany.org

North Carolina

State Associations

**Insurance Federation
of North Carolina**
3605 Glenwood Avenue, Suite 220
Raleigh, North Carolina 27612
Tel: 919-834-9773
Fax: 919-834-9802
Web: www.insurancefederationnc.com

NAIFA North Carolina
875 Washington Street, S-1
Raleigh, North Carolina 27605-3252
Tel: 919-839-5828
Fax: 919-821-5743
Web: www.ncaifa.org

No Agent Associations

Other Organizations

North Carolina Rate Bureau
PO Box 176010
Raleigh, North Carolina 27619-6010
Tel: 919-783-9790
Fax: 919-719-7400
Web: www.ncrb.org

North Dakota

State Associations

**Association of North
Dakota Insurers (ANDI)**
c/o Zuger Kirmis & Smith
316 N. Fifth Street, 6th Floor
PO Box 1695
Bismarck, North Dakota 58502-1695
Tel: 701-223-2711
Fax: 701-223-7387
Web: www.zkslaw.com

Agent Associations

National Association of Insurance & Financial Advisors of North Dakota (NAIFA—ND)
1811 East Thayer Avenue
PO Box 5010
Bismarck, North Dakota 58502
Tel: 701-258-9525
Fax: 701-222-0103
Web: www.naifa-nd.org

Professional Insurance Agents of North Dakota
1211 Memorial Highway, Suite 6
Bismarck, North Dakota 58504
Tel: 701-223-5025
Fax: 701-223-9456
Web: www.piand.com

Ohio

State Associations

Association of Ohio Life Insurance Companies
c/o Bricker & Eckler, LLP100
South 3rd Street
Columbus, Ohio 43215
Tel: 614-227-2300
Fax: 614-227-2390
Web: www.aolic.com

The National Association of Insurance and Financial Advisors — Ohio
17 South High Street, Suite 200
Columbus, Ohio 43215-3458
Tel: 614-228-4539
Fax: 614-221-1989
Web: www.naifaohio.org

Ohio Insurance Institute
172 East State Street, Suite 201
Columbus, Ohio 43215-4321
Tel: 614-228-1593
Fax: 614-228-1678
Web: www.ohioinsurance.org

Agent Associations

The Independent Insurance Agents Association of Ohio, Inc.
1330 Dublin Road
PO Box 758
Columbus, Ohio 43216
Tel: 614-464-3100; 800-282-4424
Fax: 614-486-9797
Web: www.ohiobigi.com

Professional Insurance Agents Association of Ohio, Inc.
600 Cross Pointe Road
Gahanna, Ohio 43230
Tel: 614-552-8000; 800-555-1742
Fax: 614-552-0115
Web: www.ohiopia.com

Oklahoma

State Associations

Association of Oklahoma Life Insurance Companies
c/o Kerr, Irvine, Rhodes & Ables
201 Robert S. Kerr, #600
Oklahoma City, Oklahoma 73102
Tel: 405-272-9221
Fax: 405-236-3121
Web: www.kiralaw.com

NAIFA — Oklahoma
6051 N. Brookline, Suite 124
Oklahoma City, Oklahoma 73112
Tel: 405-810-1989; 800-491-8190
Fax: 405-810-1799
Web: www.okaifa.org

Southwestern Insurance Information Service (SIIS)

See Southwestern Insurance Information Service (under Texas)

Agent Associations

Independent Insurance Agents of Oklahoma
PO Box 13490
Oklahoma City, Oklahoma 73113
Tel: 405-840-4426
Fax: 405-840-4450
Web: www.iiaok.com

Oregon

State Associations

NW Insurance Council
(Serving Oregon, Washington and Idaho)
101 Elliott Avenue West, Suite 520
Seattle, Washington 98119
Tel: 206-624-3330
Fax: 206-624-1975
Web: www.nwinsurance.org

NAIFA — Oregon
12690 NW Lorraine Drive
Portland, Oregon 97229
Tel: 503-718-0094
Fax: 866-791-3348
Web: www.oraifa.org

Agent Associations

Independent Insurance Agents & Brokers of Oregon
5550 SW Macadam Avenue, Suite 305
Portland, Oregon 97239
Tel: 503-274-4000; 866-774-4226
Fax: 503-274-0062
Web: www.iiabo.org

Professional Insurance Agents of Oregon

See PIA Western Alliance (under Washington)

Pennsylvania

State Associations

Insurance Federation of Pennsylvania
1600 Market Street, Suite 1520
Philadelphia, Pennsylvania 19103
Tel: 215-665-0500
Fax: 215-665-0540
Web: www.ifpenn.org

NAIFA — Pennsylvania
777 East Park Drive, Suite 300
Harrisburg, Pennsylvania 17111
Tel: 717-234-2523, 800-552-7258
Fax: 717-234-5190
Web: www.naifa-pa.org

Pennsylvania Association of Mutual Insurance Companies (PAMIC)
1017 Mumma Road, Suite 103
Wormleysburg, Pennsylvania 17043
Tel: 717-303-0197
Fax: 717-303-1501
Web: www.pamic.org

Agent Associations

Insurance Agents & Brokers
5050 Ritter Road
PO Box 2023
Mechanicsburg, Pennsylvania 17055
Tel: 717-795-9100
Fax: 717-795-8347

Other Organizations

Pennsylvania Surplus Lines Association
180 Sheree Blvd., Suite 3100
Exton, Pennsylvania 19341
Tel: 610-594-1340 or 888-209-3230 (in state only)
Fax: 610-594-7623
Web: www.pasla.org

Puerto Rico

No State Associations

Agent Associations

Professional Insurance Agents of Puerto Rico & the Caribbean, Inc.
PO Box 192389
San Juan, Puerto Rico 00919-2389
Tel: 787-792-7849
Fax: 787-792-4745

Rhode Island

No State Associations

Agent Associations

Independent Insurance Agents of Rhode Island
2400 Post Road
Warwick, Rhode Island 02886
Tel: 401-732-2400
Fax: 401-732-1708
Web: www.iiari.com

NAIFA – RI
1643 Warwick Avenue, PMB 128
Warwick, Rhode Island 02889
Tel: 401-739-2977
Fax: 401-727-0959
Web: www.naifa-ri.org

South Carolina

State Associations

South Carolina Insurance News Service
1301 Gervais Street, Suite 715
Columbia, South Carolina 29201
Tel: 803-252-3455
Fax: 803-779-0189
Web: www.scinsurance.net

The Association of South Carolina Property/Casualty Insurance Companies
c/o State Auto Insurance Companies
PO Box 199
Greer, South Carolina 29652
Tel: 864-877-3311
Fax: 864-879-4025
Web: www.stateauto.com

Agent Associations

Independent Insurance Agents & Brokers of South Carolina
PO Box 21000
8800 Gracern Road
Columbia, South Carolina 29221
Tel: 803-731-9460
Fax: 803-772-6425
Web: www.iiabsc.com

South Dakota

State Associations

NAIFA – South Dakota
PO Box 1820
Sioux Falls, South Dakota 57101
Tel: 605-336-3400
Fax: 605-367-8998
Web: www.naifanet.com/southdakota

Agent Associations

Independent Insurance Agents of South Dakota (IIASD)
PO Box 327305 Island Drive
Fort Pierre, South Dakota 57501
Tel: 605-224-6234
Fax: 605-224-6235
Web: www.iiasd.org

Tennessee

State Associations
NAIFA – Tennessee189 Fairmont Drive
Murfreesboro, Tennessee 37129
Tel: 615-904-6013; 888-276-4159
Fax: 615-907-6389
Web: www.tnaifa.org

Agent Associations

Insurors of Tennessee
2500 – 21st Avenue, Suite 200
Nashville, Tennessee 37212
Tel: 615-385-1898; 800-264-1898
Fax: 615-385-9303
Web: www.insurors.org

Professional Insurance Agents of Tennessee, Inc.
504 Autumn Springs Court, Suite A-2
Franklin, Tennessee 37067
Tel: 615-771-1177
Fax: 615-771-3456
Web: www.piatn.com

Texas

State Associations

Association of Fire & Casualty Companies of Texas
PO Box 15
Austin, Texas 78767-0015
Tel: 512-444-9611
Fax: 512-444-0734
Web: www.insurancecouncil.org

Insurance Council of Texas
2801 South Interregional Highway
PO Box 15
Austin, Texas 78767-0015
Tel: 512-444-9611
Fax: 512-444-0734
Web: www.insurancecouncil.org

Southwestern Insurance Information Service (SIIS)
8303 North Mopac, Suite B-231
Austin, Texas 78759
Tel: 512-795-8214
Fax: 512-795-2323
Web: www.siisinfo.org

National Association of Insurance and Financial Advisors — Texas
515 Congress Avenue, Suite 1650
Austin, Texas 78701
Tel: 512-716-8800
Fax: 512-476-1932
Web: www.naifa-texas.org

Texas Association of Life & Health Insurers
1001 Congress Avenue, Suite 300
Austin, Texas 78701
Tel: 512-472-6886
Fax: 512-476-2870
Web: www.talhi.com

Texas Coalition for Affordable Insurance Solutions

500 West 13th Street
Austin, Texas 78701
Tel: (512) 477-7382
Fax: (512) 477-6240
Web: www.tcais.org

Agent Associations

Independent Insurance Agents of Texas
1115 San Jacinto, Suite 100 (78701)
PO Box 684487
Austin, Texas 78768-4487
Tel: 512-476-6281; 800-880-7428
Fax: 512-469-9512
Web: www.iiat.org

Texas Insurance Professionals,PIA National Affiliate
PO Box 90908
Austin, Texas 78709-0908
Tel: 800-829-9838
Fax: 512-301-0265
Web: www.piatx.org

Other Organizations

Surplus Lines Stamping Office of Texas
805 Las Cimas Parkway, Suite 150
Austin, Texas 78746
Tel: 512-346-3274
Fax: 512-346-3422
Web: www.slsot.org

Texas Surplus Lines Association, Inc.
9020-I Capital of Texas
Highway North, Suite 370
Austin, Texas 78759
Tel: 512-343-9058
Fax: 512-343-2896
Web: www.tsla.org

Utah

State Associations

Rocky Mountain Insurance Information Association – UT
See RMIIA of CO, NM, UT and WY (under Colorado)

Agent Associations

The Utah Association of Independent Insurance Agents
4885 South 900 East, Suite 302
Salt Lake City, Utah 84117
Tel: 801-269-1200
Fax: 801-269-1265
Web: www.uaiia.org

Other Organizations

Surplus Line Association of Utah
(Stamping Office)
6711 South 1300 East
Salt Lake City, Utah 84121
Tel: 801-944-0114
Fax: 801-944-0116
Web: www.slaut.org

Vermont

State Associations

National Association of Insurance and
Financial Advisors (NAIFA – Vermont)
325 Ethan Allen Pkwy
Burlington, Vermont 05401
Tel: 802-660-9639
Fax: 802-862-3466
Web: www.naifanet.com/vermont

Vermont Association of Domestic Property & Casualty Insurance Companies
c/o Union Mutual of Vermont Companies
139 State Street
Montpelier, Vermont 05602
Tel: 802-223-5261
Fax: 802-229-5580
Web: www.unionmutual.com

Agent Associations

Vermont Insurance Agents Association, Inc.
PO Box 1387
47½ Court StreetMontpelier,
Vermont 05602
Tel: 802-229-5884
Fax: 802-223-0868
Web: www.viaa.org

Virginia

State Associations

NAIFA – Greater Washington D.C.
PO Box 5153
Arlington, Virginia 22205
Tel: 703-532-8778
Fax: 703-940-8393
Web: www.naifa-gwdc.org

Agent Associations

Independent Insurance Agents of Virginia, Inc.
8600 Mayland Drive
Richmond, Virginia 23294
Tel: 804-747-9300 or 800-288-4428
Fax: 804-747-6557
Web: www.iiav.com

Metropolitan Washington Association of Independent Insurance Agents
PO Box 25346
Alexandria, Virginia 22313-5346
Tel: 703-706-5446
Fax: 703-706-5445
Web: www.mwaiia.org

Professional Insurance Agents Association of Virginia & D.C.
8751 Park Central Drive, Suite 140
Richmond, Virginia 23227
Tel: 804-264-2582
Fax: 804-266-1075
Web: www.piavadc.com

NAIFA – Virginia
3108 N. Parham Road, Suite 100A
Henrico, Virginia 23294-4415
Tel: 804-747-6020
Fax: 804-965-0823
Web: www.naifanet.com/virginia

Other Organizations

Virginia Surplus Lines Association
c/o Atlantic Specialty Lines, Inc.
9020 Stony Point Parkway, Suite 450
Richmond, Virginia 23235
Tel: 804-320-9500
Fax: 804-320-7280

Washington

State Associations

NW Insurance Council
(Serving Washington, Oregon and Idaho)
101 Elliott Avenue West, Suite 520
Seattle, Washington 98119
Tel: 206-624-3330;
Helpline: 800-664-4942
Fax: 206-624-1975
Web: www.nwinsurance.org

Agent Associations

Independent Insurance Agents and Brokers of Washington
15015 Main Street, Suite 205 (98007)
PO Box 6459
Bellevue, Washington 98008
Tel: 425-649-0102
Fax: 425-649-8573
Web: www.wainsurance.org

PIA Western Alliance
Representing the affiliate chapters
of Washington/Alaska,
Oregon/Idaho, Montana and the
Group (AZ, NM, NV and CA)
3205 N.E. 78th Street, Suite 104
Vancouver, Washington 98665
Tel: 888-246-4466
Fax: 888-346-4466
Web: www.piawest.com

Other Organizations

Washington Insurance Examining Bureau, Inc.
2101 4th Avenue, Suite 300
Seattle, Washington 98121-2329
Tel: 206-217-9432
Fax: 206-217-9329
Web: www.wieb.com

Washington Surveying & Rating Bureau
2101 4th Avenue, Suite 300
Seattle, Washington 98121-2329
Tel: 206-217-9772
Fax: 206-217-9329
Web: www.wsrb.com

Surplus Line Association of Washington
(Stamping Office)
600 University Street, Suite 1710
Seattle, Washington 98101-1129
Tel: 206-682-3409
Fax: 206-623-3326
Web: www.surpluslines.org

West Virginia

State Associations

West Virginia Insurance Federation
PO Box 11887
Charleston, West Virginia 25339
Tel: 304-357-9929
Fax: 304-357-0919
Web: www.wvinsurance.org

Agent Associations

Independent Insurance Agents of West Virginia, Inc.
PO Box 1226 (25324-1226)
179 Summers Street, Suite
321Charleston, West Virginia 25301
Tel: 304-342-2440; 800-274-4298
Fax: 304-344-4492
Web: www.iiawv.org

Wisconsin

State Associations

Community Insurance Information Center
700 W. Michigan Street, Suite 360
Milwaukee, Wisconsin 53233-2470
Tel: 414-291-5360
Fax: 414-291-5370
Web: www.insuranceinfo-ciic.org

National Association of Insurance and
Financial Advisors - Wisconsin
2702 International Lane., Suite 207
Madison, Wisconsin 53704
Tel: 608-244-3131
Fax: 608-244-0476
Web: http://wisconsin.naifa.org

Wisconsin Insurance Alliance
44 East Mifflin Street, Suite 901
Madison, Wisconsin 53703-2800
Tel: 608-255-1749
Fax: 608-255-2178
Web: www.wial.org

Agent Associations

Independent Insurance Agents of Wisconsin
725 John Nolen Drive
Madison, Wisconsin 53713
Tel: 608-256-4429; 800-362-7441
Fax: 608-256-0170
Web: www.iiaw.com

Professional Insurance Agents of Wisconsin, Inc.
6401 Odana Road
Madison, Wisconsin 53719
Tel: 608-274-8188
Fax: 608-274-8195
Web: www.piaw.org

Wyoming

State Associations

Rocky Mountain Insurance Information Association – WY
See RMIIA of CO, NM, UT and WY (under Colorado)

Agent Associations

Association of Wyoming Insurance Agents
PO Box 799
Sundance, Wyoming 82729-0799
Tel: 307-283-2052
Fax: 775-796-3122
Web: www.awia.com

NAIFA – Wyoming
Hampton Insurance & Financial Services
PO Box 319
Upton, Wyoming 82730
Tel: 307-468-2635
Fax: 307-468-2415

Brief History

YEAR	EVENT
1601	First insurance legislation in the United Kingdom was enacted. Modern insurance has its roots in this law which concerned coverage for merchandise and ships.
1666	Great Fire of London demonstrated destructive power of fire in an urban environment, leading entrepreneur Nicholas Barbon to form a business to repair houses damaged by fire.
1684	Participants in the Friendly Society in England formed a mutual insurance company to cover fire losses.
1688	Edward Lloyd's coffee house, the precursor of Lloyd's of London, became the central meeting place for ship owners seeking insurance for a voyage.
1696	Hand in Hand Mutual Fire Company was formed. Aviva, the world's oldest continuously operating insurance company, traces its origins to this company.
1710	Charles Povey formed the Sun, the oldest insurance company in existence which still conducts business in its own name. It is the forerunner of the Royal & Sun Alliance Group.
1735	The Friendly Society, the first insurance company in the United States, was established in Charleston, South Carolina. This mutual insurance company went out of business in 1740.
1752	The Philadelphia Contributionship for the Insurance of Houses from Loss by Fire, the oldest insurance carrier in continuous operation in the United States, was established.
1759	Presbyterian Ministers Fund, the first life insurance company in the United States, was founded.
1762	Equitable Life Assurance Society, the world's oldest mutual life insurer, was formed in England.
1776	Charleston Insurance Company and the South Carolina Insurance Company, the first two United States marine insurance companies, were formed in South Carolina.
1779	Lloyd's of London introduced the first uniform ocean marine policy.
1792	Insurance Company of North America, the first stock insurance company in the United States, was established.
1813	Eagle Fire Insurance Company of New York assumed all outstanding risks of the Union Insurance Company, in the first recorded fire reinsurance agreement in the United States.
1849	New York passed the first general insurance law in the United States.
1850	Franklin Health Assurance Company of Massachusetts offered the first accident and health insurance.
1851	New Hampshire created the first formal agency to regulate insurance in the United States.

YEAR	EVENT
1861	First war-risk insurance policies were issued, written by life insurance companies during the Civil War.
1866	National Board of Fire Underwriters was formed in New York City, marking the beginning of insurance rate standardization.
	Hartford Steam Boiler Inspection and Insurance Company, the first boiler insurance company, was established in Hartford, Connecticut.
1873	The Massachusetts Legislature adopted the first standard fire insurance policy.
1878	Fidelity and Casualty Company of New York began providing fidelity and surety bonds.
1885	Liability protection was first offered with the introduction of employers liability policies.
1890	First policies providing benefits for disabilities from specific diseases were offered.
1894	National Board of Fire Underwriters established Underwriters' Laboratories to investigate and test electrical materials to ensure they meet fire safety standards.
1898	Travelers Insurance Company issued the first automobile insurance policy in the United States.
1899	First pedestrian killed by an automobile, in New York City.
1910	New York passed the first United States workers compensation law. It was later found to be unconstitutional.
1911	Wisconsin enacted the first permanent workers compensation law in the United States.
1912	Lloyd's of London introduced aviation insurance coverage.
1925	Massachusetts passed the first compulsory automobile insurance legislation.
	Connecticut passed the first financial responsibility law for motorists.
1938	Federal Crop Insurance Act created the first federal crop insurance program.
1945	McCarran-Ferguson Act (Public Law 15) was enacted. It provided the insurance industry with a limited exemption to federal antitrust law, assuring the pre-eminence of state regulation of the industry.
1947	New York established the Motor Vehicle Liability Security Fund to cover auto insurance company insolvencies. This organization was a precursor of the state guaranty funds established by insurers in all states to absorb the claims of insolvent insurers.
1950	First package insurance policies for homeowners coverage were introduced.
1960	Boston Plan was established to address insurance availability problems in urban areas in Boston.
1968	First state-run Fair Access to Insurance Requirements (FAIR) Plans were set up to ensure property insurance availability in high-risk areas.
	The federal flood insurance program was established with the passage of the National Flood Insurance Act. It enabled property owners in communities that participate in flood reduction programs to purchase insurance against flood losses.
1971	Massachusetts became the first state to establish a true no-fault automobile insurance plan.
1981	Federal Risk Retention Act of 1981 was enacted. The law fostered the growth of risk retention groups and other nontraditional insurance mechanisms.
	The Illinois Legislature created the Illinois Insurance Exchange, a cooperative effort of individual brokers and risk bearers operating as a single market, similar to Lloyd's of London.
1985	Mission Insurance Group failed. The insolvency incurred the largest payout by state guaranty funds for a single property/casualty insurance company failure at that time. This and other insolvencies in the 1980s led to stricter state regulation of insurer solvency.

YEAR	EVENT
	Montana became the first state to forbid discrimination by sex in the setting of insurance rates.
1992	European Union's Third Nonlife Insurance Directive became effective, establishing a single European market for insurance.
1996	Florida enacted rules requiring insurers to offer separate deductibles for hurricane losses, marking a shift to hurricane deductibles based on a percentage of loss rather than a set dollar figure. Catastrophe bonds, vehicles for covering disaster risk in the capital markets, were introduced.
1997	World Trade Organization agreement to dismantle barriers to trade in financial services, including insurance, banking and securities, was signed by the United States and some 100 other countries.
1999	Financial Services Modernization Act (Gramm-Leach-Bliley) enacted, allowing insurers, banks and securities firms to affiliate under a financial holding company structure.
2001	Terrorist attacks upon the World Trade Center in New York City and the Pentagon in Washington, D.C. caused about $40 billion in insured losses.
	New York became the first state to ban the use of hand-held cell phones while driving.
2002	Terrorism Risk Insurance Act enacted to provide a temporary federal backstop for terrorism insurance losses.
2003	In a landmark ruling, upheld in 2004, the U.S. Supreme Court placed limits on punitive damages, holding in State Farm v. Campbell that punitive damages awards should generally not exceed nine times compensatory awards.
2004	New York Attorney General Eliot Spitzer and a number of state regulators launched investigations into insurance industry sales and accounting practices.
2005	Citigroup sold off its Travelers life insurance unit, following the spin off of its property/casualty business in 2002. This dissolved the arrangement that led to the passage of Gramm-Leach-Bliley in 1999.
	The federal Class Action Fairness Act moved most class-action lawsuits to federal courts, offering the prospect of lower defense costs and fewer and less costly verdicts.
	A string of hurricanes, including Hurricane Katrina, hit the Gulf Coast, making 2005 the most active hurricane season.
	Congress passed legislation extending the Terrorism Risk Insurance Act to December 2007. The act, originally passed in 2002, had been set to expire at the end of 2005. Extended again in 2007.
2006	Massachusetts became the first state to pass a universal health insurance law.
2007	Florida passed legislation shifting more of the cost of paying for hurricane damage from private insurers to the state.
	Washington became the first state to ban the practice of texting with a cellphone while driving.
	Congress passes legislation extending the Terrorism Risk Insurance Act through the end of 2014.
2008	The Federal Reserve Bank acquired a 79 percent stake in American International Group (AIG) in exchange for an $85 billion loan, which was subsequently increased and restructured.
	Troubled Asset Relief Program established to stabilize the financial sector. Insurers that own a federally regulated bank or thrift were eligible to participate.
2010	Congress enacted an overhaul of the nation's health care system, expanding access to medical insurance.

I.I.I. Store

The I.I.I. Store is your gateway to a wide array of books and brochures from the Insurance Information Institute. Print and PDF formats, and quantity discounts are available for most products. Order online at www.iii.org/publications, call 212-346-5500 or email publications@iii.org.

I.I.I. INSURANCE FACT BOOK
Thousands of insurance facts, figures, tables and graphs designed for quick and easy reference.

THE FINANCIAL SERVICES FACT BOOK
Banking, securities and insurance industry trends and statistics. Published jointly with the Financial Services Roundtable. Online version available at www.financialservicesfacts.org

INSURANCE HANDBOOK
A guide to the insurance industry for reporters, public policymakers, students, insurance company employees, regulators and others. Provides concise explanations of auto, home, life, disability and business insurance, as well as issues papers, a glossary and directories. Online version available at www.iii.org/insurancehandbook

INSURING YOUR BUSINESS:
A SMALL BUSINESSOWNERS' GUIDE TO INSURANCE
A comprehensive insurance guide for small business owners. Special discounts available to organizations and agents for bulk orders. Online version available at www.iii.org/smallbusiness

A FIRM FOUNDATION: HOW INSURANCE SUPPORTS THE ECONOMY
Shows the myriad ways in which insurance provides economic support—from offering employment and fueling the capital markets, to providing financial security and income to individuals and businesses. Provides national and state data. Selected state versions are also available. Online version available at www.iii.org/economics

INTERNATIONAL INSURANCE FACT BOOK
Facts and statistics on the property/casualty and life insurance industries of dozens of countries. No print edition. Available in CD-ROM format. Online version available at www.iii.org/international

---

COMMERCIAL INSURANCE

A comprehensive guide to the commercial insurance market—what it does, how it functions, and its key players. No print edition. Online version available at www.iii.org/commerciallines

I.I.I. INSURANCE DAILY

Keeps thousands of readers up-to-date on important events, issues and trends in the insurance industry each business morning. Transmitted early each business day via email.

KNOW YOUR STUFF

Free online home inventory software. Available in the store and at www.knowyourstuff.org

INSURANCE MATTERS

A guide to the insurance industry for policymakers. Available at www.iii-insurancematters.org

CONSUMER BROCHURES

Renters Insurance — All renters need to know about insurance

Am I Covered? — A guide to homeowners insurance

Your Home Inventory — Instructions on how to prepare an inventory of possessions to help identify and calculate losses if a disaster strikes

Nine Ways to Lower Your Auto Insurance Costs — Tips on how to lower your auto insurance costs

Settling Insurance Claims After a Disaster — Helps you understand how to file an insurance claim after a disaster

Twelve Ways to Lower Your Homeowners Insurance Costs — Tips on how to lower your homeowners insurance costs

...and many others

I.I.I. on the Web

Visit iii.org for a wealth of information for individuals and business, from consumer brochures to issues papers to white papers to statistics.

- Become an I.I.I. fan on Facebook at www.facebook.com/InsuranceInformationInstitute
- Read about the industry in I.I.I.'s blog, Terms and Conditions, at www.iii.org/insuranceindustryblog
- Follow the I.I.I. Web site on Twitter at http://twitter.com/iii.org and on its special interest feeds:

      http://twitter.com/III_Research —
          to learn about updates to I.I.I. papers and studies
      http://twitter.com/Bob_Hartwig —
          for the latest from I.I.I. President, Robert Hartwig
      http://twitter.com/LWorters —
          I.I.I.'s media connection
      http://www.insuringflorida.org/blog —
          to keep up on Florida Insurancetrends

ACE USA	www.acelimited.com
ACUITY	www.acuity.com
Aegis Insurance Services Inc.	www.aegislink.com
Allianz of America, Inc.	www.allianz.com
Allied World Assurance Company	www.awac.com
Allstate Insurance Group	www.allstate.com
American Agricultural Insurance Company	www.aaic.com
American Family Insurance Group	www.amfam.com
American Reliable Insurance	www.assurant.com
Amerisafe	www.amerisafe.com
Arthur J. Gallagher & Co.	www.ajg.com
Aspen Re	www.aspen-re.com
Auto Club South Insurance Company	www.aaasouth.com
Beazley Group plc	www.beazley.com
Bituminous Insurance Companies	www.bituminousinsurance.com
Catholic Mutual Group	www.catholicmutual.org
Catlin Inc.	www.catlin.com
Century Surety Company	www.centurysurety.com
Chartis	www.chartisinsurance.com
Chubb Group of Insurance Companies	www.chubb.com
Church Mutual Insurance Company	www.churchmutual.com
COUNTRY Financial	www.countryfinancial.com
CNA	www.cna.com
CUMIS Insurance Society, Inc.	www.cumis.com
DeSmet Farm Mutual Insurance Company of South Dakota	www.desmetfarmmutual.com
Dryden Mutual Insurance Company	www.drydenmutual.com
EMC Insurance Companies	www.emcins.com
Employers Insurance Group	www.eig.com
Enumclaw Insurance Group	www.mutualofenumclaw.com
Erie Insurance Group	www.erieinsurance.com
Farmers Group, Inc.	www.farmers.com
GEICO	www.geico.com
Gen Re	www.genre.com
Germania Insurance	www.germania-ins.com
Grange Insurance	www.grangeinsurance.com
GuideOne Insurance	www.guideone.com
The Hanover Insurance Group Inc.	www.hanover.com
Harbor Point Re Insurance U.S., Inc.	www.harborpoint.com
The Harford Mutual Insurance Companies	www.harfordmutual.com
Harleysville Insurance	www.harleysville.com
The Hartford Financial Services Group	www.thehartford.com
Holyoke Mutual Insurance Company	www.holyokemutual.com
The Horace Mann Companies	www.horacemann.com
Ironshore Insurance Ltd.	www.ironshore.com
James River Group, Inc.	www.james-river-group.com
Liberty Mutual Group	www.libertymutual.com
Lloyd's	www.lloyds.com

Continued

Lockton Companies	www.lockton.com
Magna Carta Companies	www.mcarta.com
Marsh Inc.	www.guycarp.com
Max Capital Group Ltd.	www.maxcapgroup.com
MetLife Auto & Home	www.metlife.com
Michigan Millers Mutual Insurance Company	www.mimillers.com
Millville Mutual Insurance Company	www.millvillemutual.com
Missouri Employers Mutual Insurance	www.mem-ins.com
Munich Re	www.munichreamerica.com
Nationwide	www.nationwide.com
New York Central Mutual Fire Insurance Company	www.nycm.com
The Norfolk & Dedham Group	www.ndgroup.com
Ohio Mutual Insurance Group	www.omig.com
OneBeacon Insurance Group	www.onebeacon.com
PartnerRe	www.partnerre.com
Pennsylvania Lumbermens Mutual Insurance Company	www.plmins.com
Providence Mutual Fire Insurance Company	www.providencemutual.com
Scor U.S. Corporation	www.scor.com
SECURA Insurance Companies	www.secura.net
Selective Insurance Group	www.selectiveinsurance.com
State Auto Insurance Companies	www.stateauto.com
State Compensation Insurance Fund of California	www.statefundca.com
State Farm Mutual Automobile Insurance Company	www.statefarm.com
The Sullivan Group	www.gjs.com
Swiss Reinsurance America Corporation	www.swissre.com
TIAA-CREF	www.tiaa-cref.com
Travelers	www.travelers.com
Unitrin Property and Casualty Insurance Group	www.unitrin.com
USAA	www.usaa.com
Utica National Insurance Group	www.uticanational.com
West Bend Mutual Insurance Company	www.thesilverlining.com
Westfield Group	www.westfieldinsurance.com
W. R. Berkley Corporation	www.wrberkley.com
X.L. America, Inc.	www.xlcapital.com
XL Insurance Company, Ltd.	www.xlinsurance.com
Zurich North America	www.zurichna.com

Associate Members

Deloitte	www.Deloitte.com/us
Farmers Mutual Fire Insurance of Tennessee	www.farmersmutualoftn.com
Florida Property and Casualty Association	www.fpconline.com.
Livingston Mutual Insurance Company	www.livingstonmutual.com
Mutual Assurance Society of Virginia	www.mutual-assurance.com
Randolph Mutual Insurance Company	www.randolphmutual.com
Sompo Japan Research Institute, Inc.	www.sj-ri.co.jp/eng
Transunion Insurance Solutions	